Literary Essay: Opening Texts and Seeing More

Lucy Calkins, Series Editor

Katie Clements and Mike Ochs

Photography by Peter Cunningham
Illustrations by Marjorie Martinelli

HEINEMANN ◆ PORTSMOUTH, NH

To Lucy, our Teacher.

Heinemann
361 Hanover Street
Portsmouth, NH 03801–3912

www.heinemann.com

Offices and agents throughout the world

The authors and publisher wish to thank those who have generously given permission to reprint borrowed material:

"Shells," reprinted with the permission of Atheneum Books for Young Readers, an imprint of Simon & Schuster Children's Publishing Division, from *Every Living Thing* by Cynthia Rylant. Text copyright © 1985 by Cynthia Rylant. Cover illustration © 1985 by Simon & Schuster, Inc. All rights reserved.

Cataloging-in-Publication data is on file with the Library of Congress.

ISBN-13: 978-0-325-08886-0

Editor: Tracy Wells
Production: Elizabeth Valway, David Stirling, and Abigail Heim
Cover and interior designs: Jenny Jensen Greenleaf
Photography: Peter Cunningham
Composition: Publishers' Design and Production Services, Inc.
Manufacturing: Steve Bernier

Printed in the United States of America on acid-free paper
20 19 18 17 16 EBM 1 2 3 4 5

Acknowledgments

We ask you to pardon the cliché, but writing this book was truly a labor of love. It was written in Brooklyn coffee shops on the weekends, in the wee hours of the night after full days of staff development, and in the dark hours of the morning before we headed to schools across the city and the country. And yet every moment writing this book was a joy.

We could not share this joyous book with you without thanking, wholeheartedly, those who helped us along the way. First and foremost, we thank Lucy Calkins, our editor. She is our Teacher with a capital *T*, and we owe our best work around teaching, writing workshop, and specifically literary essay to her. Lucy led us in this project from the beginning, challenging our thinking and pushing us beyond what we could have expected from ourselves. And then, like any great teacher, she released the responsibility to us and let us write with great independence, conferring and coaching regularly. We dedicate this book to her.

Lucy is the Founding Director of the Teachers College Reading and Writing Project, the organization to which we belong. This book could not have come to fruition without the help and wisdom (and in some cases, the pens) of our colleagues. We'd like to thank Simone Fraser, whose eagerness to pilot the book in some of the classrooms she supports led to a groundswell of student work that appears in these pages. Then, too, we'd like to thank Kelly Boland Hohne, whose unparalleled brilliance shone on our book periodically throughout the process and led the way to new directions as we wrote. Ali Marron also cast her surgical eyes on this book and helped us stitch together parts into a whole to ensure that this book reads and teaches as seamlessly as we hope it does. Julia Mooney helped us guide the book home toward the end of the writing process, and Mary Ehrenworth provided us with key advice and words in all matters of teaching editing. Janet Steinberg, who is especially involved behind the scenes with PARCC and SBAC, gave us suggestions that aided us as we wrote Bend III. Kathleen Tolan helped us think smartly about the checklist and assessment system for the unit. Marjorie Martinelli crafted the gorgeous artwork you see in the book's charts. We also thank our colleagues in our literary essay think tank who helped us brainstorm ideas and pathways forward as we wrote: Hannah Arlone, Dominique Freda, Gary Petersen, and Emily Smith. We are lucky to have such intelligent and helpful colleagues and friends.

We also want to thank the people at Heinemann who helped make this the physical book you hold in your hands right now. Tracy Wells, our editor, has the eyes of an owl, a mind like an atlas, and the heart of a counselor. We thank Tracy for her ability to see the details, large and small, and to help keep us organized and moving forward. Anything in our book that appears visually accessible and easy to access gives us cause to thank Elizabeth Valway and Amanda Mullins, who organized and designed the book's artwork and digital resources.

Some of our deepest gratitude goes to the students and teachers who piloted this book. It is the work of these writers and educators who truly make this book come to life. By the time the participating classrooms had finished piloting the book, we had so much work to choose from that it took us an afternoon to sift through it all! We'd like to thank the fifth-graders and teachers at PS 267 and PS 40 in Manhattan, PS 101 in Queens, PS 449 in the South Bronx, and PS 9 in Brooklyn. Specifically, we'd like to thank Kara Fischer, Daria Agosta, and Laticia Robinson for submitting countless pieces of student work and providing key feedback all along the way. This book belongs to you and your writers as much as it belongs to anyone.

Finally, we'd like to thank you, dear reader, in advance, for making this book come to life in your own classroom. We hope you get as much joy from teaching literary essay as we had writing about it.

—Katie and Mike

Contents

BEND I Crafting a Literary Essay around a Shared Text

In this session, you'll guide students through an inquiry to explore the characteristics of essays to help them transfer previous learning to the work of the unit—writing literary essays.

In this session, you'll teach students that one way to generate ideas for a literary essay is to read with extra alertness, seeing more in the details of the text.

In this session, you'll teach students that writers can craft several possible thesis statements to see which one fits what they are really trying to say about a text.

In this session, you'll teach students that one way writers support their claim is by crafting mini-stories that are angled to highlight the writer's point and that balance storytelling as well as summarizing.

In this session, you'll teach students that writers use checklists to get ready to draft. Specifically, you'll teach that when writers flash-draft a literary essay, it helps to rehearse it in the air with the qualities of good essay writing in mind.

BEND II Lifting the Level of Interpretive Essay (and Writing One from Start to Finish)

In this session, you'll teach writers that essayists study small, specific details or the parts that feel odd or important to grow big ideas and interpretations.

In this session, you'll remind students that one way literary essayists generate ideas is to closely study the times when characters face trouble, knowing that often the character or the reader learns a lesson from those experiences.

BEND III Writing for Transfer: Carrying What You Know about Literary Essay across Your Day, Your Reading, Your Life

 Registration instructions to access the digital resources that accompany this book may be found on p. xii.

Welcome to the Unit

Fifth-graders are on the brink of an important time in their lives. Within a year or two, they'll be teenagers, with all that comes during those tumultuous times: crushes, acne, school dances . . . and yes, literary essays. In middle school and beyond, it will be standard fare for teachers to assign students to write literary essays about the theme of *To Kill a Mockingbird*, or *Animal Farm*, or other literary texts.

We remember when our teachers gave us similar assignments, and what we remember most about those assignments was the sense that we'd been given a destination without also being given a map. We knew our teachers had very specific expectations, but the assignment wasn't like others we'd been given. After all, whereas when teachers assigned us to write a poem, a mystery, a story, we could rummage around the library and find one that could serve as an exemplar, when we were assigned literary essays, such models weren't available.

In part, this book (and indeed, this unit) is the how-to guide that we were never given. In a step-by-step way, with as much clarity as possible, the unit helps kids learn how to proceed when they are asked to write a literary essay about *To Kill a Mockingbird*—or about any other literary text. You'll teach kids to draw upon what they already know about good essay writing, to think analytically about texts, and to craft claims that can be supported with evidence across texts.

But we hope that this unit goes a step further: we hope this book helps students realize the reasons to write literary essays in the first place. Certainly, writing analytically about texts matters in our current climate of high-stakes testing. Students are often called to generate ideas about texts and then write to support their ideas about those texts. Excelling on these tasks opens doors of opportunity to students. It helps give them access to the colleges and careers they are most interested in. This unit prepares students for the work of reading analytically and then writing to develop claims across a variety of texts, both narrative and non-narrative.

That said, this work being valued on high-stakes assessments is not enough to warrant an entire unit of study. What adds additional value to this unit is that it teaches the work of academics, of literary scholars. Through the act of writing an essay about a text, we are channeled to read, reread, and rethink the text in increasingly sophisticated ways. Writing about something leads you to see more in it—to notice things you might pass by otherwise and to have new and original thoughts about it. And, when you notice something new and unique in a text, it's particularly powerful to share that with others. This unit affords your writers this opportunity.

We want to convey to students the importance of literary essay, partly because the expectations for students have never been higher. Look ahead at the SAT Essay section or visit a high school English or social studies classroom to see the new writing demands that are being placed on students. The expectations can feel daunting and overwhelming, both to you and to students. In these situations, students are often called to craft a precise central claim, offer a thorough, well-considered evaluation of how an author builds an argument in a text, and develop counterclaims that anticipate the audience's knowledge level, values, and possible biases. Faced with sky-high expectations, it's easy to feel unsure where to begin.

Luckily, there is a starting point. One of the primary beliefs undergirding our thinking at the Teachers College Reading and Writing Project is that wherever you are as a reader or writer, there's a place for you to begin, and there are simple and clear steps you can take that will get you to the next step and then the next one and the next one.

In his song "Forever Young," Bob Dylan imagines building a ladder to the stars. In this unit, you build a ladder to the stars for your students. You present them with a crystal clear path that will help them craft structured literary essays and more confidently tackle any opinion writing scenario they're faced with. Across the unit, you'll teach your writers strategies to grow strong interpretations that are grounded in the text. You'll help them to craft claims that forecast what the rest of their essay will teach and then to develop each of their supports across their essay, drawing on varied techniques to do so. Throughout the process, you'll meet students precisely where they are as writers and provide next steps to help them climb that ladder to the stars.

If you are teaching from the Units of Study in Opinion/Argument, Information, and Narrative Writing or the Units of Study for Teaching Reading, you'll find that this unit nestles in neatly with the other units. This unit builds off of two foundational fourth-grade units of study in opinion writing: *Boxes and Bullets: Personal and Persuasive Essays* and *The Literary Essay: Writing About Fiction*. These units supported students in creating essays with solid organizational structures in which they developed claims, grouped related ideas, and elaborated on their ideas with specific examples. If you're teaching this after the fifth-grade reading unit *Interpretation Book Clubs: Analyzing Themes*, you'll notice many ways in which this unit builds off of your earlier instruction. Frequently, you'll reference teaching points from that unit and bring back familiar charts, supporting students in carrying what they've learned from their reading units into their new writing work. Then, too, this unit prepares students for the teaching that is to come. You might choose to follow this unit with two other fifth-grade writing units that support students in strengthening their opinion writing skills: *The Research-Based Argument Essay* and *Shaping Texts: From Essay and Narrative to Memoir*.

While this unit is ultimately a writing unit, know that you will also strengthen your students' reading skills. Your children will learn to read closely and carefully, and you'll teach them to pay attention to the details in their texts, alert that those details carry significance. Then, as the unit continues, you'll ask students to shift their focus to interpretation, so they are developing deeper ideas about the lessons and themes in their texts. You'll teach students strategies that help them determine themes, including moving from specific and concrete particulars to sky-high ideas, as well as studying times when characters face trouble to note the lessons the character or the reader learned in that situation. Then, too, you'll teach students that readers don't hold fast to their initial ideas about a text. Instead, they rethink their ideas as they read on and reread.

This unit has three main parts, or "bends." Across this unit, you will strengthen students' analytical reading skills and support them in writing well-structured, evidence-based opinion pieces across a variety of text types. In Bend I, you'll help students craft literary essays around a shared digital text.

You'll help students strengthen their skills in close reading, developing thesis statements, identifying evidence that fits a claim, and crafting angled ministories. Students will draft a literary essay to support a claim about a character or theme. Then, in Bend II, students will write a new literary essay, this time off of a text they select. One of our goals is to make sure that students make continual progress up the ladder, improving their writing so it shows their increased prowess as writers. To support this goal, you'll teach students strategies literary essayists draw on to develop interpretations and craft thesis statements that are closely tied to the text. You'll also teach new ways writers can support their claims, such as including an analysis of the author's craft, and you'll help students lift the level of their essays by strengthening their beginnings and endings and editing their writing to prepare it for publication. Finally, in Bend III, you'll help students transfer everything they've learned about writing literary essays to help them write varied opinion texts on a range of topics. Across this work, you'll set students up to be their own job captains, to take control of their own learning, so as to equip them to write well and solve their own problems in middle school and beyond.

OVERVIEW OF THE UNIT
Bend I: Crafting a Literary Essay around a Shared Text

In Bend I of this unit, students will write a literary essay in which they develop and support a claim about a character or theme in a shared text. This part of the unit is meant to be brief, and you'll take students through this process in a week from start to finish. If your students have grown up with Units of Study in Opinion/Argument, Information, and Narrative Writing, they are not new to opinion writing. To ensure students draw on all this knowledge as the unit begins, you'll tell students, "Learning how to do something new typically requires us to draw on everything we already know and to transfer what we already know to that new situation." Then, you'll recruit them to try this out as part of an inquiry into sample student literary essays, noting the big parts typically included in the literary essays that they've previously encountered.

Early in the unit, you'll introduce students to a digital text, the "Panyee Football Club" video, which they write off of across Bend I. To start, you'll teach students that people read (or watch) differently when they intend to write about their reading. They'll read with a writerly wide-awakeness, noticing details, and then write to grow ideas about the characters and themes from the tiny details in the text. Perhaps they'll notice the bent nail jutting out of the soccer field, the characters' bare feet, or the broken shutter on one of the buildings. Those small details can carry big significance in a text.

This first bend is fast-paced, and by Session 3, you'll teach students to develop claims about their texts. You'll compare the process to shopping for clothes. You'll say to students, "Just as a shopper tries on different clothes before finding the shirt or coat that fits perfectly, so too an essayist tries on different thesis statements before finding one that fits what the essayist wants to say." Then, you'll introduce students to several thesis templates they can use to build a structured essay with a thesis and supports. Specifically, you'll teach them to first state their ideas—their claim—and then to write a second sentence that forecasts their essay's structure. This scaffold will be emphasized less and less as the unit progresses. Expect students to fill a page or two in their notebook with different ways their thesis could go.

To help students prepare for drafting, you'll teach one strategy that essayists use to back up their claims about a text. You'll teach that essayists can craft mini-stories, angled to highlight their key points, that make readers pause and say, "Oh yes, I agree with the claim you're making." To lift the level of these stories, you'll return to a key theme of this unit—transfer—and ask students to recall all they know about narrative writing from earlier units.

Students will use checklists to help them remember to draw on all they know. Checklists are particularly powerful tools. They've helped pilots avoid plane crashes, helped parents remember what to pick up at the grocery store, and helped hospitals reduce their infection rates in the intensive care unit. It's only fitting that you teach students how to work with these tools well. To start, you'll teach students that they can use a familiar chart as a checklist—in this case, the "What Makes a Literary Essay?" chart they authored in Session 1—to rehearse their essay about the "Panyee Football Club" video aloud, making sure they have all the parts they need before drafting. Then, students will draft fast and furious, pouring their writing out onto the page, drafting their essay in one sitting.

Bend II: Lifting the Level of Interpretive Essay (and Writing One from Start to Finish)

Bend II focuses on lifting the level of students' interpretive writing skills. To start, you'll invite students to self-select narrative texts they want to think more deeply about, and you'll introduce your students to additional strategies to help them write to grow ideas. On the very first day of the bend, in Session 6, you'll share with them a quote by writer Richard Price: "The bigger the issue, the smaller you write." You'll tell students, "When you want to think about something really big, it helps to start with the small, specific details and think and write a lot about those." This work, of starting with the specific and then shifting up to big, in-the-clouds ideas, will help your students grow powerful interpretations about their texts. Then, you'll support students in studying times when their characters face troubles, cognizant of the fact that characters and readers often learn from those experiences. Students will draw on their growing repertoire of strategies as they write.

After a few days of work growing ideas, you'll suggest students shift their focus to their thesis statement. First, they'll revisit the thesis templates you introduced to them in Bend I and use those to craft interpretative thesis statements. Then, you'll tell students, "Essayists don't just settle for their first rough draft of a thesis; they revise that thesis statement over and over to make it stronger." Students will check their thesis statements against the text, rereading parts with their PTSs—their possible thesis statements—in mind, asking, "Does what I have claimed about the book actually go with the text? Does it actually ring true?" This process will help your writers develop thesis statements that capture a precise theme and are well substantiated by the text.

Students will then take their elaboration work to the next level. You'll support students in finding and ranking quotes that best fit their supports, and you'll teach them to weave those quotes seamlessly into their writing. Then, you'll add to students' repertoire of strategies, teaching them that they can support their claims with parallel lists and with an analysis of the author's craft. You'll help students use the Narrative Goals and Techniques cards, a favorite tool from pilot classrooms, to notice and name the craft moves that their authors make.

As the bend draws to a close, you'll help students prepare their essays for publication, teaching them to strengthen their beginnings and endings so that they draw on what's significant about the text. You'll support students as they chart their own course through a series of editing seminar stations designed to address your students' grammar and convention needs. You might offer stations on verb tense, use of commas, use of punctuation while quoting, pronoun-antecedent agreement, and others.

You'll want the bend to culminate with a celebration, so students have an opportunity to share their literary essays with a broader community. We detail several suggestions for how this celebration might go. What matters most is that you help students see the broader purpose behind this kind of writing.

Bend III: Writing for Transfer: Carrying What You Know about Literary Essay across Your Day, Your Reading, Your Life

Bend III of the unit focuses on helping students transfer all they know about crafting powerful literary essays to write any opinion text they may encounter in the future. You'll start by letting students in on a secret. You'll tell them, "This whole time, you've been thinking you were becoming stronger and stronger as literary essayists, and you were actually developing your skills as opinion writers in general. *Literary* essays are, after all, essays, and essays are a kind of opinion writing." You'll channel students to study samples of opinion and argument writing, noting the similarities between those pieces and literary essays. They'll study persuasive speeches about leadership, editorials about whether video games should be considered a sport, extended responses about rats, and others.

Noticing the similarities between literary essays and other opinion pieces will set students up to tackle any challenges that come their way. Over the next day, you'll coach students as they draw different opinion writing scenarios out of a hat, study those scenarios, and then apply all their knowledge to that new situation. To tackle these scenarios, students will draw on their narrative texts from Bends I and II and a few articles on leadership they studied at the start of this bend. Students might give advice to a character about how to become a better leader, compare and contrast the content and craft moves within two texts, or craft a petition convincing the principal to offer a course on leadership skills at the school.

During this time, you'll lift the level of students' work, teaching them that writers consider how to logically order their supports and evidence within their texts. You'll coach them as they sort and rank their reasons and evidence, choosing the order that will best convince their readers of their claim.

After students have experimented with a few different scenarios, you'll invite them to choose one and draft it, leveraging all their prior learning to make their new draft even stronger. You'll see students drafting furiously, with their tools and charts spread out in front of them, drawing on all their resources to help them. The next day, you'll teach students to be their own job captains, analyzing their writing next to the Opinion Writing checklist to see what they are doing well and to determine their goals, and then they'll work like crazy to strengthen their piece. You'll teach students to use writing checklists in a skillful way, so that they really check for evidence before checking things off.

As the unit draws to a close, you'll celebrate the expert knowledge your students have developed and then issue a challenge. You'll say, "Experts don't keep their knowledge to themselves, bottled up inside their brains. Instead, experts share what they know." After some quick preparation of what they'll teach and how they'll teach it, you'll send students off to be essay ambassadors of sorts, dispersing around the school, leading small groups for third- and fourth-graders on topics of their expertise. You'll want to scurry from room to room after them, in awe of all they've learned over a few short weeks.

ASSESSMENT

Before you start the unit, we recommend you take a bit of time to establish a baseline understanding of your students' skills as opinion writers. This assessment is crucial to help you see where your students' work lies in the trajectory of writing development. The tools that will help you do this work—the learning progressions, rubrics, checklists, and leveled exemplar texts—will help you see clearly what some steps are to improvement for the whole class. Then, too, this assessment is necessary for you to track each individual's progress—and to help your students see themselves improving.

The writing assessment referenced in this unit is part of a broader assessment system designed by colleagues at the Teachers College Reading and Writing Project to help kindergarten through eighth-grade teachers assess students' writing and track students' growth over time, as well as to empower students to identify and work toward purposeful goals across three main genres: opinion, information, and narrative writing. *Writing Pathways* was initially included as part of the grade-by-grade Units of Study in Opinion/ Argument, Information, and Narrative Writing, and it has since been published as a stand-alone book: *Writing Pathways: Performance Assessments and Learning Progressions, Grades K–8.* This book includes several chapters about the design of the assessment system, how to utilize it in classrooms, and how to turn much of the assessing work over to students in a way that empowers them. It also includes learning progressions, rubrics, student-friendly checklists, on-demand assessment prompts, benchmark student writing pieces, and leveled exemplar texts across three major genres.

The assessment system is limited to three on-demand assessment prompts: one for opinion, one for information, and one for narrative writing. This is intentional. One could certainly create checklists for every specific type of piece students create, for how-tos, lab reports, persuasive letters, speeches, realistic fiction, historical fiction, and so on. However, that would mean students would work with a new checklist and new set of expectations for each new writing piece. There would be little transfer between the personal essays students write at the start of fourth grade and the literary essays they craft at the start of fifth grade, because the tools students use and the language around those tools would differ. Instead, we've found it most effective to give students three main checklists—and to teach them how to use those checklists as they write a variety of pieces within a genre. This boosts transfer and helps students see how their learning connects from unit to unit and from year to year.

We suggest you administer an on-demand opinion writing assessment to students prior to beginning this unit. (The assessment materials—the prompt, learning progression, rubric, and student writing exemplars—are provided in the online resources.) You'll ask students to work furiously for forty-five minutes to produce the best possible opinion writing piece they can. We suggest you hold students to this time constraint, even if they have not finished their piece. You'll receive the most useful information to guide your instruction if this work is absolutely independent, with no input from you save from a few directions at the beginning.

We suggest you begin the day prior to the assessment by sharing the following prompt with students, repeating it on the day of the assessment.

> Think of a topic or issue that you know and care about, an issue around which you have strong opinions. Tomorrow, you will have forty-five minutes to write an opinion or argument text in which you will write your opinion or claim and tell reasons why you feel that way. When you do this, draw on everything you know about essays, persuasive letters, and reviews. If you want to find and use information from a book or another outside source, you may bring that with you tomorrow. Please keep in mind that you'll have forty-five minutes to complete this, so you will need to plan, draft, revise, and edit in one sitting.
>
> In your writing, make sure you:
>
> - Write an introduction.
> - State your opinion or claim.
> - Give reasons and evidence.
> - Organize your writing.
> - Acknowledge counterclaims.
> - Use transition words.
> - Write a conclusion.

Once you have administered the on-demand opinion writing assessment to your students, you'll want to assess where each writer lands on the Learning Progression for Opinion Writing. Note where the bulk of your class lands and let that information inform your plans for this unit. To do so, we suggest you read each student's on-demand piece and compare it to the exemplar texts. Don't worry too much about whether the text matches every one of the descriptors of a level. Do most students state clear claims? Do students back up their claims with specific and varied evidence? General trends will inform your whole-class teaching, and you'll also want to identify needs you'll target through small-group work and through one-on-one conferences.

Once you have a general sense of where a piece lands on the learning progression, you and your students might look to the progression's specific descriptors. These descriptors are particularly useful when you want to help students know specific steps they can take to make their writing better.

We suggest you administer the on-demand assessment again at the end of the unit. An on-demand assessment will allow you and your students to assess progress made from the beginning to the end of the unit. It can also serve as an assessment of your teaching, and of this curriculum, too. After all, you are not aiming to create perfect pieces for bulletin boards, so students' published texts are not the be-all and end-all within this unit. Instead, remember that your teaching within any one day's minilesson or conference is designed to lift the level of the work the writer does not just that day, but also other days and in other writing pieces. In this way, your focus is on teaching the *writer*, not the specific writing piece. Your goal is not to help students produce a few strong pieces, but to lift the level of the work your writers do from now on. You'll look back at the baseline data you collected at the start of the unit and at the work students produce by the end, and you'll marvel at their progress.

GETTING READY

Because this unit has a reading component, you will need to plan for the texts students will write about. Across the bends, we suggest varying the types of texts you ask students to work with, so they have opportunities to write off of digital texts as well as narrative and non-narrative texts.

In Bend I of the unit, we suggest all students work with a beautiful, brief digital text, the "Panyee Football Club" video. This engaging video is a favorite of the Teachers College Reading and Writing Project staff. It tells the story of a group of boys living on a floating fishing village in Thailand who overcome their lack of space and resources to build a floating playing field and become truly great football players. One of the reasons that the Teachers College Reading and Writing Project has made such use of this video is that we know students are being called to work with a wider variety of texts, and it's important that teaching prepares them to work with varied texts more skillfully.

To supplement the digital text, we suggest you distribute copies of the video transcript so students can mark up what they notice. You'll also want to create some digital stills of key moments in the video by taking screenshots. You'll find directions for how to do this in the online resources. Our pilot teachers reported that these materials were particularly beneficial for their students.

If you've worked with the Units of Study in Opinion/Argument, Information, and Narrative Writing, you'll note that we rarely channel all students to devote a week to writing about the same shared text, because choice is a critical tenet of writing workshop classrooms. In this unit, we made the decision to rally the class around a shared text so we could provide more support for students as they embark on this challenging, analytical work. Although there is nothing mandatory about the "Panyee Football Club" video, many teachers have piloted this unit using that text. You can, of course, choose an alternative text. The unit is constructed so that the text is almost a case in point, and another text could be substituted.

By Bend II of the unit, you'll expand choice and rally students to self-select the texts they write off of. Reading alertly is particularly difficult work, and it's important to have a range of texts so that students can read those that are a just-right level for them. We suggest a list of short, narrative texts you might ask students to write off of across this bend. We particularly recommend *One Green Apple* by Eve Bunting, *The Stranded Whale* by Jane Yolen, and *Marshfield Dreams* by Ralph Fletcher. *Marshfield Dreams* is a collection of memoirs about Ralph Fletcher's childhood, so this one story collection offers a wealth of texts students can write off of. We particularly recommend "Attack," "Last Kiss," "A Pox upon Us All," "Scuttlebutt," and "Tea Rock Lane."

Teachers piloting the unit also found that students had lots to write about other texts as well, including: *Something Beautiful* by Sharon Dennis Wyeth, *Crow Call* by Lois Lowry, *More Stories Julian Tells* by Ann Cameron, *Baseball in April and Other Stories* by Gary Soto, and *My Rotten Red-Headed Older Brother* by Patricia Polacco. Other students even brought in favorite stories from their childhood and wrote off of picture books and story collections. Of course, these texts are just suggestions. If you've read aloud several picture books or short stories to your students over the year, you might choose to substitute those texts for the ones we suggest. Regardless of which texts you choose to provide, you'll want to limit the choices you offer to students to ensure multiple students are studying the same text.

Students will write best off of texts that they've first experienced as readers, so you'll want to make sure they have an opportunity to work with the texts you select prior to Bend II. Teachers who piloted the unit took two different routes to ensure students had read the texts prior to Bend II. Some teachers decided to read the texts aloud to students, using interactive read-aloud over the course of a week to spotlight the short texts students will work with. Other teachers decided to pause the unit for the day, setting aside a special period for reading short texts. Additionally, students will benefit from having copies of the text they are writing off of so they can annotate them.

As you launch Bend III, you'll introduce students to a small packet of opinion texts. These texts are available to print and copy from the online resources. Students will pair these texts with the narrative texts they worked with across Bends I and II.

To guide their work with these texts, you'll provide students with a set of scenario cards, each representing a different opinion writing scenario. Some of the scenarios represent real-world ways students might be called to use their opinion writing skills, and others represent the kinds of prompts students encounter on high-stakes tests across the country. We encourage you to supplement the scenarios with the state-specific kinds of prompts your students will see on these assessments to better prepare them for all the ways they'll be asked to use their literary essay knowledge in the future.

You won't want to miss out on the fun of writing about texts, so we suggest a set of teacher texts. In Bend I, you'll alternate between demonstrating using the "Panyee Football Club" video and "Little Red Riding Hood." In Bend II, we use "Shells" from *Every Living Thing*, a short story collection by Cynthia Rylant. Students will work with this text often across your minilessons, so it's important they are familiar with it prior to the launch of this bend.

We recommend reading it aloud to students. In Bend III, we suggest you draw on texts you've worked with across the unit for your demonstrations, supplementing with a few of the new articles introduced in Bend III.

Additionally, you'll want to think about ways you can group students across the unit. Students will need to be matched with a writing partner for Bend I of the unit. To partner students, you might draw on data from the on-demand writing assessments, as well as your knowledge of students. You'll ask students to sit next to their writing partner when you gather them in the meeting area and to work with that partner regularly across the workshop.

By Bend II of the unit, you'll channel students into informal clubs with other students who are reading the same short text. You might, for instance, group together four students who are reading *The Stranded Whale*, three who are reading "Last Kiss," and four reading "A Pox upon Us All." These clubs will meet together regularly in Bend II, and they will support each other in developing more nuanced, text-based interpretations. You'll note that there are several days where these clubs are asked to sit together on the rug or meet together during the Share. In Bend III, students will return to their writing partnerships.

You'll find particularly helpful resources you can draw on across this unit in the online resources. Some examples are:

- samples of student work from various stages of the writing process; all the student work displayed in the unit can be accessed and printed from the online resources

- classroom charts, lists of prompts, and other teaching tools

- the Opinion Writing checklist

- homework assignments for use throughout the unit.

ONLINE DIGITAL RESOURCES

A variety of resources to accompany this unit of study are available in the online resources, including charts and examples of student work shown throughout *Literary Essay: Opening Texts and Seeing More*, as well as links to other electronic resources. Offering daily support for your teaching, these materials will help you provide a structured learning environment that fosters independence and self-direction.

To access and download all the digital resources for *Literary Essay*:

1. Go to **www.heinemann.com** and click the link in the upper right to log in. (If you do not have an account yet, you will need to create one.)

2. **Enter the following registration code** in the box to register your product: WUOS_LEVP5.

3. Enter the security information requested.

4. Once you have registered your product it will appear in the list of My Online Resources.

(You may keep copies of these resources on up to six of your own computers or devices. By downloading the files you acknowledge that they are for your individual or classroom use and that neither the resources nor the product code will be distributed or shared.)

◆ START WITH ASSESSMENT ◆

Dear Teachers,

Soon, you'll turn to Session 1 of this unit and launch your students' work with literary essay writing. Before you turn the page, we want to urge you to take one forty-five-minute period to give your students an on-demand writing assessment. We suggest you begin the day prior to the assessment by sharing the following prompt with students, repeating it on the day of the assessment. This gives students the opportunity to bring in an outside text with them to reference in their on-demand writing. It's unlikely many of your fifth-graders will choose to bring in a resource, but we felt it was important to include, because by middle school, they will be expected to cite information from trustworthy sources within their opinion pieces.

We urge you to keep the prompt as is. If your school is teaching from the Units of Study in Opinion/Argument, Information, and Narrative Writing, using common prompts across classes will allow you to compare the work students produce from class to class and from grade to grade. At the same time, keeping the prompt open-ended helps all students have an equal opportunity to be successful, since they can write about a topic they know deeply and feel strongly about.

Many teachers choose to project the prompt or display it on a chart in the room so students can access it during the assessment:

> Think of a topic or issue that you know and care about, an issue around which you have strong opinions. Tomorrow, you will have forty-five minutes to write an opinion or argument text in which you will write your opinion or claim and tell reasons why you feel that way. When you do this, draw on everything you know about essays, persuasive letters and reviews. If you want to find and use information from a book or another outside source, you may bring that with you tomorrow. Please keep in mind that you'll have forty-five minutes to complete this, so you will need to plan, draft, revise, and edit in one sitting.

In your writing, make sure you:

- Write an introduction.
- State your opinion or claim.
- Give reasons and evidence.
- Organize your writing.

- Acknowledge counterclaims.
- Use transition words.
- Write a conclusion.

You'll want this assessment to be absolutely independent, so you have a snapshot of what students can do on their own, with no input from others. While students are writing, you might use the time to jot observations. Are students appealing for help with spelling? Writing a few words and then stopping to look around? Unsure of what topic to write about? Jot these observations, as they can better inform your teaching.

Look to the "Assessment" section in the Welcome to the Unit for tips about how you can analyze your students' on-demand assessments and determine next steps for instruction. You'll want to draw on the Learning Progression for Opinion Writing, Rubric for Opinion Writing, and leveled writing samples as you do this work. These tools are provided in the online resources, and the *Writing Pathways: Performance Assessments and Learning Progressions, Grades K–8* book will be an invaluable resource as you study your writers' work.

Remember to pause again at the end of this unit, and set aside another day for assessment using the same prompt and time constraints. Your students will be able to hold their pre- and post-on-demand assessments next to one another, noting specific ways their writing has improved and setting goals to guide their future work. You'll be able to see visible ways their writing has grown stronger, reflect on your own teaching practice, and gain information about what to tackle with students in your future units.

Happy assessing!

Katie and Mike

Inquiry into Essay

IN THIS SESSION, you'll guide students through an inquiry to explore the characteristics of essays to help them transfer previous learning to the work of the unit—writing literary essays.

GETTING READY

✔ Prior to today's session, be sure you have given students the opinion on-demand assessment. Read the Start with Assessment section for more information about administering this assessment.

✔ Prior to today's session, students should read the short story "Eleven" by Sandra Cisneros, or you may choose to read it aloud (see Teaching and Active Engagement).

✔ Prepare an anchor chart with the inquiry question "What Makes a Literary Essay?" (see Teaching and Active Engagement, and Share).

✔ Provide copies of the literary essay "Eleven" by Adam to each student (see Teaching and Active Engagement).

✔ Plan small groups of writing partners by matching two sets of partners together and be ready to reveal those matches to students (see Link).

✔ For each small group of writing partners, make a packet of mentor literary essays for students to study. We recommend "Eleven" by Adam, "Fox," "The Marble Champ" by Judah, and "A Literary Essay on 'The Marble Champ'" by Ali, but you can substitute other structured literary essays (see Link).

✔ Create small cards with a few language prompts to help guide small-group talk about essays (see Conferring and Small-Group Work).

✔ Be prepared to hand back students' on-demand essays to revise this evening (see Homework).

WHEN I WAS YOUNG, I loved to visit the community pool. The pool had a high dive, and when I was finally old enough to jump off it, my father urged me to give it a go. "Go on, it will be fun. You're old enough, and you've taken your swimming lessons. Jump in," he said. I peered up to the diving board and watched kid after kid jump, squealing, into the pool. I shook my head. No thanks. The high dive wasn't for me.

My cousin, who was my age, wasn't as apprehensive. He climbed the ladder and immediately plunged off the diving board with a massive cannon ball. When I saw him emerge from the diving pool grinning and proud, I let my competitive instinct kick in. I would do it. I would jump off the high dive.

I approached the ladder and looked up. There were lots of rungs to climb, but I climbed them, one by one. As I reached the top, I clung to the rail. My cousin and father stood below, waving at me, urging me to jump. I inched toward the edge of the diving board. My toes curled over the edge. I closed my eyes.

Jump in.

At the start of this unit, you issue that same invitation to your students. "Jump in," you say to them. "Come on into the world of academic writing," you say, and then invite them to first read and then write literary essays.

The ability to compose a clear argument, one that is organized and that references texts well, is important for success in high school, college, and professional life. This unit, then, not only prepares your students for writing they'll be asked to do on high-stakes assessments—it also prepares them for writing they'll be asked to do throughout their academic lives and beyond.

This session especially invites students to read literary essays, naming the moves that the authors have made, in ways that ask your students to call to mind what they probably already know about how to write an essay well. You'll channel students to look at an essay, asking, "What makes an essay? What are the big parts? How do they fit together?" and then to answer those questions as best they can. The next session then says to kids: "Try it! Jump in!"

For today, however, you will particularly want to highlight ways in which the essays are structured. When a student says, "I see three parts that go with the big idea, and the writer thinks one of those parts is the most important of all," be ready to coach students. "That's right," you'll say. "An essayist backs up his or her claim with supports and weighs which supports will best fit with the claim." In this way, you'll alternate between channeling students to notice something that strikes them as done particularly well, urging them to use their own words to describe it, and then naming the moves in more academic language.

"The ability to compose a clear argument is important for success in high school, college, and professional life."

This constructivist method of channeling students to name and understand the process of an essay before you name it directly is at the heart of guided inquiry. This session is an act of immersion, Brian Cambourne's very first "condition of learning."

As you enter into this session, you'll want to take a look at the data from your students' on-demand writing assessments, which you will want to give prior to Session 1, to see what previous learning students have carried with them, and what elements of essay writing the class may need more support with. In that way, the data from the on-demand can guide you to highlight which aspects of essay you most want your writers to pay attention to today. See the Welcome to the Unit for more information about the on-demand assessment and suggestions for how to use the results to guide your teaching across this unit.

This unit stands on the shoulders of other writing units, particularly the Grade 4 units *Boxes and Bullets: Personal and Persuasive Essays* and *The Literary Essay: Writing About Fiction*, part of the Units of Study in Opinion/Argument, Information, and Narrative Writing. If your writers did not experience this unit in fourth grade, then you will need some minor adjustments to fit your writers' needs. You'll find tips for tailoring this session in the italics in the margins of the session.

In this first bend of the unit, students will conduct an inquiry into noticing the big parts of the essay and how they go together. Then, you'll spend the next four sessions guiding students to write their own essay off a shared text. We've chosen a wildly popular video about the Panyee Football Club. With this video text, you'll channel students to read closely to grow ideas, and to write long about those ideas. Then you'll teach students to craft a thesis with supports. After that, you'll show students how writers can use mini-stories and lists to reveal examples of those supports. Finally, the bend ends with writers flash-drafting their essays off the shared video text.

Inquiry into Essay

CONNECTION

Use common examples to highlight how learning something new typically requires us to transfer everything we already know.

"Remember earlier this year when I taught you to multiply fractions? We didn't just start over from scratch, forgetting everything we already knew. Instead, we had to first think, 'What do I know about multiplication? And, what do I know about fractions?' and then we used all that information to help us. Or, think about when the gym teacher was teaching you how to shoot layups. You didn't just pick up a basketball and shoot perfect layups in an instant. Right? Instead, you had to put together everything you know about shooting, dribbling, and aiming together to help you take on that new work.

"Learning how to do something new typically requires us to draw on everything we already know and to transfer what we already know to that new situation. In this way, our understanding builds, as we attach our new learning onto the things we already know."

Introduce the new work of the unit. Rally students around the importance of literary essay and how it is valued in the world of schooling.

"Today we're launching a new unit. You'll be crafting literary essays. This is a kind of writing that schools really care about. Here's the thing about a literary essay—kids who not only can write well but also can read well. To write a good literary essay, a writer needs deep, thoughtful ideas about a text. *And* the writer needs to be able to use writing to put an idea, not just an experience, onto the page. That's hard.

"Writing literary essays is big work. High school students do that all the time! But luckily, you aren't starting from scratch. I was talking to your fourth-grade teachers last night, and it turns out you already know quite a bit about writing essays. To show me what you already know, your fourth-grade teachers started pulling out all these mentor essays that you studied last year. I've borrowed those essays so that today, you can study them to remind yourself of everything you already know about essay writing. Are you game?"

You are referencing the student sample essays, originally included in the fourth-grade unit The Literary Essay: Writing About Fiction, *part of* Units of Study in Opinion, Information, and Narrative Writing. *If your students have not experienced this instruction, you'll want to modify this bit of your minilesson. For example, you could highlight that whenever writers begin a new project, it is helpful for them to have a vision of the end product in mind. You might say, "Writers, whether you are learning to multiply fractions, shoot a layup, or embark on a writing project, it's helpful to know what the end product is supposed to look like so that you can envision your progress along the way."*

❖ **Name the inquiry question.**

"The question we'll be researching today is, 'What makes a literary essay? What, exactly, are the big parts, and how do they fit together?'"

TEACHING AND ACTIVE ENGAGEMENT

Introduce the inquiry to students. Set students up to listen and annotate the text, marking up the essay's characteristics, as you read the text aloud.

I quickly distributed copies of Adam's literary essay "Eleven" to the students. "Readers, I'm hoping we can study this essay, 'Eleven,' written by Adam, like an architect might study a building. Architects construct buildings, and when they look at other buildings, they study how they are made, how the building parts go together to make a whole structure. Will you study this essay like an architect, thinking about our inquiry question, 'What are the big parts of literary essays?' Jot notes as we go, annotating the text with what you notice, or draw boxes and arrows that help you keep track. I'll pause along the way so we can share our thinking." I started reading.

"Eleven" by Adam

In literature, authors write a lot about one character being upset and taking it out on another person. Sandra Cisneros's essay "Eleven" is about a girl named Rachel who is mistreated by her teacher and in return mistreats her classmates.

Alternate between reading a small passage of text and asking students to jot notes, turn and talk while you coach, and share what they've found with the class.

"Readers, we've just read a small passage, and there's already a lot to notice about our inquiry question, about the big parts of essays. Go back with your partner and reread this part, marking it up with what you notice." While students worked, I knelt to coach, reminding students to point to evidence in the text that matched what they were describing.

I gave students a minute to talk and then said, "Let's chart what you're already noticing about the big parts of essays." I asked Rafael to share. "It starts with an introduction," he said.

"Be specific. What do you notice about the parts of the introduction? Turn and talk with your partner." As students talked, I began adding the anchor chart Post-it notes.

Readers, you needn't choose this text—you could instead select one from students in your own school, or another text from the book. We thought the essay "Eleven" might be especially helpful since this is a text that students studied in Narrative Craft, *the first unit for fifth grade in* Units of Study in Opinion, Information, and Narrative Writing. *"Eleven" is also a brief and enormously popular text—one you could read aloud quickly if your students don't already know it. Hopefully you won't need to do that reading aloud within this minilesson but could get it done another time.*

If none of your students share the big parts of essays listed on the exemplar chart, you might choose to say, "I heard you saying . . ." and then chart the responses as if students said them. Or, you might coach into a partnership that is approximating the work, helping them generate the language needed to name different parts of the essay.

What Makes a Literary Essay?

- Starts with an introduction
  - Hooks the reader
  - Names the author and text
  - States a claim and some supports

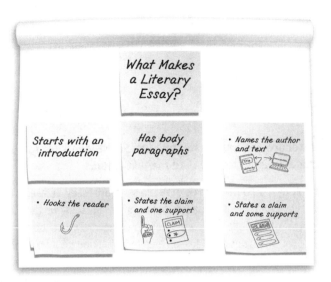

"Let's read a bit more with our question in mind, pushing ourselves to notice the big things the author is doing—like including an introduction—as well as the smaller parts—hooking the reader, naming the author and text, and so on." I read the next passage aloud, pausing to remind students to jot when I noticed their pens were down.

> Rachel is mistreated by her teacher. Mrs. Price finds an ugly, old sweater in the coat room and forces Rachel to put it on. Rachel says "That's not . . . mine," but Mrs. Price moves on to the next math problem without understanding Rachel, saying "Of course it's yours." Mrs. Price says "I remember you wearing it once." This is mistreatment because Mrs. Price isn't respecting Rachel. Mrs. Price doesn't care about what Rachel has to say. Later, right before the bell rings, Mrs. Price pretends as if everything's okay, ignoring the real pain Rachel is feeling.

"Are you noticing a ton more now? Turn and study this like an architect, noting the big parts and how they're held together."

I coached students as they talked, then I asked Julia to share what she and her partner had noticed. "He gave the claim again. And he gave the first support, that Rachel is mistreated by her teacher." I added to our chart and said, "As we read on, we'll have to see if *all* the body paragraphs go that way—does the author usually start a new body paragraph by repeating the claim and then giving another support that fits with the claim?"

If your students have not experienced essay work prior to this unit, you might channel them to name what they see in their own words. Then, once they strike upon something in the essay that matches your goals, give students the academic vocabulary that matches what they noticed. For instance, if a student says, "The writer has a big idea at the beginning," you might reply, "Exactly! And the fancy word for the big idea in an essay is a claim."

What Makes a Literary Essay?

- Starts with an introduction
  - Hooks the reader
  - Names the author and text
  - States a claim and some supports
- **Has body paragraphs**
  - **States the claim and one support**

Marco chimed in. "There's also a ton of evidence to back up the claim."

"Go back to that paragraph and notice what kinds of evidence this author is using to back up his claim. Be specific. Turn and talk!" After a minute, I called students back and recorded what they noticed. "What I am hearing you saying is that the author uses different kinds of evidence. Did any of you notice that the author used a story to support his claim?" I asked, marking off the story that was embedded in the first body paragraph. Students nodded.

"What do you notice the author doing here?" I read a bit of the text aloud. "Adam wrote, 'Rachel says "That's not . . . mine," but Mrs. Price moves on to the next math problem without understanding Rachel, saying "Of course it's yours."' What might the author be doing here?"

The kids noticed the writer was using words directly from the text. I said, "Oh, it must be that he's quoting the text, choosing the words that really support his claim. Let's add that to our chart."

> **ANCHOR CHART**
>
> ### What Makes a Literary Essay?
>
> - Starts with an introduction
>   - Hooks the reader
>   - Names the author and text
>   - States a claim and some supports
> - Has body paragraphs
>   - States the claim and one support
>   - **Gives evidence that shows the support is true**

> - Gives evidence
>   that shows the
>   support is true

LINK

Set students up to work in small groups, annotating a set of mentor essays to note their characteristics.

"Writers, look at how much you've already noticed! You're noticing and marking up the big parts of this essay and how they fit together, things that you learned how to do when you were in fourth grade last year. This kind of close, careful looking can help you recall all that you already know, which will help you as you take on these more challenging literary essays.

"When you head off today, I've matched you and your partner with another partnership, and I've prepared a little folder of literary essays I borrowed from your fourth-grade teachers for all of you to read. You'll want to read them with our question in mind, marking them up to capture what you're noticing about the big parts of each essay and how they fit together. You can design your own system to help you—annotating in the margins, using sticky notes to flag what you're noticing, or some other system you choose.

"And push yourself to look closely as you do this, the same way that an architect reads plans for a building. Get the big picture, but also look at the small parts, so you can make sense of how each essay is held together."

You'll want to keep an eye on the clock as you move through this minilesson. It's easy for the turn-and-talk intervals to run long and for time to pass as you solicit responses from different students. To keep the inquiry minilesson to ten minutes, you might ensure the turn-and-talk intervals are brief. After the brief turn-and-talks, you might also say, "I heard you saying . . ." and then name what you heard instead of calling on individual students to share.

For students who did not experience an essay unit in fourth grade—in addition to charting what you notice in the inquiry—it may be helpful to annotate an enlarged version of Adam's essay (or the mentor essay you choose) with colored pencils, highlighters, or small sticky notes with labels that name the different parts of the essay. Then you could display the annotated essay while students are working in groups for reference.

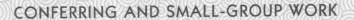

Analyzing Mentor Texts

ODAY'S SESSION LAUNCHES THE WORK OF THIS UNIT, so you'll want to be sure that the conferring and small-group work you do today has some extra fanfare, rallying students to the new work of this unit. You might linger near a group of writers who are analyzing an essay and read aloud an introduction, saying, "Doesn't that writing just pull you in and make you want to read more?" At the next table, you might pause near writers in the midst of an essay, read some particularly beautiful lines of evidence and say, "Wow! It feels like that writer chose precisely the right evidence to support her claim. Out of all the stories she could have chosen from "The Marble Champ," she chose that one. That must have been a tough choice." Your tone of voice and the language you use will help students see the beauty in the essays they're studying and begin thinking about the effect that essay writers can have on their audience.

Join the group as a proficient partner to model the work you want students to emulate.

Your major work of today will be to support the work that students are doing analyzing mentor essay texts to determine their characteristics. If you notice a group of students on a scavenger hunt, simply noting where the characteristics you charted are showing up across different essays, you might coach them to be more specific as they name what they notice. You could join the group as a proficient partner, becoming a member of the conversation to model some particular work you notice students could use support with. The key to effective, proficient partner teaching is to alert students that you are taking on the role and that part of their job is to notice the moves you make to be a strong group member.

For example, when one group member says, "Here's the introduction!" and is ready to label it and move on, you might interject, saying, "Let's look at it more closely. What are the different parts of this introduction?" Or, if students are talking about a part superficially, perhaps naming and circling all the transitions in the piece, you might model how you think deeper about the transitions, saying, "I wonder if all

---

MID-WORKSHOP TEACHING   **Make Your Study Comparative**

When I saw most groups analyzing a second essay, I paused the class. "Writers, eyes up here for a minute. I want to give you a tip. As you move from studying one essay to studying the next essay, you may find it helpful to lay the second alongside the first and to ask, 'What's the same? What's different?' You know the content of each essay is different, so you'll want to push yourselves beyond that as you compare.

"You can do this for the entire essay, noting what's the same and what's different about the ways the two essays are structured. Or, you might read more closely, go smaller, looking at specific parts of the essays. You could lay the two introductions alongside each other, asking, 'What's the same? What do both these introductions have in common?' Also, push yourself to notice what's different. What do only some literary essays have?

"Try this out right now with your group, choosing the parts you want to compare. Talk a lot about what you notice and jot notes about the similarities and differences."

Your students are apt to notice that essays include varied numbers of body paragraphs and that the length of those body paragraphs can really vary, with some essays including large amounts of evidence as supports and others giving very little. Students might notice that some essays mention the author quite a bit, while other essays mention the author only once. They might note that essays have different focuses: some are about characters, whereas others are about themes.

---

these transitions are the same. Some of them sound like *one reason*, *another reason*, but these sound like *one example*, *also*, and these say *this shows*. It feels like different transitions do different work. Let's think more about that." Your prompting, as a proficient partner in the group, will help students notice more in the essays than they had before.

You may need to shift back into direct instruction to make it obvious to students that essays have an overarching structure, that the heart of an essay is its thesis and supports—its trunk and branches, so to speak. You might say to a group, "You noticed that the introduction names the claim and supports, but did you also notice that the claim and each single support is repeated each time a new support is introduced? For instance, take a look here," you might say, pointing explicitly to the first support. "Do you see where the other supports are introduced? What do you notice?" In this way, and across countless other opportunities, you'll want to push writers to notice that essays have a clear structure that is sometimes structured as a claim supported by examples that appear at different times across the story. In other words, you'll push students to see the structure of literary essays that are organized, 'So-and-so is this or that early in the story, in the middle of the story, and most importantly, at the end of the story.'"

Provide students with support in describing the similarities and differences between essays.

It's likely you'll encounter other groups in your class who are able to spot the characteristics of different essays, but who need additional language to describe the ways the essays are similar and different. You might provide these groups with a small card of language prompts, giving them some questions and stems to guide their talk. For example, you might give them a simple tool that says:

Name the similarities.
How are they the same?
What's the same is _____. For example, _____.

Name the differences.
How are they different?
What's different is _____. In this text, _____, but in this text, _____.

To introduce the tool, consider placing it in the center of a group. As you observe the conversation, tap the tool if you notice students could be using prompts from the tool to make their conversation more comparative.

Support students who did not experience a fourth-grade essay unit.

If your students did not experience an essay unit of study in fourth grade, then they may need extra support identifying the same characteristics in the mentor essays that you named in Adam's essay during the minilesson. If you annotated a copy of the mentor essay with the parts of the essay that the class noticed in the inquiry, be sure that essay is displayed for students to reference. This way, students can use the mentor essay as an exemplar for the part of the essay they will be looking at together. It is also helpful to direct students to the kinds of things you want them to notice. If you want to get students to notice transitions, you might feign ignorance and tap on one part of an essay and ask, "What's this? What's going on here?" or "What is the author doing? Do you see that anywhere else?" and then when a student says something like, "It's like the writer is using words to move between different parts of the essay," you might connect the students' noticing to the academic language, saying, "Precisely! And the fancy word for that is *transitions*."

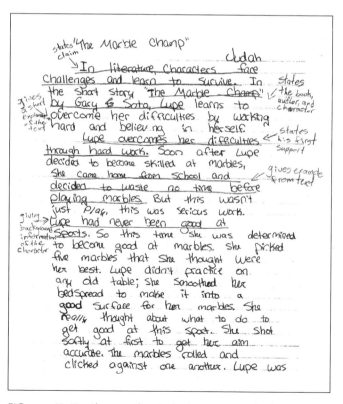

FIG. 1–1 Notice the way the student annotates the literary essay by underlining and labeling the parts.

Determining Literary Essay Characteristics

Collect and chart students' findings about the characteristics of literary essays.

"Writers, let's gather together for our share." Once all the students were seated at the meeting area, I said, "It's pretty incredible what your studies have revealed. Let's share for a few minutes and collect what your groups noted about the characteristics of essays overall and also about the ways essays might be similar or different from one another."

As students shared, I added sticky notes to our chart and occasionally asked the students to turn and talk to elaborate further on a key point. I drew attention to parts of the text the students weren't discussing, reading the part aloud and asking students, "What is *that part* doing?" I restated points the students made. For example, if a student said, "It's got an ending," I said, "It does. It ends with a conclusion, where the writer restates the claim and supports." There were a few parts that students did not mention, and I added them to the chart to fill it out, saying, "One important part I noticed is . . ."

Eventually, our chart looked like this:

REVISING TO STRENGTHEN YOUR ON-DEMAND ESSAY

Writers, you'll remember that we started this unit with an on-demand essay. Tonight you'll be revising your on-demand to make sure your essay has more of the features of the essays we studied today. I'm including a copy of the chart we created in class today that you can use to guide your revision. To start, spend a few minutes rereading your essay, annotating it like you did the sample essays today. Notice ways your on-demand already matches the essays you have studied—and ways it doesn't, but could. Revise your on-demand in big ways, adding or changing whole sections, not just adding in a word or two.

Growing Ideas Means Reading with a Writerly Wide-Awakeness

IN THIS SESSION, you'll teach students that one way to generate ideas for a literary essay is to read with extra alertness, seeing more in the details of the text.

GETTING READY

✔ Be sure students have their writing notebooks with them in the meeting space (see Teaching and Active Engagement).

✔ Prepare to play the "Panyee Football Club" video for students. You may wish to watch the video ahead of time so that you may practice reading the subtitles aloud to students (www.youtube.com/watch?v=jU4oA3kkAWU search terms: Panyee FC short film). A link is available in the online resources (see Connection, Teaching and Active Engagement, and Link).

✔ Begin a "To Craft Powerful, Interpretive Essays . . ." anchor chart (see Link and Share).

✔ Copy the "Panyee Football Club" transcript for each student (see Link).

✔ Prepare sets of the "Panyee Football Club" digital stills for each table. Instructions for creating the stills are available in the online resources (see Link).

✔ If possible, make laptops or tablets available to students so they can view snippets of the "Panyee Football Club" video (see Link).

✔ Prepare a sample of your written work, showing how you generated a lot of thinking off of one sentence in the video (see Conferring and Small-Group Work).

✔ Distribute to students mini-copies of the "To Understand/Interpret a Story, Readers Pay Attention To . . ." chart from the *Interpretation Book Club* unit (see Mid-Workshop Teaching and Share).

I N THEIR BOOK *Falling in Love with Close Reading: Lessons for Analyzing Texts and Life*, Christopher Lehman and Kate Roberts write, "We believe that, as human beings, we already know how to read something closely . . . . You may not always realize you are doing these things, but that is just the point—we already know how to study what we love closely, it is a process, a method, of falling in love. The work, then is to transfer this human ability to the texts we are reading, the texts that surround us, and to some of the areas in our life that go unnoticed" (2013, 8).

Isn't this what the students you teach do every day? They study the emotions on their parents' faces, using the information to decide if this is the precisely best moment to ask for a puppy. They notice when their best friend, who usually pulls up right next to them on the carpet during the read-aloud, suddenly positions himself a few inches further away. And if you, for some reason, forget to change the date on the board before your students walk in, you know they'll scurry right up to you and let you know, while also questioning why you failed to change the date in the first place.

This careful study in which your students are constantly engaging helps them to make more of the world around them. Your major work, then, as Roberts and Lehman remind us, is to help students learn how to transfer this natural ability to the texts they are reading.

Analyzing texts is difficult work, so we're suggesting that, just for the first few days of this unit, you limit choice, and channel all your students to work off of a brief and powerful video text. We recommend the "Panyee Football Club" video, which tells the story of a group of boys living on a floating village, Koh Panyee, in southern Thailand. These boys have loved football for years but have never had the space to play. The boys band together to build a floating playing field, using whatever resources they can secure, and overcome obstacles as they work toward their goal of becoming truly great football players. Of course, you could substitute another short text that has had a particularly strong impact on your writers, but the classes who piloted this unit found that this text resonated deeply with their students, and you'll see it has been woven across the first bend of the unit.

Students will have opportunities to work with the short film during your minilessons, but they'll benefit from having additional access to it as well. If you are able to make a few laptops or iPads available, students will benefit from being able to view the video repeatedly, pausing at key scenes and writing off of those scenes. To supplement the video text, you'll want to provide all students with a transcript of it. We also recommend that you create folders filled with screenshots from key moments in the film. You'll find directions for how to create these in the online resources.

"Students can craft powerful literary essays off texts that matter deeply to them."

If you and your students are working with Units of Study for Teaching Reading, Grade 5 (2015), you will appreciate ways in which this unit builds off of Unit 1, *Interpretation Book Clubs*. In Session 3 of that unit, "Writing about Reading Means Reading with a Writerly Wide-Awakeness," you taught students to push themselves to see more, notice more, think more about the text, cognizant that any details could become grounds for a deeper idea. Initial ideas in hand, you channeled students to read on, carrying those sparks of an idea with them to later parts of the text. This session references that work.

This bend provides a fast-paced introduction to literary essay. Over the next four sessions, you'll teach students to write a clearly structured literary essay. This work will prepare your students to craft powerful literary essays off of texts that matter deeply to them and to respond in quick, on-the-run ways to the essay prompts set out on the standardized tests your fifth-graders are called to take.

Growing Ideas Means Reading with a Writerly Wide-Awakeness

CONNECTION

Introduce the touchstone text for the bend, the "Panyee Football Club" video, and invite students to watch the video straight through, thinking about the plot and characters.

"Have you found a video on YouTube that is so good—maybe it is hilarious or maybe intriguing or maybe important—but in any case, it is so good that you watched it again and again, and shared it with practically everyone you know? Last night I came across one such video—it is called the 'Panyee Football Club,' and it tells the story of a group of boys who start their own football team against a ton of odds. I'm going to play it for you now. The movie has subtitles, and I'm going to read them aloud to you so you can really follow what's happening. And as you watch, note who the characters are, what happens to them, and how their problems are resolved (if they are)." I pressed play and then read the subtitles to students when they appeared. We watched the entire four-minute film.

We recommend reading the subtitles aloud to students while the video plays. This will give them an opportunity to study the images and actions in the story. Alternately, if your workshop is pressed for time, you might dedicate a bit of read-aloud time prior to this lesson to watching this video, avoiding the need to do so in the Connection.

Explain how students will use the video across the bend to craft initial literary essays.

"Wow! That's powerful stuff, isn't it?" The kids agreed. "Right now, will you think about the ideas it stirs up in you?" I let the silence feel prolonged, and did my own thinking at the front of the room.

Speaking into the silence, I said, "I thought that for the next few days, you might be game to do some work with this video, so that four days from now, you'll be ready to draft interpretive literary essays about a claim you feel really captures something essential about the characters or about what this text teaches, about the lessons and themes in this text. It will mean we have to watch the video a bunch of times, and study the text and images from the video really closely. Are you up for it?" The students nodded enthusiastically, and a few even cried out, "Yes!"

"Great! Let's get started by drawing on some work we did together earlier this year in reading workshop."

❧ Name the teaching point.

"Today I want to remind you that people read differently when they intend to write about their reading. Writers see more, notice more . . . and everything becomes grist for the thinking mill. When you read as a writer (or watch videos as a writer), you bring an extra-alertness to your reading, noticing stuff others pass by."

If you launched your year with Interpretation Book Clubs, *from Units of Study for Teaching Reading, then it's likely this teaching point is a reminder for your students and you'll want to name it as such. If, however, you launched the year in a different way, simply change the wording of the teaching point, saying, "Today I want to teach you . . ."*

TEACHING AND ACTIVE ENGAGEMENT

Rally students to try the work with you, watching the "Panyee Football Club" video like writers, noting its details.

"Let's try it. I'll replay the 'Panyee Football Club' video. Let's all watch it as writers, with an extra alertness, seeing more, noticing more in the details of the text. Open your notebooks to a new page and be ready to jot about what you see." I pressed play to show the beginning of the video, from 0:00 to 0:25.

To tell the story of our football team, we need to go back to the very beginning.

Koh Panyee, 1986

On our island we loved to watch football. But no one had actually ever played it. You see, we live on a small floating village. And space can be hard to find. The only sports played here are boat racing . . . And telling tales about the size of fish you caught.

I noticed the majority of students were not yet writing, so I paused the video. "We could just speed through this part, thinking, 'There's nothing to see here. This is just some boys on an island in the middle of nowhere who want to do something and they aren't able to. But we're trying to see more, to notice stuff others would pass by, to read this video with an extra-alertness.

"So, what feels important? I'll replay the beginning again, and this time, watch as writers and really notice the details." I cued the video back up to the beginning and hit play.

Coach students to write to grow their thinking off of the details.

"Did you notice more?" I asked, nodding vigorously to suggest that I surely had. "Did any of you notice something during this second viewing that you think other kids might have passed right by?" Again, I knew the answer would be yes, and concurred. "You are doing what essayists do—paying attention to things that at first seem like nothing, but that with some thinking, can become something more.

"Let's get some of those observations onto the page. Ask yourself, 'What is a detail that I notice—one that for some reason seems sort of important? What might be especially meaningful about what I'm noticing? How might this detail connect to earlier parts or later parts?' Pick up your pen and start writing."

After a minute of silent writing, I said, "Let's watch a bit more of the video with that same alertness, again trying to notice stuff others pass by. Try to notice details that in some way seem like they could be important to your thinking about this story. Get ready to jot after you watch a bit—I'll hit pause again soon." I played another segment of the video, from 0:25 to 0:52.

One day one of the boys had an idea. He suggested we form a team of our own. When the other villagers heard our plan they thought it was ridiculous.

The words that you use here refer back to the day's teaching point. You'll want to repeat these words several times across a minilesson, almost like a refrain, so students launch into their independent work with a clear sense of what you taught.

If you feel that the kids aren't getting the details you hoped they'd notice, you might voice over while the video plays the second time, saying, "I love how you are noticing moments that seem important to the whole text." Or, you might say, "Did you notice how the boys were throwing their hands up in the air and cheering when the soccer game was on? That feels important!"

Villager (yelling): *"What are you noisy kids doing? You are scaring all the fish away!"*

Boy (yelling): *"We're starting a football team. We're going to be world champions."*

Villager (laughing): *"Look around you. Look where you live."*

"There's so much to jot about. Narrow in on a detail and start writing." As students worked, I voiced over. "Keep your pen moving down the page," I prompted. "If you run out of things to say about one detail, think about another detail from that same part and write all about it."

Set students up to share their writing with a partner, talking off of their initial entries.

"I'm going to give you some time to talk, as talking is another way to grow your thinking. Get to it!"

I listened to Adam and Helen as they talked. "It looks like after the boys have an idea, they are voting or volunteering for different roles or something," Adam said.

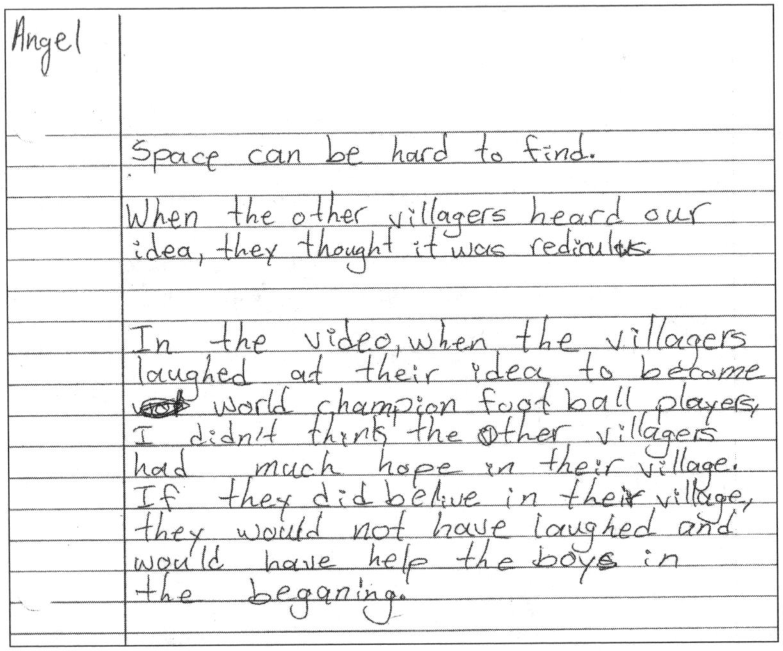

Angel	
	Space can be hard to find.
	When the other villagers heard our idea, they thought it was rediculus.
	In the video, when the villagers laughed at their idea to become world champion football players, I didn't think the other villagers had much hope in their village. If they did belive in their village, they would not have laughed and would have help the boys in the beganing.

FIG. 2–1 Angel quickly jots about details she noticed during the minilesson.

As you coach students, encourage them to notice details in the words and in the images. Students might notice the crooked shutters on one of the houses on the island or the bare feet on so many of the characters in the video. These details carry significance, just as the details in the text do.

"It's like they are all agreeing and working together. Like they are really getting along," Helen said.

I interrupted, gesturing for the whole class to listen: "Don't forget to ask yourselves *why* the details you are noticing might be important."

Helen continued. "Maybe it's important because in places like that—where you don't have a lot of stuff—you really have to get along with others and work together to get things done." I gestured for them to say more and moved on to coach other partnerships, asking others, "Why might that be important?"

LINK

Emphasize that as writers read on in texts, they carry their initial ideas with them as lenses. Prepare students to carry their initial ideas with them as you play the next snippet of video.

"Writers, I want to give you one more tip. When you read alertly and write to grow ideas, you often develop ideas you didn't have before you started to write. Bring those ideas with you as you read on. That way, you 'read' the next scene in your text a little differently, because you've got your initial idea in mind.

"Sometimes you'll find that the new scene gives additional evidence for your idea, or helps you refine your idea to make it stronger. Other times, the new scene might cause you to revise an idea you're carrying.

"Let's try it. Think about some of the ideas you'll be bringing with you as you watch. Call out one if you have it." The students called out a few ideas:

The boys seem super close to each other.

The boys and the other villagers don't have much but they make do with what they have.

Not everyone believed in the boys' dream.

"Okay, now I'll play the next snippet of the video for you. Watch the next part of this video with those ideas in mind, noting details and trying to make more of them." I played a segment from 0:52 to 1:12.

> *We realized they were right, we had nowhere to play or even practise. [sic] We had ourselves a football team, but we didn't have a pitch. This was a real problem because where we live space wasn't something we had. We figured we'd have to create our own space.*

"There's so much to think about, right?"

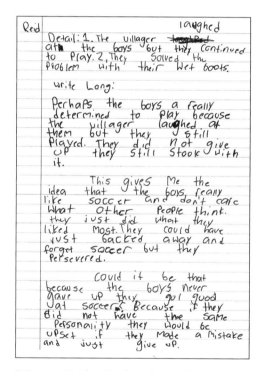

FIG. 2–2 Reid writes long to consider different possibilities. See additional student writing samples on the online resources.

Restate the teaching point. Send students off to closely read the video, transcript, and images.

"Writers, remember you need to read differently when you want to write about your reading, seeing more, noticing stuff that others might pass by. Then too, it helps to write to make something of what you see. Later, you'll be able to mine these entries to get ideas for claims for your literary essays." I gestured toward a new anchor chart.

"Usually when I send you off, I'll give you lots of choices over the text you study. But instead, for the next few days, we'll all study this text of the 'Panyee Football Club' video. You've got copies of the transcript of the video at your desks, and that will be incredibly useful to study. I'm also going to leave a laptop with the video cued up on it at each of your tables. You might decide to watch little snippets of the video together—just thirty seconds or less at a time—noting details others might pass by and then write as long as you can off of that snippet in your writing notebooks. I also captured a few images of key moments we discussed the first time we watched the video. You might pore over those and notice all the details with them. Off you go!"

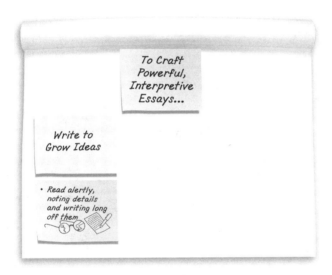

You'll notice that we encourage students to look at images from the video to help them grow ideas. Teachers who piloted this unit said that the digital stills they provided were incredibly helpful in directing students to powerful images from which to grow those ideas. In the online resources, you'll find specific instructions for creating your own digital stills to hand out to students for today's workshop.

> Panyee Football Club   Sana
>
> In the story/video, the matter of space showed up a lot. This is important because the shortage of space was a problem, but it still didn't stop the boys from following their dreams→being able to play soccer. The boy(s) even admitted that space wasn't one of the things that the village had. As I'm saying/writing this, I'm realizing that the boys had enough imagination and determination to create things that people thought weren't possible. Also, when they finally built they're small pitch, people such as the old man were pessimistic to them and said that they weren't "going to become champions on that thing." Before the boys came up with their idea, nobody actually even played soccer in their village because it was too small. They only watched it on T.V. This shows me that space was very limited in the village. However, the boys found out a way to "fix" that problem.

FIG. 2–3   Sana writes to explore her thinking about details in the text.

Launching the Work of Writing with Volume and Stamina

Supporting Volume and Stamina

You'll divide your time today between supporting writing volume and helping students grow ideas off of the text. Writing volume matters. You'll want to see your fifth-graders producing about two pages of writing a day and sustaining engagement in writing for upward of forty-five minutes. If you notice that most of your class needs support writing with these levels of volume and stamina, consider using voiceovers to increase the volume of students' writing. Otherwise, you might choose to target these reminders to table groups or individuals. To voice over, you'll interject writing workshop with your encouragement from time to time, particularly when you notice volume or stamina are waning, to keep your class writing with full steam.

Consider using these voiceovers across the workshop to support your students:

◆ "Keep your pens and pencils moving fast and furious!"

◆ "If you're stuck and unsure what to write next, reread your writing. Often rereading will fill you up with ideas of what to write next."

MID-WORKSHOP TEACHING   Broadening Attention to Other Story Elements

"Eyes up, writers. I can see how alert and engaged you are in growing ideas off this video! I wanted to pause to remind you to bring everything you know about reading stories to your reading of this text. The 'Panyee Football Club' video is a *story*, after all. Don't forget that it can pay off to think about the elements of stories: about characters and their traits and motivations, the problem the characters face, their responses to the problem, the setting, the repeated objects . . ." I distributed a familiar chart from the *Interpretation Book Clubs* unit to each student.

"Take a minute with your partner to glance over this list I'm giving you—it is one you already know well—and then check to see which of these you've already written about. If you notice one you haven't addressed—perhaps setting, for example—try jotting some quick thinking about that.

"And remember, keeping different story elements in mind will help you notice details in the text you might otherwise have passed by."

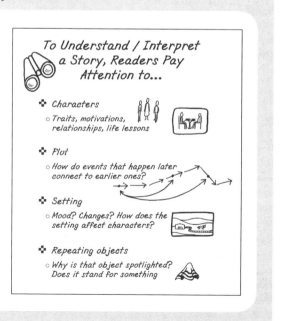

To Understand / Interpret a Story, Readers Pay Attention to...

❖ *Characters*
  o *Traits, motivations, relationships, life lessons*

❖ *Plot*
  o *How do events that happen later connect to earlier ones?*

❖ *Setting*
  o *Mood? Changes? How does the setting affect characters?*

❖ *Repeating objects*
  o *Why is that object spotlighted? Does it stand for something*

- "This is writing workshop! Make sure you're just doing a *tiny* bit of reading or watching, just thirty seconds or so, and then writing long and strong."

- "If you're stuck, try writing off a new detail."

- "There are fifteen minutes left in writing. See if you can write an *entire page* in these last fifteen minutes."

- "Try to write as long as you can without looking up, without taking a break."

Growing an Idea, Not a Summary

You might find that some of the students who are writing volumes aren't doing much more than retelling the plot of the text—not growing ideas off the text. For example, when studying the "Panyee Football Club" video, a student might write, "The kids want to be part of a football team, but they've never played and they don't have space. They get the idea to build a football pitch. The villagers laugh at them and their idea." Gather students who are retelling and say, "I want to teach you that when you're writing about your reading, it helps to zoom in on one small part of the text, maybe even one sentence, and to write a lot about that one part." Remind students of how you did this work in the minilesson with the "Panyee Football Club" video. You might even share a sample of your written work with students, showing how you took one sentence, perhaps, "And space can be hard to find," and generated a lot of thinking off of it.

Sample entry

The text says, "And space can be hard to find." It seems like this is the kind of place where space is hard to find for everyone. It's hard for the adults to find space to do their work. It's hard for the kids to find space to be kids, to run around and play and have fun with each other. And it's particularly hard for them to find space to play soccer. I think this makes what the Panyee Football Club did all that much more remarkable. They could easily have sat back and said, "It's just too hard. We'll never get to play." But instead, as soon as one kid got an idea, they launched into it, and they didn't give up, even when things got tough. I think this shows how dedicated the football club members are to what they believe in.

Then, as quickly as possible, launch all the students you've gathered into their work, and then coach students individually and briefly as they reread, zoom in on a detail, and try writing and talking long off of it.

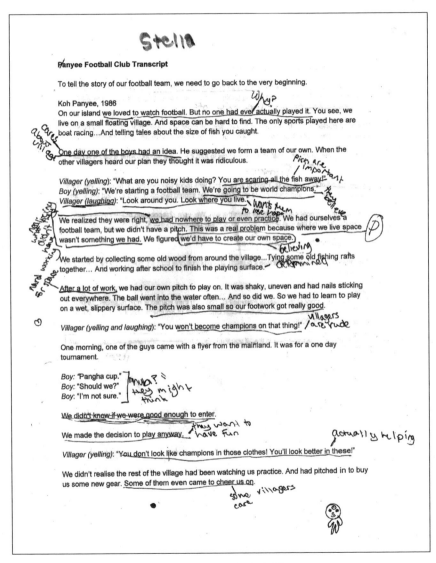

FIG. 2–4 Stella annotates the "Panyee Football Club" transcript.

Noticing Patterns

Explain that another way writers grow ideas from a text is by noticing patterns.

"Writers, eyes up here. I want to share one tip that can help you move from thinking about the details in the text to growing ideas about the text. Here it is: you can look for patterns in the text—in the characters, plot, setting, and repeating objects. For instance, in the story 'Little Red Riding Hood'—a text I've been reading closely—the red hood that Little Red Riding Hood wears is an object that seems to appear again and again. Studying those patterns can help us grow ideas about the text.

"To find a pattern, start by finding a detail you wrote about earlier today—maybe something about relationships or setting or a repeating object. Reread that part to each other, and then look for places where that detail repeats, maybe in exactly the same way or maybe in a slightly different way. Mark any pattern you find in your text and talk with your partner about what you're noticing." I added the tip to our anchor chart.

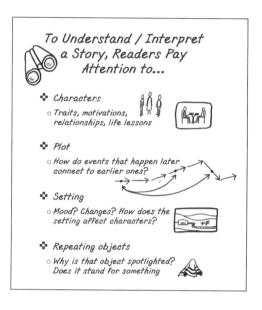

To Understand / Interpret a Story, Readers Pay Attention to...

❖ *Characters*
  ○ *Traits, motivations, relationships, life lessons*

❖ *Plot*
  ○ *How do events that happen later connect to earlier ones?*

❖ *Setting*
  ○ *Mood? Changes? How does the setting affect characters?*

❖ *Repeating objects*
  ○ *Why is that object spotlighted? Does it stand for something*

ANCHOR CHART

To Craft Powerful, Interpretive Essays . . .

- Write to grow ideas for possible essays:
  - Read alertly, noting details and writing long off them.
  - **Notice details that repeat and think about patterns.**

• *Notice details that repeat and think about patterns*

 IDENTIFYING PATTERNS IN THE TEXT

Writers, today you studied a text as a writer, expecting to see more, notice more, and make more significance out of the details in the text. One way you did this was by noticing patterns, studying details in the text that repeat. Tonight, continue this work. Notice a few patterns in the text, and write to grow new ideas about them. Use a "To Study Patterns in the Text . . ." chart to help you.

To Study Patterns in the Text . . .

1. Choose a text detail that seems to repeat (characters, plot, setting, repeating objects).

2. Reread one place where that detail shows up.

3. Find and reread other places where that detail shows up. Ask yourself, "What goes together? How do they go together?"

4. Write to grow a new idea. You might begin by writing, "This is important because . . ." or "This makes me think . . ."

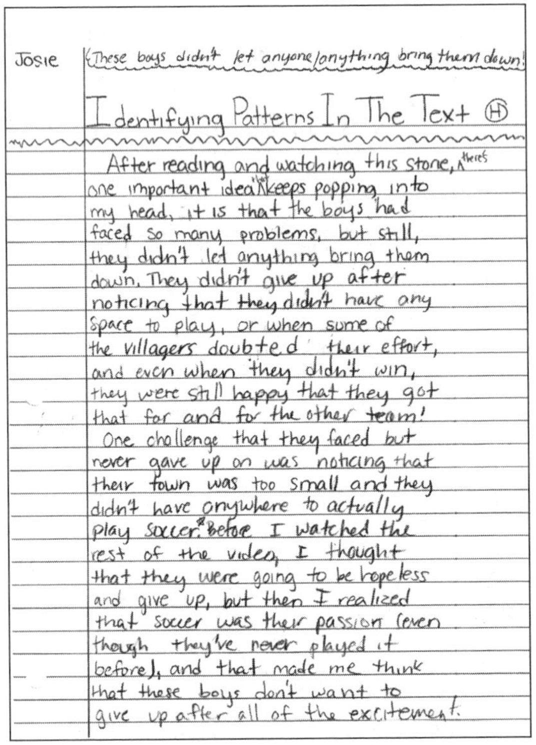

Josie | (These boys didn't let anyone/anything bring them down!)

Identifying Patterns In The Text ⊕

After reading and watching this stone, there's one important idea keeps popping into my head, it is that the boys had faced so many problems, but still, they didn't let anything bring them down. They didn't give up after noticing that they didn't have any space to play, or when some of the villagers doubted their effort, and even when they didn't win, they were still happy that they got that for and for the other team!

One challenge that they faced but never gave up on was noticing that their town was too small and they didn't have anywhere to actually play soccer. Before I watched the rest of the video, I thought that they were going to be hopeless and give up, but then I realized that soccer was their passion (even though they've never played it before), and that made me think that these boys don't want to give up after all of the excitement.

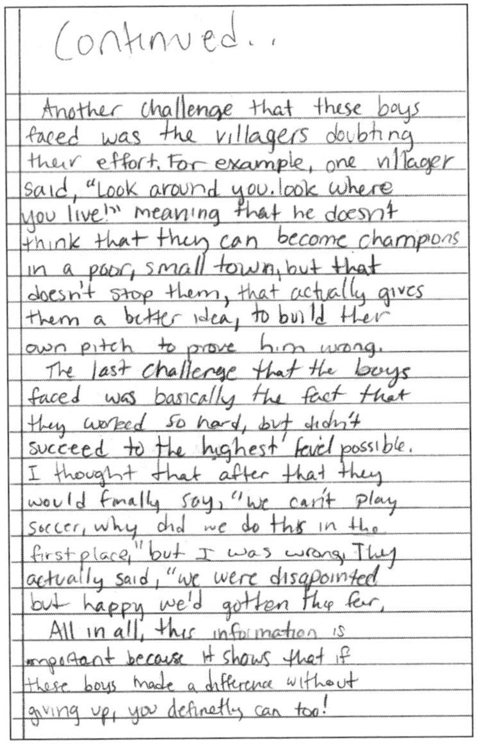

Continued..

Another challenge that these boys faced was the villagers doubting their effort. For example, one villager said, "Look around you. Look where you live!" meaning that he doesn't think that they can become champions in a poor, small town, but that doesn't stop them, that actually gives them a better idea, to build their own pitch to prove him wrong.

The last challenge that the boys faced was basically the fact that they worked so hard, but didn't succeed to the highest level possible. I thought that after that they would finally say, "we can't play soccer, why did we do this in the first place," but I was wrong. They actually said, "we were disappointed but happy we'd gotten this far.

All in all, this information is important because it shows that if these boys made a difference without giving up, you definitely can too!

FIG. 2–5 Josie noticed patterns in the videos and wrote to grow new ideas about those patterns.

Trying On Various Theses for Size

TODAY YOU TEACH STUDENTS to plan a blueprint for a literary essay by equipping them with templates for building an essay structure according to the traditional thesis and supports, or as we like to call this, a boxes-and-bullets structure. One way to do this is by teaching writers to first state their idea—their claim—and then to write a second sentence that forecasts the essay's structure. By the end of today's workshop, writers will have a thesis about the "Panyee Football Club" video that may sound something like "The character illustrates this trait" or "The text teaches this lesson" followed by "It does it through one way, another way, and most of all, another way."

Of course, developing a solid outline or frame for an essay is often a more complicated, iterative process. Here, we push students to develop clear theses and supports so that they can focus on supporting those claims with text evidence. Later, in Bend II, you'll show students that the process of developing that initial frame is actually a more complex process. If you are uncomfortable with the idea of giving kids a template for their thesis statements, know that soon you'll expand the repertoire of possibilities. And if you decide to do so, you can soon emphasize this scaffold less and less.

In the share of today's lesson, you'll introduce students to one way they can collect evidence to support a claim: by setting up booklets with a page for each of their supports. To create these booklets, students will need to write their idea and one of their supports on the top of each page. It's important that students restate their idea—the first part of their thesis statement—so that as they collect evidence, they are reminded to make sure all their evidence fits with their idea, not just their support. In Bend II, you'll give students more choice over the system they use to collect evidence, inviting them to choose between files, mini-folders, and booklets. For now, though, we recommend you channel students to create booklets, since this is a quick essay, and students will not have much time to collect or revise their evidence.

IN THIS SESSION, you'll teach students that writers can craft several possible thesis statements to see which one fits what they are really trying to say about a text.

GETTING READY

✔ Students' writing notebooks and pens (see Teaching and Active Engagement)

✔ Prepare a chart titled "Templates for Trying Out Possible Theses to Find the Perfect One" (see Teaching and Active Engagement and Homework).

✔ Be prepared to show two clips from the "Panyee Football Club" video, from 1:09 to 2:05 and from 3:30 to 4:35 (www.youtube.com/watch?v=jU4oA3kkAWU search terms: Panyee FC short film). A link to the video is provided in the online resources (see Teaching and Active Engagement).

✔ Chart paper and markers to create a list of possible thesis statements (see Teaching and Active Engagement)

✔ Be ready to add to the "To Craft Powerful, Interpretive Essays . . ." anchor chart (see Link).

✔ Create booklets for students by stapling three pieces of lined paper together; students will use them to collect evidence for their thesis statements (see Share).

✔ Prepare to show students pages in a booklet where you recorded the thesis statement you'll support across this bend. We chose to craft a thesis about "Little Red Riding Hood," but you could choose any familiar text (see Share).

Trying On Various Theses for Size

CONNECTION

Pose a question to the class about a common experience—shopping for clothes—and relate it to today's work of trying out different theses.

"Writers, I have a question for you. By a show of hands, how many of you have ever gone shopping for clothes?" Hands, predictably, shot up.

"Next question: How many of you have had to go to a dressing room to try on one piece of clothing, then another, then another?" Hands stayed up. "How many of you have sometimes needed to try on a whole bunch of different sizes or different brands of clothes?" Most of the hands stayed up, accompanied by smiles and a couple giggles.

I feigned shock. "Well, why is this? Why can't you just waltz into a clothing store and pull out what you need directly from the rack and pay for it? Turn and explain this to your partner, quickly." I gave students a moment to explain their reasons to one another.

"I heard many of you say you have to try on different sizes and kinds of clothes to get the perfect fit and the perfect look, yes? Well, I must tell you: shopping for clothes and writing an essay have some things in common, especially when it comes to what you *really* want to wear, or what you *really* want to say."

"Once essayists have studied a text, they craft a big idea—a thesis—capturing what they *really* want to say about a text."

❖ **Name your teaching point.**

"Today I want to teach you that just as a shopper tries on different clothes before finding the shirt or coat that fits perfectly, so, too an essayist tries on different thesis statements before finding one that fits what the essayist wants to say."

You could, of course, use another analogy that relates the ideas of thesis writing to a common experience, perhaps trying on shoes or hats or any experience that requires multiple iterations before getting something "just right." If you choose a different analogy than the one described here, be aware that we repeat and extend the analogy of trying on clothes in Bend II, Session 8, "Developing Stronger Thesis Statements."

TEACHING AND ACTIVE ENGAGEMENT

Explain to writers that there are a few familiar prompts essayists can draw on that provide templates for writing a thesis.

"My friends, when you go shopping for clothes, you don't just grab a bunch of random items of clothing and toss them into the dressing room. Instead you usually have an idea of a particular kind of clothing you want to wear, and you then search for and consider a few variations on that kind of clothing. It's the same when you want to try on different thesis statements. You generally have an idea of the kind of thing you want to say about the text, and then you try a few different ways to say it.

"Yesterday, you started growing ideas about the 'Panyee Football Club' video, and today I thought you could try writing different theses to help you discover what it is you really want to say about the text. I've listed a few thesis templates here." I gestured to a chart I had prepared.

"You'll notice that the first step is to state an idea about the text. Is your idea something about the character and his or her traits?" I pointed to the template as I talked students through it. "Or maybe something about what the character learns, or something about what the text is really teaching us?

"The next step is to forecast your essay's structure, telling how the organization of your essay will go. Forecasting an essay's structure is similar in some ways to a weather forecaster telling us about tomorrow's weather. You set people up to know what will be coming, what to expect. Perhaps your claim is supported by different parts of the text. Or maybe your claim is supported in different ways throughout the text. Or perhaps your claim is supported by different reasons. Or maybe you support it in some other way!

"Those two sentences (and they are sometimes combined into one)—stating your idea and forecasting your essay's structure—let readers know your claim, and your plan for how you will support that claim.

Template for Trying Out Possible Theses to Find the Perfect One	
1) First state one idea about the text.	**2) Then forecast the essay's structure.**
• The character is...	• (The character) shows this through (one part of the text), (another part of the text), and most of all, (another part of the text).
	• (The character) shows this through (one way), (another way), and most of all, (another way).
	• (This is the claim) because (one reason), because (another reason), and most of all, because (a third reason).
• The character learns...	• (The character) shows this through (one part of the text), (another part of the text), and most of all, (another part of the text).
	• (The character) shows this through (one way), (another way), and most of all, (another way).
	• (This is the claim) because (one reason), because (another reason), and most of all, because (a third reason).
• The text teaches (or is really about)...	• (The text) shows this through (one part of the text), (another part of the text), and most of all, (another part of the text).
	• (The text) shows this through (one way), (another way), and most of all, (another way).
	• (This is the claim) because (one reason), because (another reason), and most of all, because (a third reason).

Here, you introduce students to three ways they can support their idea: through parts, ways, or reasons. Students might choose to support the idea that the boys are dedicated to their goal with three general parts from the story. This could be the beginning, middle, and end of the story. Or, students might choose to zoom in to three more specific parts: building the pitch, playing on the pitch, and playing in the big game. Alternately, students could support an idea with three ways that idea is true. For example, one way we see the boys are dedicated to their goal is they're willing to play in tricky situations. Thirdly, students could try out reasons why their claim is true. For instance, one reason why the characters are really hard-working is they want to play football badly, and so on.

Try not to get too hung up on the semantics of whether students are supporting their idea with parts, ways, reasons, or developing their own supports. We have found that what matters most is that students choose three supports that are parallel to each other, and that students choose supports that help them defend their idea.

"What I have given you is a few templates that you can work from as you try to find what it is you want to say at the start of this essay. You'll have to try out several templates (and several ways of working with a template) to see which fits best what you really want to say about the text."

Play a clip from the "Panyee Football Club" video, and ask students to consider what they want to say about the text. Coach students as they generate potential thesis statements.

"Ready to try this? I'm going to play a few snippets of the 'Panyee Football Club' video, and as I do, will you think about what you *really* want to say about the characters or themes in the text? When I pause the film, you'll try using these templates to write a bunch of possible thesis statements. Open your notebooks so you can jot your ideas."

I cued the video to 1:09 and pressed play. I paused the video at 2:05.

> *We figured we'd have to create our own space.*
>
> *We started by collecting some old wood from around the village . . . Tying some old fishing rafts together . . . And working after school to finish the playing surface.*
>
> *After a lot of work, we had our own pitch to play on. It was shaky, uneven and had nails sticking out everywhere. The ball went into the water often . . . And so did we. So we had to learn to play on a wet, slippery surface. The pitch was also small so our footwork got really good.*
>
> Villager (yelling and laughing): *"You won't become champions on that thing!"*

"Go for it, writers! Take those first templates and try stating some ideas about the characters or themes. Think about what you *really* want to say about the text." The kids jotted for a minute.

Collect and chart students' possible theses statements. Set students up to forecast the supports in their essay, and coach in to lift the level of their work.

"Let's hear some of your ideas." I gestured for a few kids to share, and I quickly scrawled their ideas on chart paper.

Possible Thesis Statements

- The text teaches that if you work hard, you can achieve.
- The text is really about how working as a team helps you to do hard things.
- The characters are really hard working.
- The characters learn there's always a way to solve a problem if you search for it.

"Once you've got an idea that could work, you've got to forecast what's to come in your essay. Do you want to use scenes to support it? Ways? Reasons? Something else? Work with your partner to try out some possibilities."

There are no characters explicitly named in the video. If you notice students who are spending significant time trying to determine a character's name, you might explain that students could name one specific character or describe a group or team, using the same template. That is, they could say, "The Panyee Football Club learns . . ." or "The soccer team is . . ."

You'll notice that several of the minilessons in this first bend apply the guided practice method of teaching. This is unusual, and it is also intentional. Our intent is to harness the fun and the power of the video, and to keep the sessions lively and clear. We thought the best way to do this would be through guided practice. You could, of course, demonstrate the teaching point before channeling writers to try it with the video. If you make that choice, consider demonstrating with "Little Red Riding Hood," a text we reference across the bend.

If your kids need additional support, you might instead choose to say, "I saw you writing . . ." and then record these thesis statements on chart paper, providing students with a vision for how their thesis statements could go.

As students worked, I noticed some were trying to combine different kinds of supports, using one scene, one way, and one reason to support a single idea. I paused the class and said, "Writers, when you're forecasting your essay, it is usually important to use the *same* kinds of supports. You might support your essay with two or three parts *or* tell about a few ways that the text supports this. Make sure you're using all the same kinds of supports and not mixing them up. You can check yourself by repeating the sentence stems on our chart," I gestured toward our chart. "'This is the claim because . . .' and say your first reason. 'This is the claim because . . .' and say your second reason."

I gave students another minute to work, and then asked Khalid to share a possible thesis. "I was thinking I could say, 'The Panyee soccer team video teaches that when you work together, you can overcome the challenges. The text shows this through the beginning, the middle, and end of the story.'"

"See how Khalid supported his idea with three parts across the story? He could also try out three *ways* the characters work together to overcome challenges, or maybe even three reasons why."

Set students up to try this with another section of text. Coach them as they generate possible thesis statements and supports, then set them up to share.

"Here's the thing: just like you try on a bunch of clothes at the store to find the right fit, you've got to try on a bunch of thesis statements to figure out what you're really trying to say about the text. I'm going to skip ahead a bit to the scene with the big game. As you watch, think about what you really want to say about this text, and get ready to jot some thesis statements, your ideas and supports."

I played the video from 3:30 to 4:35, stopping after the award ceremony.

> *The other team were two up by halftime.*
>
> *With our spirits down, we couldn't work out how to turn the game around. After a bad first half we needed to do something.*
>
> *So we got rid of our wet boots. Playing in bare feet was more comfortable for all of us. We were light on our feet and could move much faster. We scored two goals and evened the score.*
>
> *But a last minute goal gave the other team the win. We were disappointed but happy we had gotten this far. And the rest of the village were really proud of us.*

"You've got this, writers!" I tapped the first step on our "Template for Trying Out Possible Theses to Find the Perfect One" chart. As students started jotting, I whispered in to remind them to try out prompts about themes and about character.

Once most students had jotted an idea or two, I said, "You're ready to move to our second step: forecast the essay's structure. Try this out. See if you can try two different ways of supporting one idea. Can you come up with several *ways* the text supports your idea? Can you think of several *parts* of the text that support your idea? Regardless, whatever type of supports you choose should belong to the same category." I gave students a minute to jot.

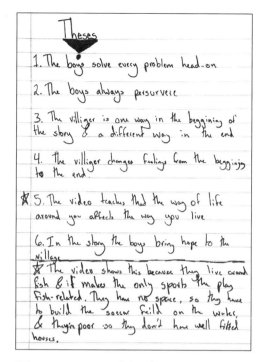

FIG. 3–1 Emmy used the thesis template to jot a few possible thesis statements for the text.

This work of thinking of the kinds of evidence that will best support a claim is tricky work. When you make a claim about a text, and then do the work of seeing what kind of evidence best supports the claim, sometimes you need to go back and revise your claim to fit with the best evidence. And once you revise your claim, you need to go back and tweak your supports again. This back-and-forth work of revising a thesis and supports begins here in Bend I, and you'll lift the level of that work in Bend II.

Channel students to share their theses statements with a partner.

I asked students to share with a partner. "Listen first for your partner's idea and then to hear how your partner forecasts how he'll support that idea."

Marco said to his partner Latisha, "I'm thinking that idea from before, that *obstacles can actually be good things*, is still true here, because the water was an obstacle, but it turned out well for the team. So I wrote, 'The text teaches that obstacles can be good things. The text shows this through the soccer field, through signing up for the soccer tournament, and through the tournament itself." I gave them a thumbs up and moved on to coach another partnership.

LINK

Reiterate the teaching point and send kids off to try on different theses for size. Encourage them to create their own thesis statements.

"Remember, writers: it's rare that the first time you try on new clothes, they fit exactly right or look exactly right. The same is true for theses. To find the best clothes and the best theses, you have to try some on for size."

Notice the analogy you used in the connection is repeated in the link. This repetition gives a minilesson a circular structure, which aids in students' memory and retention of the material you are teaching, and gives your class a language with which to talk about writing.

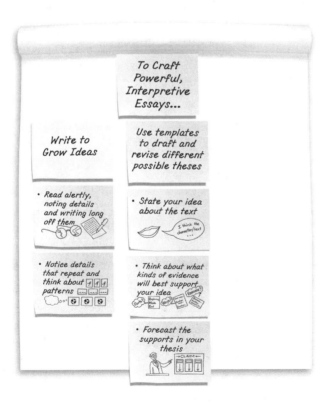

To Craft Powerful, Interpretive Essays...

Write to Grow Ideas
- Read alertly, noting details and writing long off *them*
- Notice details that repeat and think about patterns

Use templates to draft and revise different possible theses
- State your idea about the text
- Think about what kinds of evidence will best support your idea
- Forecast the supports in your thesis

Josie — Possible Themes Date 2/4

*At least 6 new theses!
me: 6/6

This text teaches ~~me~~ that hard work pays off. It teaches ~~the~~ this when they made the pitch, when they took their cleats off, and most of all when they got an overall of third place.
|Scenes| #1

These characters are learning that if you really want something in life, you have to work towards it. They work hard to make a pitch, to get their villager's respect, and most of all, they work hard to become champions 6 years in a row.
|Ways| #2

These characters are learning that they shouldn't give up after all of their hard work to get so far. They learned this when they were building a pitch, when they didn't know how to tie the game again, and most of all, when they got third place.
|Ways| #3

Continued... Josie Date 2/4

The characters learn to keep looking forward to follow your dreams, don't give up, ever. They learn this when they realize that they don't have space to play, when they don't know how to tie the game again, and most of all, when they don't win, but are still happy that they got so far.
|Scenes| #4

This text is really about how these kids couldn't have gotten this far by themselves, they had to work together. They had to work together because none of them could've built a pitch all by themselves, they had to team up to ignore the villagers, and most of all, because you can't play soccer with one player!
|Reasons| #5

This text is really about how anyone can make a difference in life. They made a difference by showing the world not to give up, looking forward, and keep thinking over & over. |Ways| #6

Pangee football club — Themes + Theses Date 2-4

Ways:
Thesis #1 | In this story, the members of the football club learn that what you have as a person is more important than what you have as possessions. The characters show this by saying how they have no space, saying how they have to create their own space, and most of all by being more workers to build their own pitch!

Parts:
Thesis #2 | This story teaches how to always believe in yourself. It teaches this when the boys don't give up after hearing the villagers mean words, when the boys decide to go to the tournament, and most of all when the boys took on the opposition at the semi-finals without hesitation.

Reasons/actions:
Thesis #3 | In the story about the Pangee football club, I think the leader of the teams determined. I think this because he doesn't give up when he finds out there is no space, he deals with the small pitch and even lets it make him...

FIG. 3–2 Josie developed thesis statements by trying out multiple ideas and supports.

"Today, writers, you'll need to try out a bunch of possible thesis statements, where you state your idea, think about what kind of evidence will best support your idea, and then forecast your supports." I added the strategy to our anchor chart. "To do this, you can watch and rewatch little scenes from the video or pore over the transcript for ideas. You'll probably fill two pages in your notebook with your ideas and supports. Off you go."

Coaching to Develop Strong Claims

A SOLID THESIS STATEMENT creates a strong foundation for a literary essay, so today you may want to focus your energy on helping students strengthen their claims. Without a strong claim and supports, your students may struggle to find relevant evidence to back up their supports or to really convince readers that their idea is true. Here, we've detailed the most predictable issues we've seen in classrooms, and we use the familiar text "Little Red Riding Hood" to illustrate the issues. We've also detailed for you ways to address those problems. Based on your class, some of these might become small-group teaching points and others may be better addressed through one-on-one conferences.

Students write theses that are facts, not opinions.

Little Red Riding Hood wanders off the path into the woods.

Some writers might take a fact from the text and record it as a thesis statement. To address this, you might encourage students to check their thesis, thinking, "Is this my opinion about the text? Could someone have a different opinion about this than I do?" You could use a familiar example—fruit—to model the difference between facts and opinions. You could say, "Apples are often red. That's a fact. Red apples are the best. That's my opinion. You could feel differently. Maybe you think red apples are just the worst." Then, you could coach students to rewrite their thesis statement as an opinion, not a fact.

Students struggle with interpretation.

Little Red Riding Hood learns not to pick flowers in the woods.

MID-WORKSHOP TEACHING   Testing Thesis Statements in Partnerships

"You know how when you're trying to find the perfect outfit, you can't just look at an outfit on a hanger and know it will fit perfectly. You've got to actually try it on to see if the sleeves are the right length or if the pants are dragging on the floor. The same is true of your thesis statements. Once you've got a thesis statement that seems strong, that might work, you've got to try it on for size. Of course, you can't *actually* try it on, but you can look back across the text and think, 'Can I find a lot of evidence to support this idea?' and 'Is there evidence from different parts of the text to support this idea?' The strongest thesis statements usually have lots of evidence from different parts of the text."

"With your partner, share a possible thesis and then really test the thesis statement together to see if you can find enough evidence for it at different points in the story."

As kids worked, I coached partnerships with tips for finding evidence across the text.

After a few minutes, I said, "In the next fifteen minutes, you'll need to choose a thesis and test it to see if it can be supported across a text, asking yourself these questions. You'll want to bring your chosen thesis and supports—your boxes and bullets—with you to the meeting area for our share in a few minutes."

At this point in the unit, some kids will be writing theses that are more interpretive, while many others will be writing essays about character traits and how they are revealed across the story. Either is fine, but if you see students struggling with interpretive theses, you might steer such writers to first write an essay on character rather than theme. Fifth-graders will know how to name a character in the text, and can be channeled to name the character's predominant trait. A sample thesis with supports could go like this: "(Character) is (trait) because A, because B, and most of all, because C." You might show writers how you come up with the idea that "Little Red Riding Hood is immature" and then generate three possible supports.

Students cannot find many supports to back up their claim.

> The story teaches that it's okay to use violence to solve a problem.

- The huntsman uses violence to free the grandmother from the wolf.

Realize that when students are writing about very short texts, it is almost inevitable that there won't be tons of evidence to support their claims. You could teach them three things. First, it could be their thesis doesn't actually work. Bravo! If they discover that and revise their thesis, they are doing the hardest and smartest work that an essayist can do. You might teach them to reword their thesis so it fits with the evidence in their text. Or, channel these writers to reread their earlier notebook entries and to be on the lookout for ideas that can be more strongly supported across the text.

On the other hand, perhaps if they look more closely, realizing the exact words in the text and the tiny details matter, they will see specifics that *do* support their point. And finally, they should realize that the way they discuss their evidence is an important part of making the evidence convincing. Give them an example that comes from real life, one that is not at all nuanced. You could say, "If my claim is that fifth grade is challenging, and I want to find evidence for that, I could say, 'Lunch isn't until 12:15.' That evidence might not sound like it is that convincing, but watch how I can spin it so that it is: 'One way fifth grade is challenging is that a late lunchtime means kids are trying to learn while they are starving.'"

Students write supports that are too specific—the supports are really examples, not buckets of examples.

> The text teaches that you shouldn't talk to strangers.

- The wolf recommended Little Red Riding Hood go off the path and search for flowers.
- Little Red Riding Hood talks to the wolf right away when she sees him.

You might teach these writers the difference between supports and evidence. To do this, you might say, "Writers, supports are like buckets. They're bigger categories that lots of evidence from the text can fit into." Coach writers to make their buckets bigger by thinking, "This fits inside the larger idea of . . ." Then, they can rewrite their bullet with that answer in mind.

Students write supports that are not parallel.

> "Little Red Riding Hood" teaches that you should follow advice from loved ones.

- Her mom gives great advice.
- One way Little Red gets in trouble is by following bad advice.
- This is true at the beginning of the story.

Not all literary essays contain parallel supports. Strong essays could be organized with supports that follow in logical sequence but are not parallel. However, using parallel supports can make an essay feel cohesive.

If students are not supporting their ideas with parallel supports (e.g., all reasons, all ways, all parts, all characters, all kinds), and if their plans do not feel cohesive, you might coach students as they check each bullet, asking, "Do these supports match?" You might provide a tip. "It helps if your bullets begin the same way. They might all begin with *because* . . . or *one way* . . . or *one part* . . . ."

Students write supports that overlap.

> Little Red Riding Hood learns to listen to advice from her loved ones.

- She learns this by ignoring her mom's advice.
- She learns this by not doing what her mom recommends.

Teach these writers to ask, "Can the same example fit under more than one bullet?" If so, one bullet can be cut. Then, you could coach writers as they come up with a second, more distinct bullet. You might encourage them to think about a whole other part of the text or a whole other reason to generate a new support.

Students write supports in a random order, rather than a logical order.

> The text teaches that you should think before you act.

- Little Red Riding Hood stays even though her grandma seems odd.
- Little Red Riding Hood takes the wolf's advice without pausing.
- Little Red Riding Hood ignores mom's advice.

Most world-class standards expect fifth-graders to logically order reasons to support a claim. To address this, you might teach writers to avoid stating their supports in any random order, and teach students to instead order their supports in a way that will best convince their reader of their claim. For instance, you might channel a student to order his supports from least strong to most strong. Then coach the student to signal which support he believes is the strongest by writing *most of all* just before it.

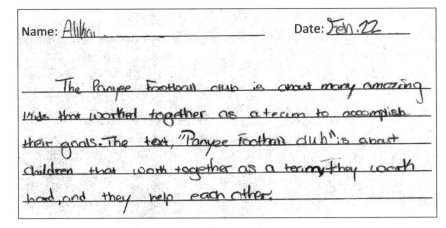

Name: Alikrii   Date: Feb. 22

The Panyee Football club is about many amazing kids that worked together as a team to accomplish their goals. The text, "Panyee Football club", is about children that work together as a team, they work hard, and they help each other.

FIG. 3–3 Alikrii jotted a thesis statement with a predictable problem: supports that overlap.

Setting Up to Collect Evidence

Introduce a system to collect and organize writing. Explain how the system works by using your own example, and ask students to create their own booklets to collect evidence.

Once students had gathered, I said, "Now that you've got your boxes and bullets finalized, you'll need to set up a system to collect and organize all your evidence." I held up my own organization system, which was a booklet—a few sheets of paper stapled together. On the top of each booklet page, I had written my thesis and one support.

"Like all of you, I spent time developing my thesis and supports, playing around with different ways my thesis could be worded. My essay is about 'Little Red Riding Hood.' You know the fairy tale, yes? Here's the version I settled on." I showed each page of the booklet under the document camera. "See how each booklet page has my claim and one of my supports? See how my supports all fit under the same category of parts of the story?"

Claim (on all pages): Little Red Riding Hood learned not to take advice from strangers.

Support (on page 1): She learned this at the start of the story.

Support (on page 2): She learned this in the middle of the story.

Support (on page 3): She learned this at the end of the story.

"Will you spend a few minutes creating a plan for your own boxes and bullets? I'm thinking you'll want to use booklets, but if you'd prefer folders or if you have another way of keeping yourself organized, you can do that instead. If you use booklets, make sure that each booklet page includes your claim and a support." I passed out sheets of paper that I had already stapled together to the students and circulated as students jotted their boxes-and-bullets plan.

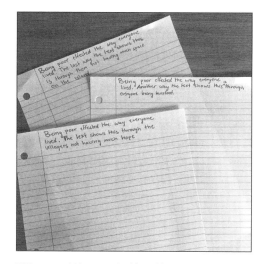

FIG. 3–4 Mica created booklets to capture her claim and supports. Notice how she repeated her claim and one support at the top of each page.

GENERATING THESIS STATEMENTS

Writers, one way to get really good at something is to do that thing a variety of ways, multiple times. The fancy words for this are *deliberate practice*. This means you practice something over and over, trying each time to get a little bit better.

Tonight, try getting good at the skill of trying on templates to generate a bunch of possible thesis statements for a folktale of your choice. For instance, one thesis for "Little Red Riding Hood" might be, "Little Red Riding Hood learns the lesson not to take advice from strangers, but from loved ones. She learns this in the beginning of the story and especially at the very end of the story."

Or, you might choose to do this work with your independent reading book, using the same thesis templates. Remember to make sure your thesis statements state an idea and name supports that belong to the same category: parts, ways, reasons, times, and so on.

Template for Trying Out Possible Theses to Find the Perfect One

1) First state one idea about the text.	2) Then forecast the essay's structure.
• The character is...	• (The character) shows this through (one part of the text), (another part of the text), and most of all, (another part of the text). • (The character) shows this through (one way), (another way), and most of all, (another way). • (This is the claim) because (one reason), because (another reason), and most of all, because (a third reason).
• The character learns...	• (The character) shows this through (one part of the text), (another part of the text), and most of all, (another part of the text). • (The character) shows this through (one way), (another way), and most of all, (another way). • (This is the claim) because (one reason), because (another reason), and most of all, because (a third reason).
• The text teaches (or is really about)...	• (The text) shows this through (one part of the text), (another part of the text), and most of all, (another part of the text). • (The text) shows this through (one way), (another way), and most of all, (another way). • (This is the claim) because (one reason), because (another reason), and most of all, because (a third reason).

Session 4

Angling Mini-Stories to Support a Point

M Y FOURTH-GRADERS AND I sat cross-legged on the floor on the Brooklyn Museum, pulled in close to Charles Willson Peale's 1776 painting *George Washington*, listening to our tour guide. She told us a story about how President George Washington's pants were specially made in Europe. You might think the docent would talk about Washington's commanding posture, or his leadership talents—but no, she told us stories about his pants! Her details, carefully chosen, brought the story to life.

The docent asked us, "Do you sometimes order clothes online—and have them come through the mail?" She added, "Well George Washington did a version of that. He ordered pants from a tailor in England. One time he sent his measurements over and the tailor in England thought the measurements were so crazy—not possible—that he sent the president typically sized pants instead of following the measurements. Washington couldn't wear them at all," the docent had said, pantomiming putting on too-small, too-tight pants. The class and I laughed, and she continued, "So Washington ordered another pair of pants and this time included a note saying 'The measurements are not a joke.'"

We were captivated by her storytelling. I'd seen this painting a half-dozen times before, but now, through the stories told by a skilled docent, the image seemed to come alive. It has been years since that visit to the museum, and I have long since forgotten what I read on placards around the museum, but I still remember her story about George Washington's pants.

Stories are memorable. Stories are important. In her famous TED Talk on the power of vulnerability, research professor Brené Brown began by talking about the importance of stories and said, "stories are just data with a soul." In Carmine Gallo's (2014) best-selling book *Talk Like TED: The 9 Public-Speaking Secrets of the World's Top Minds*, "Master the Art of Storytelling" is the second secret. As Gallo claims, "Ideas are the currency of the 21st century and stories facilitate the exchange of that currency. Stories illustrate, illuminate, and inspire" (74). Stories can convince. If well developed, the stories your students weave into their writing to support their claims can be similarly effective. To facilitate this, during today's minilesson you'll teach your students that one way literary essayists support their

IN THIS SESSION, you'll teach students that one way writers support their claim is by crafting mini-stories that are angled to highlight the writer's point and that balance storytelling as well as summarizing.

GETTING READY

✔ Have a copy of "Little Red Riding Hood" ready to reference (see Teaching).

✔ Prepare a mini-story related to "Little Red Riding Hood" or another story of your choice, to read aloud and to display to students (see Teaching).

✔ Prepare the "To Craft an Angled Mini-Story . . ." chart (see Teaching, Active Engagement, and Link).

✔ Prepare to play the first 1:30 of the "Panyee Football Club" video (www.youtube.com/watch?v=jU4oA3kkAWUi or use the search terms: Panyee FC short film) (see Active Engagement).

✔ Be prepared to add to the "To Craft Powerful, Interpretive Essays . . ." anchor chart (see Link).

✔ If possible, make computers or tablets available to students so they can view snippets of the "Panyee Football Club" video (see Link).

✔ Make sets of the "Panyee Football Club" digital stills available for each table (see Link).

thesis is with carefully crafted mini-stories. By including tiny stories that are written in ways that advance a writer's main points, the essayist solidifies his or her point. The most powerful mini-stories help readers understand the writer's claim and help ensure the claim will stick with readers long after they put down the essay.

To help your students accomplish this, you'll teach them that when literary essayists craft mini-stories, they choose which details to story-tell—the details tied into the main points they're trying to make—and they also choose which parts of the text they will summarize because they provide important background information but are less central to readers wanting to grasp the main point. This requires writers to look across all the parts of the text that could possibly serve as supports and to think, "Out of all these possible parts, which *best* supports my main point?"

Over and over again throughout their academic (and professional) lives, your students will need to draw on their abilities in narrative writing to help communicate their ideas. But more importantly, the work of being able to guide someone to understand the point you're trying to make matters deeply in literary essays, and in life. The world is fraught with enough miscommunication between countries, between political adversaries, and sometimes between families and friends. Today, you help your students develop the ability to support their points with clear mini-stories as evidence. This is a worthy and honorable goal in a democratic society.

The challenge in writing this minilesson was to be sure that kids grasped the gist of the work, first learning to choose moments from a story that illustrate their point, before coaching them to do the finer points of this work. The lesson we ultimately settled on here is derived from one that Lucy wrote when showing Teachers College Reading and Writing Project colleagues how to make complicated minilessons more accessible for students, particularly English language learners. The goal here to be sure, early in the unit, is that the foundational work of writing a literary essay is accessible to all your students.

Angling Mini-Stories to Support a Point

CONNECTION

Tell a story to the class, one that is entirely made up but that displays the ingredients of good storytelling.

"Writers, hurry over to the meeting area. I have a story to tell you." Once the kids were settled, I began. "I have to tell you this really creepy thing that happened last night. Long after you guys had all left school, when I was sitting here all alone, just reading your work, I heard a scratch on the window—this one, over here. I looked up, didn't see anything, so I went back to reading Raymond's notebook. Then a minute later I heard a little child's voice, saying 'Heerrre, here . . .' I thought, 'Oh my goodness, what—who—could that be?' and I raced to the window, my heart pounding . . ."

Then I stopped. A few of the students' eyes were wide as saucers, and I broke into a warm smile. "Guys, none of that was true. But I was starting to tell you a pretty good story, wasn't I? Here's my question. What made it a good story? What are the ingredients in a good story? What's the recipe? Turn and talk."

I listened as children talked, then I called them back and summarized some of their major points: writers tell their stories in order, show feelings and don't tell them, add in details, and include a beginning, middle, and end.

Then I said, "Remember those ingredients later today, and whenever you write essays about literature, because here's an important tip: Literary essayists use a special kind of storytelling to provide support for their claim."

Name the teaching point.

"Writers, today I want to teach you that one way to make your essay memorable is to insert stories into it. Essayists try to support their points in ways that will move readers to agree with their points, to nod, 'Yes, yes.' To do that, essayists sometimes tell a story to support a point—and they try to tell the story well."

◆ COACHING

Your fifth-graders will need to draw on all they know about crafting powerful narratives, ones that are filled with rich description, action, dialogue, and thinking. If you are teaching from Units of Study in Opinion/Argument, Information, and Narrative Writing, it's likely you launched the year with the Narrative Craft unit. You taught your students to ground their writing in specific, concrete details and to stretch out important parts, telling what happened bit by bit. Today's teaching supports students in transferring over these skills.

TEACHING

Demonstrate how you do this work step-by-step, by first showing how you take one idea and then by how you identify and then rank moments that could offer support. Use a familiar text: "Little Red Riding Hood."

"This is big work. Once essayists come up with their ideas about the text, they find parts of the text that support their idea. As you know, I am writing about 'Little Red Riding Hood,' and I've already got my claim: that Little Red Riding Hood learns not to take advice from strangers, but from loved ones. Now, I have to think about a part of the text that shows this. I have to skim the text, trying to find the parts that *best* show she learned this lesson."

I picked up the text and glanced at the opening scene. I said. "Oh, here, it says that everyone who met Little Red Riding Hood liked her, especially her grandma. Does that fit?" The kids shook their heads no.

I tried another part. "Or what about here: Little Red Riding Hood's mom is telling her what she should do on the journey: look straight ahead, not stray from the path, say good morning. Does that fit?" The kids all nodded yes, and I said, "That's one part we *could* use. Let's make sure we have the strongest part.

"Here it says that the wolf gives Little Red advice, telling her she should go into the forest. What do you think?" The kids nodded to signal that the part also fit.

"Oh, I've got two parts now. When essayists find a few parts that fit, they think about which part best fits their claim. Quick, talk with your partner, and make a case for which of these parts best fits our claim: that Little Red Riding Hood learns not to take advice from strangers, but from loved ones." I gave them a minute to talk, and then called them back. Most kids agreed I should start with a mini-story about Little Red's mom, who was one of Little Red Riding Hood's loved ones giving her advice. That would fit with my first support: Little Red Riding Hood learned this at the beginning of the story.

Shift to telling the part like a small moment story, stretching it out bit by bit. Recruit students to finish the remainder of the mini-story.

"Writers, you helped me do the first part. I found parts that showed my claim and you helped me choose that part that *best* fit. Once essayists have found a part, they work to tell that part well, using all the ingredients in a good story, so their readers will nod and think, 'Oh, yes, yes! I agree.' Watch me try this. First, I'll need to state my idea about the text, then I'll shift into the story. Here goes." I started saying the mini-story aloud.

> At the beginning of the story, Little Red Riding Hood learns it's better to get advice from a loved one than a stranger. One example is that she gets advice from her mother when she starts off on her trip. Her mother says that when she is walking in the woods, Little Red Riding Hood should "look straight ahead like a good girl."

We use a common fairy tale in our demonstration, "Little Red Riding Hood," as it is generally well known. You could substitute this text for another text your students know well, such as a short picture book you've read aloud, or a different fairy tale or folktale. If you choose to go with "Little Red Riding Hood" and you are concerned that some students don't know or don't remember the text, you might read it aloud to the class at a time outside writing workshop. You can find a copy of the fairy tale in the online resources. Whatever you use, be aware that we use this text not only in this session, but also in demonstrations throughout this unit. If you choose a different text, you'll want to weave that same text throughout your unit as well.

Notice the varied ways we engage students across the teaching portion of the minilesson. These brief moves help ensure students are cognitively engaged across your demonstration.

"Writers, remember that at first, Little Red Riding Hood is listening to all her mom's advice, and then she promises she'll do everything her mom said, but then she doesn't actually do any of it. Will you and your partner keep telling that story, using specific details that tie in to the big point you're trying to make? I'll get you started." I continued writing-in-the-air.

> Little Red listens really carefully to her mom as she's sharing her advice. "And don't go off the path and into the woods," her mom tells her. Little Red Riding Hood promises that she'll do that, but then a little later when she is in the woods, a wolf . . .

I projected a copy of the mini-story I had prepared earlier as a guide for students. Then, I signaled to the kids to get started writing-in-the-air, and listened to a few partnerships as they tried the work.

Debrief, naming the replicable steps you just demonstrated.

"Writers, do you see how literary essayists first work to find a moment that really supports their claims? Then, they tell the story of that time, using all the ingredients that make up a good story. These carefully crafted stories lead their readers by the hand, helping them to understand their claims. Let me list out the steps I took." I listed them across my fingers as I revealed a new chart.

To Craft an Angled Mini-Story . . .

- Choose a point to support.
- Identify and rank moments that support a point.
- Begin by naming the point you're making.
- Retell the mini-story.
  - Weave in specific details tied to your point.
  - Pop out the parts to show your claim.
  - Choose which parts to story-tell (fit with your point) and to summarize (provide background information).

ACTIVE ENGAGEMENT

Invite students to try the work in a shared text, the "Panyee Football Club" video, using their own claims.

"It's your turn to try this work with the 'Panyee Football Club' video. You decided on your claim and supports yesterday. So, look at our chart—what do you need to do next?" The kids agreed that they needed to identify and rank moments that supported their point. "It helps to revisit the text to do this. I'll replay the beginning of the video. Will you look for a few parts that *might* show your claim? Pop your thumb up when you find one so I'll know."

I hit play, and I paused the video about a minute and a half in when most kids had their thumbs up. "Do you have at least one moment in mind? If you've got a few, it helps to rank them to make sure you know which is best.

The teaching portion of the minilesson typically ends with a debrief, where you name out in a step-by-step fashion the work you just demonstrated. This gives students another opportunity to hear the teaching point.

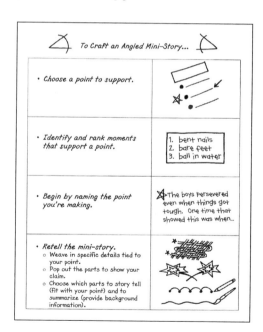

"Now, get ready to write that bit in the air to your partner. Look at our chart. It helps to start by saying your claim, and then to jump into your example, to tell the story bit by bit, really popping out the parts that show your claim. Partner 1, you get started first, and Partner 2, you listen to see how your partner pops out his or her claim."

I knelt to coach partnerships as they worked. To one partnership, I said, "Start by saying your idea, just like I did, and then go to an example."

To another partnership, I coached, "Weave in more specific details. Really bring this point to life for your readers!" To some other writers, I said, "Link it back to your point. Use words from your claim to make it really clear to your readers."

You might assign one member of each partnership to be Partner 1 and another to be Partner 2. That way, you can vary the work you ask partners to do. You can also vary which partner you ask to go first during the active engagement. This is particularly useful on days like today where you likely won't have time for both partners to try out ministories.

Highlight the work one writer did. Ask the other writers to listen and share their observations.

After a few minutes, I asked Saul to share his mini-story with the class. "Listen for how Saul pops out the part of his mini-story that fit with his claim: that the characters never give up." I said. Saul got started.

> The characters never give up. One way they show this is through building their own soccer pitch. They had to find spare wood from everywhere around the village, even though they're in the water. It took a few kids to carry each piece of wood. Then, they had to use fishing rafts to keep it all together, which was not easy at all. They wobbled all over while they tied the rafts. They worked together and they never gave up until they built the pitch.

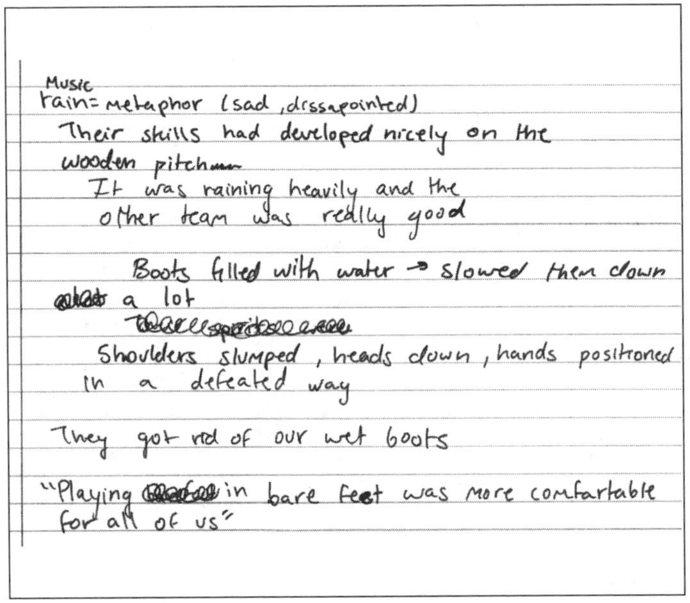

Music
rain= metaphor (sad, dissapointed)
Their skills had developed nicely on the wooden pitch
It was raining heavily and the other team was really good
Boots filled with water → slowed them down a lot
Shoulders slumped, heads down, hands positioned in a defeated way
They got rid of our wet boots
"Playing in bare feet was more comfartable for all of us"

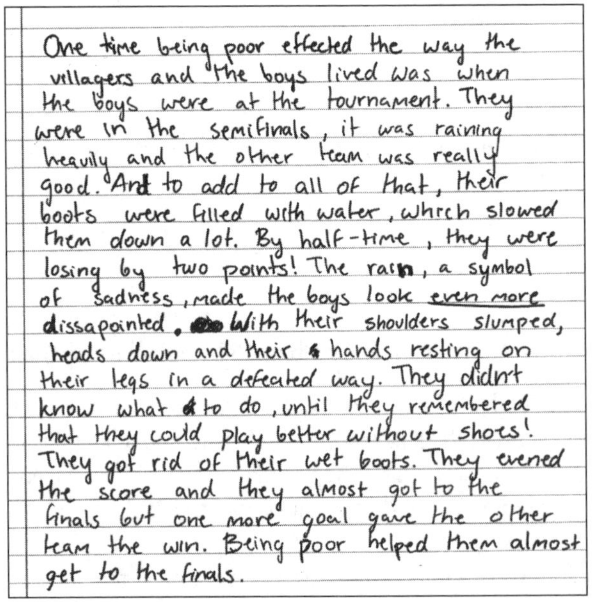

One time being poor effected the way the villagers and the boys lived was when the boys were at the tournament. They were in the semifinals, it was raining heavily and the other team was really good. And to add to all of that, their boots were filled with water, which slowed them down a lot. By half-time, they were losing by two points! The rain, a symbol of sadness, made the boys look even more dissapointed. With their shoulders slumped, heads down and their hands resting on their legs in a defeated way. They didn't know what to do, until they remembered that they could play better without shoes! They got rid of their wet boots. They evened the score and they almost got to the finals but one more goal gave the other team the win. Being poor helped them almost get to the finals.

FIG. 4–1 Mica first took notes on a powerful moment from the video, then she used those notes to generate a mini-story.

"Tell your partner what you noticed about Saul's mini-story." I listened, and then signaled for a few students to share what they had noticed. "You used words from the text, like *spare wood* and *fishing rafts*," Julia said. I signaled for Adam to add on. "Yeah, and you popped out parts that showed they never gave up. Like, you said they helped each other tie the rafts together, and they found old wood."

Keep a careful eye on pacing. If your minilesson is approaching ten minutes, you might decide to skip highlighting the work of one writer and instead move directly to the link, prioritizing your students' independent work time.

LINK

Connect the work students just did crafting mini-stories to the work they'll do across all the literary essays they'll write.

"Writers, I'm about to send you off. Remember that literary essayists work hard to convince their readers of their claims, and angled mini-stories help them to do that. A powerful mini-story can make your reader pause and say, 'Oh yes, I agree!' If you choose to try this today, your first job will be to remind yourself of the claim you're trying to support, and then to reread the text, finding parts that make the point you're trying to make. If you find a few, it helps to rank the points to choose the best one. Then, reread to see whether you could tell that part as a story, bit by bit. If you write mini-stories today, you'll write that story in your booklet under the bullet it fits with, just as you would place any other evidence under the appropriate bullet." I added this to our anchor chart.

"You'll probably find a couple of stories to support a couple of your points. Off you go, literary essayists!"

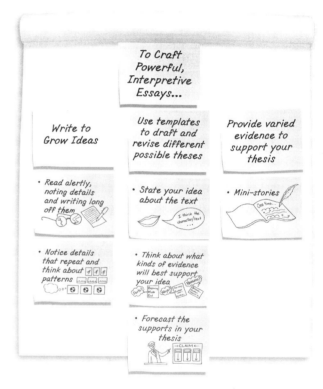

Tackling Predictable Problems with Mini-Stories

TODAY, you introduced your students to one way they can support their claim, by crafting mini-stories. This is serious and important work with long-lasting implications, so you'll want to be sure some of your conferring and small-group work today addresses this. A well-crafted narrative has the power to bring moments to life, convince readers of a claim, and linger with the reader for years to come. As students identify significant moments and craft those moments into mini-stories, they may benefit from some predictable support, either in small groups or one-on-one in conferences.

As always you'll want to be sure your conferring and small-group work is not bound by the minilesson. That is, you'll want to make sure students are drawing on all the strategies you've taught so far in this unit, as well as strategies they should be carrying over from other units, as they work today. For instance, if you find a few students who are not writing with volume, you might gather them together and remind them of the importance of writing long and strong. Or, if you see students who are crafting mini-stories without correctly spelling the words that are stated in the text, you might remind them of how essayists use all their resources to spell words correctly, particularly checking in with the text in front of them.

Writers are having trouble identifying moments that support their claim.

When writers are having trouble identifying moments that support their claim, it often means their claim is only true for a portion of the text. Despite the conferring and small-group work you did as part of Session 3 to help students shore up their thesis statements, you may find a few students who are working with thesis statements that pertain to only part of the text. Gather these students and remind them that their thesis statement must be one that can be supported across the entire text. Refer them to the "Template for Trying Out Possible Theses to Find the Perfect One" chart from Session 3 if they need to develop a new thesis statement. As you're coaching, keep in mind that stories are often written in a problem-solution way. Instead of, "You should hold tight to friends," the best way to make a thesis more encompassing might be to include the problem as well as the solution. Now the thesis might be: "Especially when it seems like the world has turned against you, you should hold onto friends." In such a thesis, the first part—the problem part—pertains to the start of the book, and the last part—the solution part—pertains to the end of the book.

Writers are telling, not showing.

A quick survey of the room may identify another group of students who are telling, not showing in their mini-stories. Instead of writing with details, a student's writing might sound more like, "They wanted a place to play football, and so they built a court,

---

MID-WORKSHOP TEACHING

Storytelling with Relevant Details

"Writers, eyes on me for a moment. You know to use the ingredients of good storytelling to tell a mini-story. You already know that telling a mini-story bit by bit and stretching out the important parts are important ingredients, but the point is that you retell just the details from a text that connect to and provide evidence for your thesis and supports.

"If you are writing to show how people work together to overcome hard times, you probably don't need to say, 'The boys were wearing gray tank tops . . .' but you might well decide to suggest that when they worked, 'sweat was dripping from their foreheads.' The gray tank tops don't support your point—but the sweat dripping from their foreheads does.

"You might take a moment right now to reread your mini-stories and ask yourself, 'Is this detail just extra, superfluous? Does this detail connect to my claim?' In several minutes you'll be meeting with your partner to look more closely at your evidence, so you might take this time to get ready for your partner."

---

and then they had a place to play." Sometimes students cut out the start to the story altogether, so their story sounds more like reporting a fact: "They made a soccer field on a raft."

Either way, gather these students together and begin by complimenting what they have done. They have found evidence in the text to support their claim. What they have done is entirely acceptable in a literary essay. However, they have not written that evidence as a story, which should be something they know how to do and can choose to do some of the time in their literary essays.

To help them see the difference between what they have done and what you have been trying to teach in today's minilesson, you might bring a copy of the Grade 5 Narrative Writing Checklist and suggest students look between that checklist and what they had been thinking was a small story written to support their claim. You may want to channel them to study the Elaboration category especially, noting the expectations for writers when they craft narratives.

Then, remind writers that essayists do similar work with their mini-stories, blending together description, action, dialogue, and thinking to bring their mini-stories to life. You'd probably want to channel them to get started working on their mini-stories right there in the small group, so you can coach students to lift the level of their work. Push them to try writing out the mini-story in a bit-by-bit way, and let them know they can decide later if they want to include that version or the shorter summary of the part in their essay.

Writers are including all the details of a moment without prioritizing.

You may see students who are stretching out their stories so they are no longer *mini*, by including every possible detail they can. You might find these students pausing the video and recording everything they see. Gather these students together, first complimenting them on the specific details they've woven in to bring their mini-stories to life.

Then, shift into your teaching point. "To make your mini-stories as strong as possible, it helps if all the details you include advance your claim. You can look at each detail and ask, 'Does this fit with or help show my claim?' If not, you'll want to cut it out or revise it so it does." Then, you might show students how you try this with a mini-story that's a bit exaggerated, laden with additional details to make the point.

Sample writing to model revising to ensure all details fit with the claim.

The boys were incredibly hard working. One part that shows this is when a boy in a long, gray tank top got an idea. They could build their own football pitch! The other boys cheered. Then, they got to work. There were some long, skinny pieces of wood down below their floating village. One boy passed the wood up to another boy who was on a tall wooden ladder. The bigger boys collected longer wooden planks. They put them over their shoulders.

Demonstrate how you read through that story thinking, "Does this support my claim?" When you find details that don't fit, cross out many of them, and show how you revise one or two to fit. Then, coach students as they read through the mini-stories they've already drafted or craft additional mini-stories, making sure each detail they include advances their claim.

Analyzing Mini-Stories with Partners

Set students up to analyze their mini-stories with partners, giving one another feedback as to whether their mini-story fits with their claim.

"Writers, to make your mini-stories as clear as possible, it helps to make sure they're focused and that every single part you include connects in some way to your claim. To do this, it helps to remove details that don't fit with the specific claim or aren't necessary.

"Take a couple of minutes to meet with your partner to see if your evidence *really* goes with your claim and your support. Partner 2, will you be first to display one of your mini-stories? Tell your partner what claim and bullet you're hoping that mini-story supports, and then read it aloud to your partner. Partner 1, you'll need to listen carefully to determine whether the mini-story *totally* fits the claim, is *starting to* fit the claim, or *does not yet* fit the claim.

"After Partner 2 shares, Partner 1, you'll provide feedback. You might say, 'Well, this first part totally fits your claim, but I'm not sure how the second part fits it. Can you explain it to me?' or you might say, 'It seems like this part fits, but I'm wondering if there's a way to say it to help your readers understand *how* it fits.' Ready? Get started."

I coached students while they worked. "Look at each sentence," I whispered to a listening partner. "Listen to see if each sentence fits." To another student I said, "Help your reader choose which parts are really important to storytell."

FIG. 4–2 Emmy uses her knowledge of narrative craft to strengthen her mini-story.

SESSION 4 HOMEWORK

 COLLECTING ADDITIONAL EVIDENCE

Writers, tomorrow you'll be laying out all your evidence and drafting a powerful, interpretive literary essay. Use tonight to collect more evidence. Collect additional mini-stories and add them to the files you set up in your writing notebook. You might also collect quotes, lifting really powerful lines from the text that support your ideas and adding them to your notes. Make sure you have at least two or three pieces of evidence for each of your supports.

Flash-Drafting a Literary Essay

SOMETIMES, TO DRAFT, writers need a little guidance, a reminder for how their writing could go. Today, you'll provide that guidance by reminding students of the work they did on the first day of the unit, when you conducted an inquiry into the characteristics of literary essay writing. You'll teach kids that the chart you made in the first session can be used as a sort of checklist, and you'll demonstrate how writers can rehearse their essays by saying them in the air, referencing the checklist along the way to make sure they have all the necessary parts.

Using the checklist as a guide, you'll channel partners to rehearse an essay in the air that is organized into a clear, predictable structure. Then you'll send them off to flash-draft, writing fast and furious down pages of loose-leaf paper outside of their notebooks, so they draft a majority of their essay in one single session of independent writing. This goal is entirely attainable, and to encourage it you'll want to spend a bit of your conferring and small-group work time encouraging students to write with greater volume and stamina.

Writing literary essays can seem like a complex activity, while checking items off a checklist can seem rather mundane—but it is no small fries. In 2001, doctors at Johns Hopkins Hospital started using daily checklists as a part of their intensive care unit procedures. The items on the checklist seemed incredibly routine: (1) Wash your hands with soap. (2) Clean the patient's skin with antiseptic. (3) Put sterile drapes over the patient. (4) Wear a sterile mask, hat, gown, and gloves. While some doctors chafed at having to check off commonplace aspects of caring for patients, when the checklist was put into practice, the infection rate of ICU patients plummeted, and lives were saved.

Checklists work: they make what is complex doable, and they help what is doable to be done well. The checklist you'll share with students today will function similarly. It will make their essay feel writable, and it will ensure their first literary essay of the unit is written well.

During today's homework you'll invite students to choose a text they want to write about texts. To do this, you'll send home a short list of familiar titles. On this list,

IN THIS SESSION, you'll teach students that writers use checklists to get ready to draft. Specifically, you'll teach that when writers flash-draft a literary essay, it helps to rehearse it in the air with the qualities of good essay writing in mind.

GETTING READY

✔ Have an image of a plane's cockpit ready to display (see Connection).

✔ Display the "What Makes a Literary Essay?" anchor chart from Session 1 (see Teaching).

✔ Have your booklet handy, complete with the mini-stories you've created for your demonstration text. We use "The Little Red Riding Hood" (see Teaching).

✔ Prepare mini-copies of the "What Makes a Literary Essay?" anchor chart for each writer (see Active Engagement).

✔ Have lined paper ready for students to use to flash-draft their essays (see Link).

✔ Be ready to add to the "To Craft Powerful, Interpretive Essays" anchor chart (see Link).

✔ Print a few copies of "A True Friend" to support students with paragraphing (see Conferring and Small-Group Work)

✔ Prepare mini-copies of a "Transitions that Spiff Up Essays" chart to distribute to students (see Mid-Workshop Teaching).

✔ Distribute copies of the Grade 5 Opinion Writing Checklist to students to keep in their writing folders (see Share).

✔ Be ready to hand out a short list of texts you recommend students choose to write off of for Bend II. We provide a list as part of today's homework, but you could choose your own texts (see Homework).

✔ Before the next session, you will want to read to the class a narrative mentor text you'll use to demonstrate writing a literary essay in Bend II. We've chosen "Shells" by Cynthia Rylant from *Every Living Thing*.

consider including during Bend II you've read aloud so far this year: short stories, literary nonfiction, picture books, and others. Keep the list short, because in the next session you'll channel students into clubs around the texts they've chosen. In the homework, you'll see a list of titles that pilot classrooms had great success using, but you can certainly substitute other short texts. If your students have not yet read the titles we recommend, you might choose to pause the unit for a day and invite students to read some of those recommended texts to help determine which one they want to write about. The suggested texts span a wide range of levels, and you might do some behind-the-scenes engineering to direct kids toward texts they can read independently.

Students also need to be familiar with a shared text you will work with in Bend II. We've chosen the story "Shells" by Cynthia Rylant, from her short story collection *Every Living Thing*. This text is woven deeply into the work of Bend II. You might choose to substitute another narrative text, but doing so will require you to modify many minilessons across the bend. You will want to read aloud "Shells" or whatever other mentor text you choose prior to tomorrow's minilesson.

Flash-Drafting a Literary Essay

CONNECTION

Announce to writers that by the end of writing workshop, they will have completed their first literary essay of the year.

"Writers, today is a big day! By the end of writing time today, you will have flash-drafted your very first literary essay of the year. I know your notebooks are brimful of the evidence you have been collecting and sorting, and that you've worked hard to make sure your evidence matches your claim and is varied. All this helps set you up for a successful draft."

Create an analogy between a complex operation that requires a checklist—flying a plane—and the act of drafting an essay.

"Have any of you flown in an airplane?" Heads nodded, and I continued. "Did you ever peek inside the cockpit, where the pilots sit? Have you ever seen all those buttons and dials that pilots have to use to be able to fly a plane?" I briefly displayed the image of a cockpit.

"Looks pretty complex, huh? Almost a hundred years ago, people started making bigger and faster planes, kind of like the planes some of you have flown in. But guess what? Few people could fly these planes very well. Pilots kept crashing the planes, which was very dangerous and life-threatening. So how did people solve the problem? They created a *checklist* for pilots, easy steps for pilots to follow so that they could operate these big, complex flying machines safely. And do you know what? It *worked*. Pilots stopped crashing planes, and people could fly safely like we do today.

"It may sound a little silly, but flying a plane is actually a lot like drafting an essay. Both are pretty complex operations. Both flying planes and writing essays can seem really hard to do, but with the right checklists to help you, both flying planes and writing essays can be done well."

❖ **Name the teaching point.**

"Today I want to teach you that essayists, like pilots, use tools to help them do complex operations. A familiar checklist can help you lift your essay off the ground. It can help you to rehearse your essay aloud, making sure you have all the parts, and then help you draft your entire essay, fast and furious."

◆ COACHING

As is true for most connections, today's connection is rather brief for a reason. You'll want to devote much of your time in today's minilesson to your demonstration and to the oral rehearsal students will practice in the Active Engagement, all to keep the entire minilesson under ten minutes.

TEACHING

Briefly review the information you compiled from the Session 1 inquiry. Explain that this chart can also be used as a checklist, reminding writers of what they need to include in their draft.

"Writers, I know you remember our inquiry from the first day of the unit. Take a moment to reacquaint yourself with the contents of this chart."

I paused for a moment and then said, "You can use this chart we created together as a sort of checklist. You can use this after you draft an essay to see if it has the parts it should, but the checklist can also be almost a recipe, a step-by-step guide as you write."

Demonstrate for writers how you rehearse with a structure in mind by writing-in-the-air, referencing each of the key points from the chart as you go.

"I'm going to say my essay about Little Red Riding Hood in the air, just the first part, so you can get an idea of how using a checklist and rehearsing a draft in the air could go. Will you imagine you're holding an imaginary pencil and make a big check mark in the air each time you see me check off a different part on the checklist?"

"Let me gather my notes so I can use them to remember what I want to say." I collected my bearings and tapped the *hooks the reader* bullet to signal where I was starting. "Hmm, . . . I usually hook the reader a bit like I try to hook you guys into a minilesson. I try to come up with something interesting like the bit about pilots flying a plane needing checklists. Let me see . . . How about this?

> "In this day and age, there is peer pressure everywhere, and it's not all positive. Sometimes students forget that the people who love them most, their family, have the wisest advice on life."

I mimed checking off the first bullet.

> "In the folktale 'Little Red Riding Hood,' the girl learns the lesson that people should listen to the advice of loved ones, not strangers. The folktale shows this in the beginning, the middle, and the end of the story."

I paused and looked at the class. "How am I doing so far? Good? Okay, let me keep going down the checklist." I pointed to the "has body paragraphs" bullet point on the checklist, and then I shifted back to writing-in-the-air. "Keep checking off what I include!" I continued writing-in-the-air.

> Early in the story, Little Red Riding Hood learns that people should listen to the advice of loved ones, not of strangers.

In Bend I, your primary teaching method in the minilesson was guided practice. In Bend II, you'll vary your methods to include more demonstration and explanation as well. Grant Wiggins claims that one of the most powerful ways for students to transfer their learning is for them to see a lot of powerful demonstration and thinking aloud.

I paused for a moment to think aloud. "To give evidence, I look across all the stuff I've collected and decide which evidence might best convince readers of my idea." I scanned my notes. "Which of these do I want to start with? Oh, I've got it. Here goes:

> For instance, the girl's mother gives her very clear advice: not to wander in the forest and to go straight to her grandmother's house. And does Little Red Riding Hood do any of those things? No! One example of this is when Little Red Riding Hood disregards her mother's advice and wanders off the trail. The flowers on the side of the trail catch her eye, and she decides she will pick her grandmother a fresh bouquet of flowers. Each new flower seems prettier than the last, and she follows the flowers, one after another, deeper and deeper into the woods.

I traced my finger down the checklist to the "includes explanations of evidence" bullet point.

> She doesn't follow her mother's instructions at all! As a result of this, the wolf has time to find and attack her grandma. This evidence shows that people should listen to what family members have to say, not strangers.

Debrief your demonstration, naming the steps so students can emulate what you just modeled.

"Writers, did you see what I just did? See how I moved my way down this chart as if it were a checklist, making sure I mentally marked off each bullet on the list as I went down the chart? Are you ready to try this with your partner?"

ACTIVE ENGAGEMENT

Channel writers to write their drafts in the air with a structure in mind. Invite one member of each partnership to do this, then the next.

I distributed mini-copies of the chart to students. "Partner 2, you go first. Take a moment to make sure your evidence is at hand, and move your way down the checklist, saying your essay in the air. Partner 1, will you keep an eye on the checklist too? Check off the things your partner does along the way, and if your partner needs help, give a tip about what to say next. Ready? Get to it!"

Some partners got started right away, but others stared at each other as if unsure of what to say first. I prompted them, saying, "Try hooking your reader with a sentence about why the theme or character trait matters."

Notice how you tuck in brief tips along the way in your demonstration. This helps spotlight why you are making particular decisions.

FIG. 5–1 Students can turn an anchor chart into a checklist.

After a couple minutes, I channeled writers to switch roles and continued coaching and prompting students.

LINK

Send students off to draft with their organizational structures and their checklist in mind. Reiterate that each writer should have a flash-draft literary essay completed by the end of the day's session.

"Today and every day, remember that having a checklist of what you're trying to create can help you do better work. This is true whether you're about to fly a plane, perform surgery, or flash-draft a literary essay.

"Writers, I'm not going to keep you here much longer because I want you to hold onto what you just wrote-in-the-air to your partner. Each of you has rehearsed the first part of your essay, using our 'What Makes a Literary Essay?' chart as if it were a checklist. Take a few more minutes to rehearse if you didn't get to finish, and then get started drafting fast and furious on loose-leaf paper." I added a bullet to our anchor chart.

Most days we suggest students choose among a repertoire of strategies. Today, you send kids off to get started on one thing: drafting. Often it is the case that the last words students hear is what they transfer most readily. Be aware of the last words you send kids off with in your link. Are you repeating a variation of the teaching point, offering suggestions for how kids might self-assign their work each day, or are you giving rote directions for managing transitions? There is a big difference between saying "Get started drafting fast and furious on loose-leaf paper," and saying, "If you need your pencil sharpened or extra paper, go to the Writing Center."

ANCHOR CHART

To Craft Powerful, Interpretive Essays . . .

- Write to grow ideas for possible essays:
  - Read alertly, noting details and writing long off them
  - Notice details that repeat and think about patterns
- Use templates to draft and revise different possible theses.
  - State your idea about the text.
  - Think about what kinds of evidence will best support your idea: Parts? Ways? Reasons?
  - Forecast the supports in your thesis.
- Provide varied evidence to support your thesis.
  - Mini-stories
- **Draft fast and furious, using tools to help you.**

Draft fast and furious, using tools to help

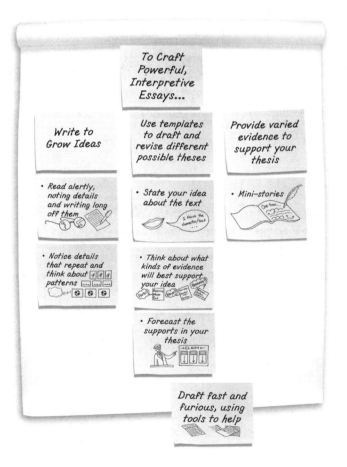

To Craft Powerful, Interpretive Essays...

Write to Grow Ideas

Use templates to draft and revise different possible theses

Provide varied evidence to support your thesis

- Read alertly, noting details and writing long off them
- State your idea about the text — I think the character/text . . .
- Mini-stories
- Notice details that repeat and think about patterns
- Think about what kinds of evidence will best support your idea
- Forecast the supports in your thesis — CLAIM
- Draft fast and furious, using tools to help

Supporting Volume, Stamina, and Revision

TODAY, as writers disperse to draft, your initial role may be one of cheerleader. You'll want to get as many writers drafting as soon as possible, and you'll want that drafting to happen quickly, with writers' pens and pencils flying down the page. One way you might support this is to scurry from table to table, encouraging writers to set their organizing structure right away and then get started drafting, and by reminding students of what they already know about good essay writing. You might lean in to one table and say, "Notice how Marco has begun right away, crafting a lead to get his readers' attention!" or "Remember to begin each body paragraph by restating your claim" or "Keep going! You have almost drafted two entire sections!" Alternately, you may decide to voice over to the entire class with these supports, sharing a bit of encouragement every few minutes to keep writers writing. You'll want to send the message that your writers can flash-draft an entire literary essay in one writing period, and that you expect everyone to have flash-drafted their essay by the time you meet for the Share.

Revising as You Draft

You may see some writers who think their job today is to simply copy what they wrote in their booklets the same way a clerk might copy numbers into a ledger. This is not the case, and today's workshop provides an ideal opportunity to teach that revision can occur across the writing process, especially during the drafting stages.

You might notice writers copying their evidence directly from their booklets to their drafts. These students will probably benefit from small-group teaching. Begin by naming your teaching point, saying, "I want to give you a tip: drafting is not copying. In fact, drafting is *revising*, seeing your writing again and making it better." It could help to explain to students that one way to flash-draft is to reread the evidence you've collected, get it in your head, then put that writing out of sight and begin flash-drafting down the page, trying to make your writing even stronger as you go. If you think an example might help, you could pull out your booklet and show students how you revised a portion of a mini-story while you were drafting it. Then, ask students to try

---

MID-WORKSHOP TEACHING
Using Transitional Phrases to Link Parts of an Essay

"Guys, you are doing great with including all the parts of an essay. If you can take a moment to think about one more thing: Remember also to glue your parts together. Using some of these transition words can spiff up your essay and make it seem really professional." I distributed a tiny cheat sheet of transitions. "Some of them are transitions that you can use when you want to zoom in to a specific example in the text, and others will help you when you want to explain what caused something or what happened as a result. Try to use some of these to glue the parts of your essay together as you keep writing. Now, get back to drafting fast and furious!"

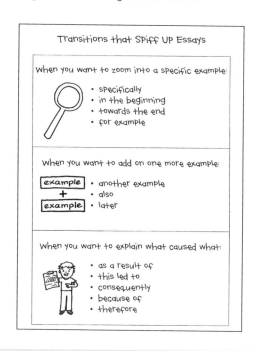

this work with you in the small group. You might ask them to reread their notes and then close their notebooks to try redrafting a section. Or, you could channel students first rewrite a section in the air to rehearse it before they put pen to paper. Leave students with a link at the end, reminding them that this is work they can do any time they are drafting, whether they are drafting an essay, an information text, or a story.

Paragraphing within a Literary Essay

As students begin drafting their support paragraphs, it's important they understand that the writing around each support does not necessarily constitute one single paragraph. That is, a thesis that includes, say, three supports will not necessarily result in a five-paragraph essay, with an introduction, a paragraph for each support, and a conclusion. Instead, you'll want to teach students that essayists are more flexible. For instance, students might find that one support requires lots of elaboration and make the decision to divide that elaboration over several paragraphs. Or, students might incorporate a mini-story into their essay and paragraph each time a new character speaks within the story.

To teach this, you might gather a group of students ready to experiment with paragraphing, and then reference an essay titled "A True Friend," an essay students may have read if they experienced the *Boxes and Bullets: Personal and Persuasive Essay* unit in Grade 4, and also available in the online resources: You could use this essay as an example to explain the paragraphing decisions Sophie made in her essay and possible reasons why she made those decisions. You will also want to highlight the obvious transitions Sophie uses to make her reasons stand out (*The first reason . . .* , *Perhaps the most important reason . . .*). Such clear transitions become a critical tool for a writer experimenting with paragraphing. Then, coach students as they reread their essays, helping them consider where to insert paragraphs before they continue drafting with paragraphing in mind.

Celebrating Growth

Celebrate the work writers have done so far. Ask students to study their writing next to the Opinion Writing Checklist and to reflect on areas of growth and next steps.

I asked students to bring their flash-drafts with them to the meeting area, and quickly distributed copies of the Grade 5 Opinion Writing Checklist. "Friends, I must congratulate you. In one week, you have gone from noticing what essayists do well to writing your own literary essays. This is no small feat.

"And, I'm thinking your writing has gotten a *ton* better in this short time. A few days ago, you studied your on-demand writing to see what parts of an essay it had. Right now, will you and your partner do similar work? Will you and your partner place your drafts next to the opinion writing checklist? Look for evidence of what you're doing well as an essayist, and also look for what you're doing better now than you were a few days ago."

After a few minutes, I voiced over, "Don't stop at your strengths! You also want to ask, 'What's something I could do even better?' Scan your piece and the checklist to come up with a goal or two." I asked students to jot their goals in their writing notebooks.

"Tomorrow, we'll start working on new literary essays off of texts you know and love. Instead of everyone writing off of the same text, you'll be able to choose from a ton of different texts. Tonight, you'll be choosing the one text you most want to study and write about. If you have a favorite short story or picture book or memoir, let me know—or bring it in tomorrow so you can use it for your essay."

If the checklist is new to students, you'll find chapters on how to introduce and use writing checklists in Writing Pathways: Performance Assessments and Learning Progressions, Grades K–8 *(Heinemann, 2015).*

Opinion Writing Checklist

	Grade 5	NOT YET	STARTING TO	YES!
	Structure			
Overall	I made a claim or thesis on a topic or text, supported it with reasons, and provided a variety of evidence for each reason.	☐	☐	☐
Lead	I wrote an introduction that led to a claim or thesis and got my readers to care about my opinion. I got my readers to care by not only including a cool fact or jazzy question, but also figuring out was significant in or around the topic and giving readers information about what was significant about the topic.	☐	☐	☐
	I worked to find the precise words to state my claim; I let readers know the reasons I would develop later.	☐	☐	☐
Transitions	I used transition words and phrases to connect evidence back to my reasons using phrases such as *this shows that*	☐	☐	☐
	I helped readers follow my thinking with phrases such as *another reason* and *the most important reason.* I used phrases such as *consequently* and *because of* to show what happened.	☐	☐	☐
	I used words such as *specifically* and *in particular* in order to be more precise.	☐	☐	☐
Ending	I worked on a conclusion in which I connected back to and highlighted what the text was mainly about, not just the preceding paragraph.	☐	☐	☐
Organization	I grouped information and related ideas into paragraphs. I put the parts of my writing in the order that most suited my purpose and helped me prove my reasons and claim.	☐	☐	☐
	Development			
Elaboration	I gave reasons to support my opinion that were parallel and did not overlap. I put them in an order that I thought would be most convincing.	☐	☐	☐
	I included evidence such as facts, examples, quotations, micro-stories, and information to support my claim.	☐	☐	☐
	I discussed and unpacked the way that the evidence went with the claim.	☐	☐	☐
Craft	I made deliberate word choices to had an effect on my readers.	☐	☐	☐
	I reached for the precise phrase, metaphor, or image that would convey my ideas.	☐	☐	☐
	I made choices about how to angle my evidence to support my points.	☐	☐	☐
	When it seemed right to do so, I tried to use a scholarly voice and varied my sentences to create the pace and tone of the different sections of my piece.	☐	☐	☐

Panyee Football Club Essay

Sometimes in life, we will have a dream. A goal that is so big, so strong, that it never fades away. However, we will find that to get to those goals, those dreams, we will face challenges. Challenges as big as our dream. Some will back down, let their dream fade away and crumble. Yet some will stand strong, and work and push through these challenges. The story of the Panyee Football Club is a story of just that. In the story, the Panyee FC learn that in life, you will have to face challenges to achieve a goal. A dream. That you must not back down. They show this in the beginning, middle, and end of the story.

The story of the Panyee FC is really about how in life, you will need to push through challenges to get to your dream. While the characters show this throughout the story, a strong example of this is in the beginning. The story shows this when the team first has their dream to become soccer champions. However, it isn't that easy. The boys have never played soccer. In their water surrounded village they call home, they have hardly any space or materials to practice - a vital to becoming champions. On top of that, the elders of the village scoff at their big dreams. ["Look around you. Look where you live."] It seems as if all of their dreams are going down the drain. The team could have backed down, they could have given up. They could have taken the easy way out. Yet the team didn't back down, or give up. Not at all. As a result, the team worked hard to push through the challenge at hand. They found old wood and fishing boats to

make a pitch. They worked hard after school to get it done. They took it in to their own hands, and didn't let anybody bring them down, not even the doubting villagers. Because they pushed through their challenge, they were able to get one step closer to achieving a goal.

The story of the Panyee FC is really about how in life, you will have to push through challenges to achieve your dream. While the team shows this in the beginning and end, the story escpecially shows this in the middle of the story. The Panyee FC has already faced a big challenge, but that isn't the end of their troubles. The Panyee boy's pitch is shaky, uneven, and has nails growing everywhere, like ivy. The pitch was small and slippery, as the ball would splash in the surrounding water often. Also, the villagers are still not giving any support to the dreaming, hardworking boys. ["You won't become champions on that thing!"] Some people may have given up. They may have become too fed up and overwhelmed about all of the challenges. Some may have doubted, just as the villagers had. However, the Panyee FC team didn't give up. Not at all. All of the imperfections about the pitch don't make them stop believing in their dream. All of the doubting villagers don't stop them, either. In fact, these challenges just made the team stronger.

The story of the Panyee FC is really about how in life, you will need to push through challenges to achieve your goals. The story shows this in the end, when the team faces more challenges.

They face a challenge that will test their strength, determination, and hope - The Pangha Cup. The biggest challenge of all. First, they faced this challenge by signing up for the competition in the first place, and by believing in themselves. Nevertheless, the real challenge comes later. The team had made it to the semifinals. It was downpouring hard, and the other team was "really good." The opponents were winning, up by two points by halftime. It seemed as if all of their hardwork really was for nothing. But it wasn't. Once again, the young boys from panyee proved everybody wrong, facing their challenge. They took of their water filled boots. Even though the other, opposing team ended up stealing the game, the importance is, the Panyee FC pushed through another challenge - and achieved their goal in the end.

To sum it all up, the story of the Panyee FC is one of hardwork, determination, and strength, inside and out. This story inspired and taught me many things, shown all throughout the story. One big lesson that the legend of the Panyee FC taught me was that in life, you will push through challenges to get to your goal.

Now, go out, and achieve your dream.

FIG. 5–2   Olivia's final draft. Notice how she repeats her claim at the beginning of every paragraph, followed by supporting evidence.

GRADE 5: LITERARY ESSAY

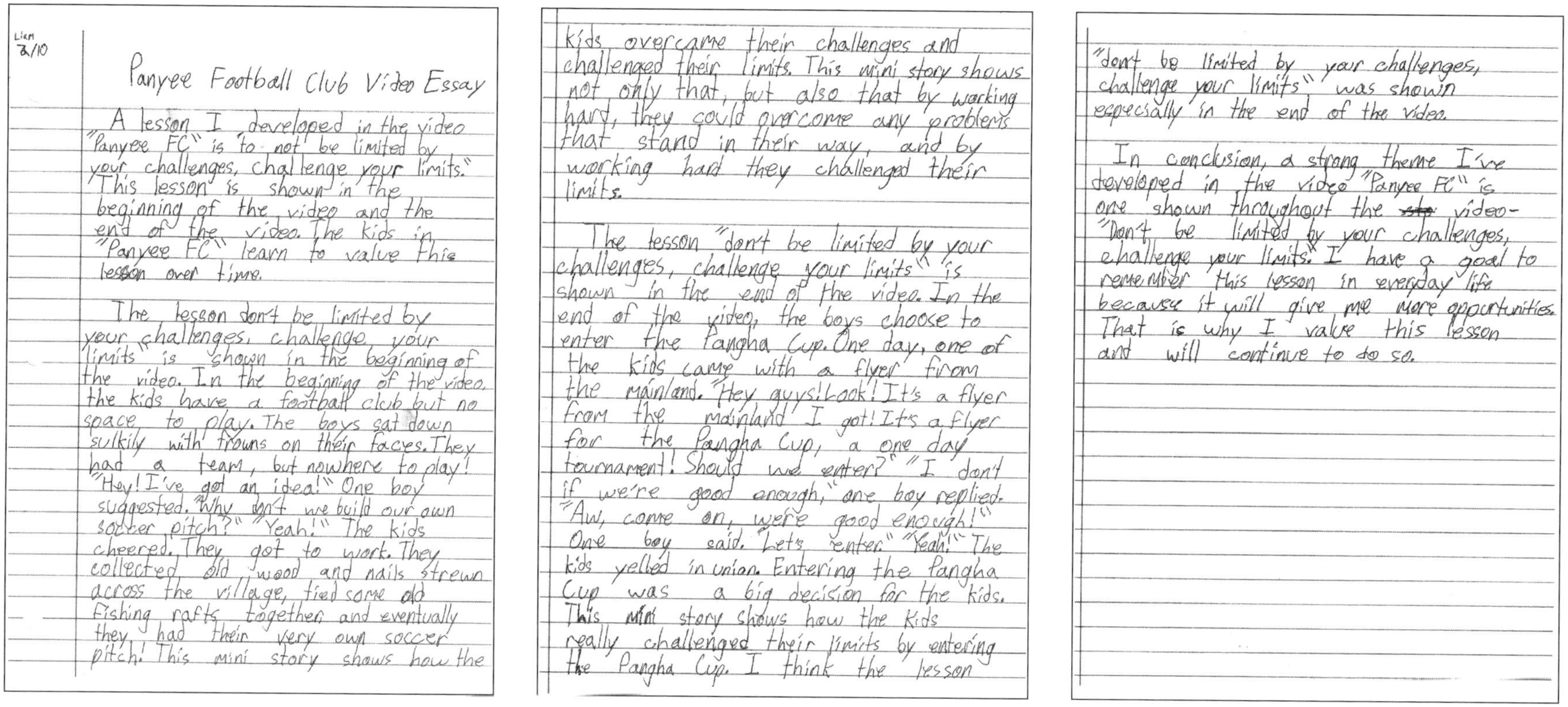

Liam
2/10

Panyee Football Club Video Essay

A lesson I developed in the video "Panyee FC" is "to not be limited by your challenges, challenge your limits." This lesson is shown in the beginning of the video and the end of the video. The kids in "Panyee FC" learn to value this lesson over time.

The lesson don't be limited by your challenges, challenge your limits" is shown in the beginning of the video. In the beginning of the video, the kids have a football club but no space to play. The boys sat down sulkily with frowns on their faces. They had a team, but nowhere to play! "Hey! I've got an idea!" One boy suggested. "Why don't we build our own soccer pitch?" "Yeah!" The kids cheered. They got to work. They collected old wood and nails strewn across the village, tied some old fishing rafts together and eventually they had their very own soccer pitch! This mini story shows how the kids overcame their challenges and challenged their limits. This mini story shows not only that, but also that by working hard, they could overcome any problems that stand in their way, and by working hard they challenged their limits.

The lesson "don't be limited by your challenges, challenge your limits" is shown in the end of the video. In the end of the video, the boys choose to enter the Pangha Cup. One day, one of the kids came with a flyer from the mainland. "Hey guys! Look! It's a flyer from the mainland I got! It's a flyer for the Pangha Cup, a one day tournament! Should we enter?" "I don't if we're good enough," one boy replied. "Aw, come on, we're good enough!" One boy said. "Let's enter." "Yeah!" The kids yelled in union. Entering the Pangha Cup was a big decision for the kids. This mini story shows how the kids really challenged their limits by entering the Pangha Cup. I think the lesson "don't be limited by your challenges, challenge your limits" was shown especially in the end of the video.

In conclusion, a strong theme I've developed in the video "Panyee FC" is one shown throughout the video— "Don't be limited by your challenges, challenge your limits." I have a goal to remember this lesson in everyday life because it will give me more opportunities. That is why I value this lesson and will continue to do so.

FIG. 5–3 Liam's final draft. His thesis forecasts how the essay will be organized.

FLASH DRAFTING AND SELECTING A TEXT

Writers, today you started flash-drafting a literary essay to prove your claim about the "Panyee Football Club" video. Tonight, you've got two big jobs. First, you'll want to finish flash-drafting your essay so that your entire essay is finished when you return to school.

Your second big job is to select a text you want to write about for your next literary essay. Choose a text from the list. You might rank your top two or three choices. It's best if you choose a text you love that is also written well. You will also want to be sure the text you choose will be a good text off of which to write long and grow ideas. Tomorrow I'll put you into clubs with other readers who chose the same text to write about.

I'm sending home a short list of familiar texts you might choose, which is filled with favorites we've read together. Read it over carefully, remembering what moved you about each text. But, if you have a favorite short story, picture book, or memoir that's not on the list, bring it in with you tomorrow if you're interested in writing about it.

Some of Our Favorite Shared Texts to Choose From

- *One Green Apple* by Eve Bunting
- *The Stranded Whale* by Jane Yolen
- Selections from *Marshfield Dreams* by Ralph Fletcher, especially:
  - "Attack"
  - "Last Kiss"
  - "A Pox upon Us All"
  - "Scuttlebutt"
  - "Tea Rock Lane"

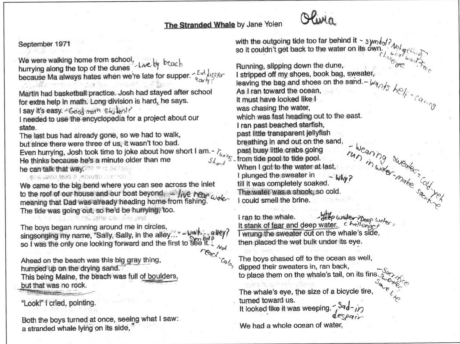

FIG. 5–4 The first page of an annotated student essay. The full essay is available on the online resources.

Lifting the Level of Interpretive Essay
(and Writing One from Start to Finish)

BEND **II**

Writing to Grow Ideas

IN THIS SESSION, you'll teach writers that essayists study small, specific details or the parts that feel odd or important to grow big ideas and interpretations.

GETTING READY

✔ Before starting this bend, each student will need to have read at least one of the short texts you'll have invited them to work with across this bend. We recommend *One Green Apple* by Eve Bunting, *The Stranded Whale* by Jane Yolen, and short stories from *Marshfield Dreams* by Ralph Fletcher, including "Attack," "Last Kiss," "A Pox upon Us All," "Scuttlebutt," and "Tea Rock Lane." Alternately, you may decide to choose a few of your own favorite texts.

✔ Before this session, you will need to have read aloud "Shells" by Cynthia Rylant, or another touchstone text that you choose, to your students.

✔ Be sure students have their **reading** notebooks with them in the meeting space (see Connection).

✔ Provide each student with a copy of "Shells" and be ready to display the first few paragraphs to the class (see Teaching and Active Engagement).

✔ In your writing notebook, write to grow ideas connected to your demonstration text, and be ready to project the page to show to students (see Teaching).

✔ Provide students with a copy of the short text they've chosen to study across this bend (see Link).

✔ Be ready to add to the "To Craft Powerful, Interpretive Essays" anchor chart (see Link and Share).

✔ "To Develop Ideas, Readers . . ." and "Ways to Push Our Thinking" charts (see Conferring and Small-Group Work)

✔ Group students into informal clubs of kids who are reading the same short text (see Share).

THIS SESSION KICKS OFF the second bend of the unit, and therefore this is an important time for you to rally your students to invest in the new work they'll be doing over the next few weeks: writing interpretive essays that advance well-supported claims. To convince them that it is important to learn to write effective literary essays, you need to have an answer to the question, "Why write literary essays?"

Our hunch is that your first response is that this is a high-stakes genre. Chances are good that for years to come, writing to support ideas about texts will continue to be prevalent on high-stakes assessments. Let's face it—that matters. It is important to equip young people to excel on the tasks that can open doors for them, giving them access to the colleges and careers they are most interested in.

Having said that, we want to encourage you to realize that there is a reason why literary essays are highly valued on high-stakes tests. This is a genre that matters to academics—to scholars. Why? For us, literary essays matter because the act of writing within an essay structure channels us to read, reread, and think about texts in increasingly complex ways. This reading and rereading helps to open those texts up to us and makes them vastly more interesting. When we seriously and deeply and closely engage with a short story, that story becomes "ours" in a way that matters. And equally importantly, when we write essays about a text, we learn to look, theorize, check our theories, look again, refine our ideas . . . in short, to think analytically. So yes, this portion of the unit, and this unit, matters.

Just as a bend in the road brings new vistas, so too does this bend of the unit bring a new set of skills for writers to learn as they craft literary essays. You'll start this bend by channeling students to celebrate their best writing about reading thus far in the year, and you'll use that mini-celebration as a springboard into the bend's new work. Specifically, you'll teach writers that one way to generate ideas for essays is to note small, specific details in the text, or parts that jump out to the reader as odd or important. Then, readers can linger with those details, talking and writing and thinking a lot about them. Lingering with the nitty-gritty in the text can help readers grow ideas up in the clouds, reaching toward possible themes and lessons in the text. This is writing to learn, and you should expect that many students will fill their notebooks today with pages where they write long about details in the text. This writing will not resemble students' published essays.

"Lingering with the nitty-gritty in a text can help readers grow ideas, reaching toward possible themes and lessons in the text."

Across this bend, you'll teach students to lift the level of their essay writing and to craft powerful, interpretive essays on self-selected texts. You channeled students to select these texts as part of the homework in Session 5. Kids will be regularly working in informal clubs across this bend, grouped together with other students studying their same text. To facilitate this, it will help if there are at least two students in the class studying each text, with ideal groups numbering between three and five students. Prior to today's session, collect a list of the texts students are interested in studying, and group students together into informal same-text clubs. Students will carry these texts with them into Bend III, pairing them with other texts and articles to write a variety of opinion texts.

In this bend you'll teach students additional ways writers generate ideas for literary essays, by studying the small, specific details in the text and growing ideas off of those details and by studying scenes where characters respond to trouble or where something related to the problem shifts. In this bend, you'll also teach writers way to provide evidence for supports by finding and ranking precise quotes from a text and by crafting powerful lists. Then you'll show students how to analyze a text through the lens of the craft moves an author uses, and to use those craft moves as supports for a claim. Expect to see your students' essay-writing skills grow dramatically across this bend.

If you're teaching from Units of Study in Opinion/Argument, Information, and Narrative Writing, you'll see great reciprocity between the Grade 5 *Narrative Craft* unit and your teaching today. For instance, in Session 4 of that unit, "Telling the Story from Inside It," you taught your writers to only include the truest details, the ones a character would have actually experienced in the moment. And in Session 16, "Catching the Action or Image that Produced the Emotion," you taught students that they could include a character's precise actions or images on the page, weaving in the kinds of details that would lead readers to think more deeply about a character's thoughts or feelings. Today, you'll help them consider the significance of those same kinds of details in the texts they read.

Writing to Grow Ideas

CONNECTION

Invite students to bring their reading notebooks to the meeting area, and set students up to study them, noting the characteristics of their best writing about reading.

"I saw some of you giving me funny looks when I asked you to bring your reading notebooks to the carpet. A few of you even said, 'Reading notebooks? Are you sure? This is *writing*.' But, I think there's actually a ton you can learn from studying your reading notebooks. Remember how you started the year with an intense focus on lifting the level of your writing about reading? You learned to read with that *writerly wide-awakeness*, noting things others would just pass by, to ground your thinking in the text, and then, rather than leaving those ideas behind, you learned to carry them with you. Your writing about reading grew leaps and bounds.

"Before we start writing today, will you spend a little time admiring the writing about reading work you've done, and recalling all you've learned about strong writing about reading? Take a minute to skim and scan your notebook right now, studying all you've done from the beginning of the year, and ask yourself, 'Out of all these entries, which one represents my very best writing about reading?' When you find it, name what it is that makes it so strong." I allowed a short moment to pass while pages turned and students read their own work, and then I spoke again over the silence.

"Now, will you share that entry with your partner? Brainstorm what makes that particular entry so strong. Really admire the work you've done as writers. Get to it!" I gave students a couple minutes to study.

Explain that crafting literary essays requires writers to begin with powerful writing about reading—and close reading.

"I'm sharing this with you because we're launching a new bend in this unit. You'll be crafting interpretive essays about texts *you* select—and writing strong, interpretive essays requires you to write about your reading in these same ways you do in reading workshop—noting significant details, writing to explore and to make more of those details, even writing to capture how your possible interpretations evolve as you move across the terrain of a text. This work also requires a lot of rereading, diving into passages of text again and again to try to make more of them, just as you did in your book clubs.

◆ COACHING

Here, you're referring to the work students did as part of the Interpretation Book Clubs: Analyzing Themes *reading unit, specifically the first bend of the unit, "Writing about Reading with Voice and Investment." If you chose to launch the year differently, you might instead ask students to study the writing about reading work they've done with you, or you might choose to project the powerful samples of writing about reading shown in Figs. 6–1 and 6–2 and ask students to study them, noting their characteristics.*

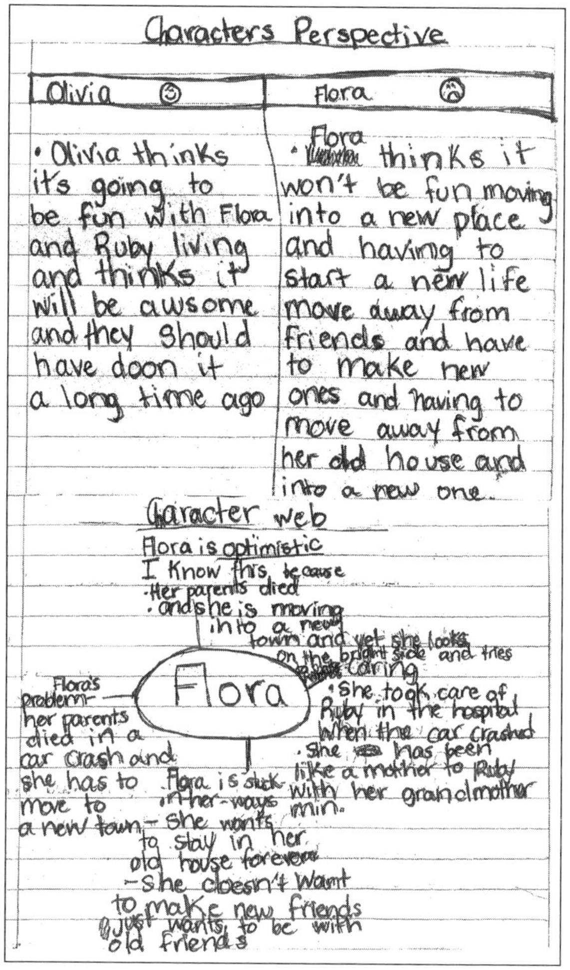

FIG. 6–1 A student shares a page from her reading notebook where she grew ideas about characters.

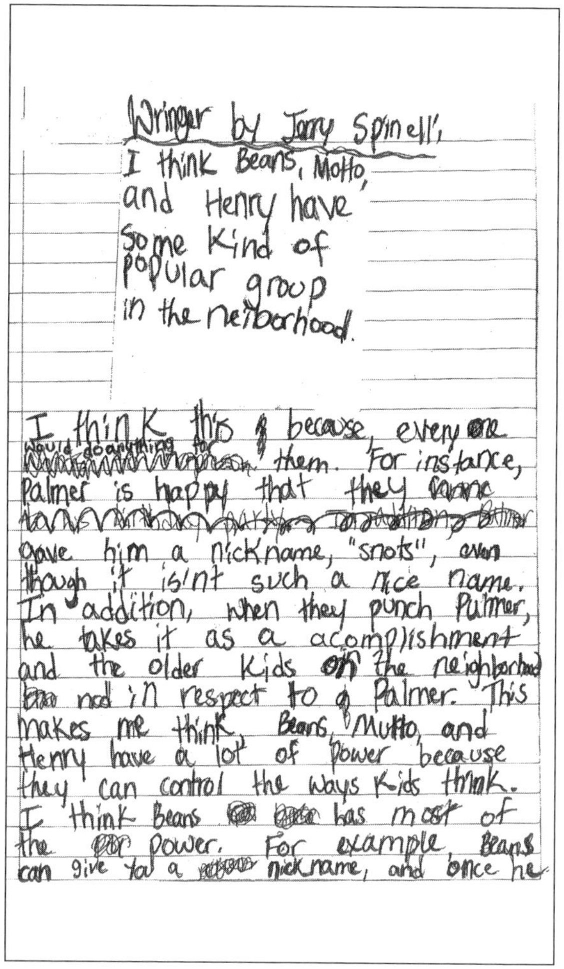

FIG. 6–2 A student showcases a page from his reading notebook where he wrote about power issues.

"In this next bend of our unit you'll have to carry with you all you know, but I also want to teach you some strategies that help literary essayists grow particularly poignant ideas."

❖ **Name the teaching point.**

"Today I want to remind you that to grow ideas, literary essayists often study the small, specific details in the text, or the parts that feel odd or important. They know that studying these tiny details can lead them to big ideas and interpretations."

TEACHING

Explain to students that the best writing about reading starts with noticing concrete details in the text or parts that feel odd or important.

"The writer Richard Price once said something that relates to this. He said, 'The bigger the issue, the smaller you write.' Now, Price didn't mean that you make your handwriting really, really tiny when you're writing about big things, like themes in a text. Instead, he meant that when you want to think about something really big, it helps to start with the small, specific details and think and write a lot about those. He even said, 'You don't write about the horrors of war. No. You write about a kid's burnt socks lying on the road. You pick the smallest manageable part of the big thing, and you work off the resonance'—or the meaning or significance of that small part."

Demonstrate how you read a passage from your demonstration text, noting the small details and the bigger ideas the text sparks for you.

"Like all of you, I chose a text for us to study. The text I've selected to work with across this bend is 'Shells,' by Cynthia Rylant. Ever since we read it yesterday, the text has just been lingering with me. I keep thinking about how weird Michael and Aunt Esther's relationship seems. I'm hoping that as I do some more rereading and writing about it, I'll understand the text even more. And, I thought, you could try some of this work with 'Shells' too.

"Will you watch me try this? What I usually do is I reread, looking for parts of the text that grab me, that draw me in. Sometimes they are details, sometimes they are just parts that feel odd or important."

I projected the beginning of "Shells" and read it aloud.

> *"You hate living here."*
>
> *Michael looked at the woman speaking to him.*
>
> *"No, Aunt Esther. I don't." He said it dully, sliding his milk glass back and forth on the table. "I don't hate it here."*

"Like now—there is a line that feels really odd to me: 'Michael looked at *the woman* speaking to him.' It's his aunt, right? A member of his family? So it feels really odd when she is described as *the woman* instead of his aunt." I paused to give students time to think with me. "It makes her sound almost like a stranger." I underlined the phrase and jotted, "Why 'the woman'?" in the margin.

Write-in-the-air to show students how you move from a small detail in the text to a big idea. Recruit students to signal when it's time to move from the particulars to big ideas.

"I'll start and try this, then you can take a turn. As I do this, I'm going to try to say a lot about the details, the particulars, then shift to the big ideas . . . and how about you help me know when to shift? I'm going to start and talk about the

It matters that students select texts they feel passionate about, texts they want to spend a bend exploring. Their literary essays will be better because of their engagement. Note how we tuck in the reasons why we selected this text to help students begin thinking about the texts they might select.

Notice that you read aloud just a few lines of the text during your demonstration. It's important to show students that big thinking can spring from a tiny passage from the text, even from a single phrase an author includes. Reading aloud a tiny passage from the text also helps to keep your demonstration brief and your mini-lesson under ten minutes, which helps you prioritize that students write independently for a majority of the workshop.

gritty specifics of this. Listen, and when you think it's time for me to shift to talk about the big ideas, point up in the air, to the big ideas in the clouds.

"Okay, here goes":

> In this story, the boy, Michael, is sitting at the table with a glass of milk in front of him and his aunt is nearby. He looks at her, but in the text the author describes this by saying "Michael looked at the woman speaking to him."

At that point, a few students pointed up, suggesting I shift to talk about the big ideas in the clouds, but I gestured that no, I should stay at the gritty level longer. I wanted to show the kids how they could do that. I repeated what I'd said so far and continued:

> In this story, the boy, Michael, is sitting at the table with a glass of milk in front of him and his aunt is nearby. He looks at her, but in the text the author describes this by saying "Michael looked at the woman speaking to him." He calls her Aunt Esther when he says her name, but he's not enthusiastic about it. In the text it says, "He said it dully, sliding his milk glass back and forth."

At this point I appealed to the students who again pointed toward the sky and I shifted, talking in big, airy concepts.

> This makes me think that just because people are family, they aren't always close. You can live with someone and that person can still feel like a stranger to you.

Debrief, naming the transferable work you just demonstrated.

"Writers, do you see how it helps to first reread, noting details or places that feel odd or important? Then, you can grow some ideas off of what you noticed, starting in the particulars, the nitty gritty, and then moving to big ideas, up in the clouds."

ACTIVE ENGAGEMENT

Read aloud a little more of the text, and set students up to notice details or parts that feel odd or important.

"Ready to try this? I'll read a bit more of the text—follow along on your copy as I read—and will you be on the lookout for any details, or any odd or interesting parts, that stand out to you? Underline them or mark them with a symbol if you find them. After I read, you'll try growing your idea with your partner, moving from the nitty gritty details to big ideas."

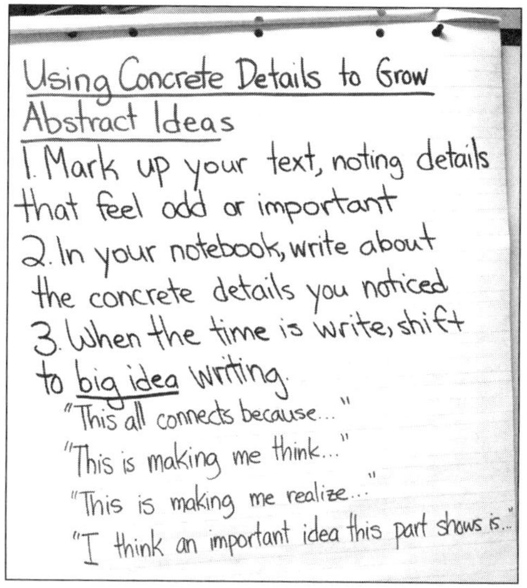

FIG. 6–3   One teacher created a chart to help break down the steps involved in growing abstract ideas.

If you think students would benefit from seeing a visual representation of what you wrote-in-the-air, you might prewrite the words you just said aloud and then project them for students at the end of your demonstration so students have a visual of what the work looks like.

I projected the next passage of the text and read it aloud.

"I don't hate it here."

Esther removed the last pan from the dishwasher and hung it above the oven.

"You hate it here," she said, "and you hate me."

"I don't!" Michael yelled. "It's not you!"

The woman turned to face him in the kitchen.

"Mark up a detail you're noticing, or an odd or interesting part."

Set up partners to write-in-the-air, channeling them to shift from the particulars in the text to big ideas about the text. Coach partnerships to write-in-the-air and to give each other feedback.

"You've got some details or lines marked up. Will you try this with one of Partner 1's lines? Partner 1, you get started talking about the details you noticed in the text. Partner 2, listen for when it's time for your partner to think big and move your hand up high, into the clouds, to signal to your partner. Go for it!"

I noticed most students weren't looking at their texts, so I voiced over. "Use the text to help you. When you're thinking small, ground your thinking in the details, the exact words, that are in the text."

Then, I knelt next to Joanna and Mohammed. Mohammed was writing-in-the-air. "I put a star by where it says, 'The woman turned to face him in the kitchen.' I thought that was a weird detail to include." He paused.

I coached. "That is weird, right? Sometimes it helps to start by talking about what the line means."

"I guess it means she had to turn around to look at him, right? So she must not have been looking at him before. She was looking away from him," Mohammed continued.

"Now, think about why Cynthia Rylant might have included that detail," I added.

"Maybe . . . I guess it's kind of rude not to be looking at someone when they're talking to you, 'cause it said Michael was looking at her. And, it's hard not to look at someone when they're yelling at you."

I whispered to Joanna, "I love the way he's paying attention to the specific words on the page. You could say he's writing 'small,' right?' Help him go big." She moved her arm up to signal to Mohammed. He nodded, paused to think, and then shifted, saying, "I guess maybe a big thing is their closeness. They must not be that close to each other." I gave them a thumbs up and moved on.

To keep your minilesson moving along and prioritize time for students to write independently, you'll notice we choose to have just one partner, in this case, Partner 1, share a line he found in the text. Both partners still play an active role and have opportunities to engage with this work.

LINK

Emphasize that writers should add today's strategy to their growing bank of strategies for developing ideas for interpretive essays.

I gestured toward the "To Craft Powerful, Interpretive Essays" anchor chart, where I had added the day's strategy. "Writers, this strategy you learned today—that writers start by rereading and noting tiny details, the nitty-gritty, and then grow their thinking to big ideas—it's just one strategy that you can draw on today. You know other strategies too. Remember that in the last bend of the unit, you learned that writers read with extra alertness, paying close attention to the details that other people pass right by, and then they write a lot about those details. And you learned that writers notice repeating details and write a lot about the patterns. You can try all of these strategies as you write about your new texts today. Off you go!"

Across this bend, you'll want to look for opportunities to help students transfer what they've learned in Bend I to the new work in Bend II. Regularly referencing strategies you taught earlier and charts you developed earlier in the unit will help the student transfer of learning you expect to see.

ANCHOR CHART

To Craft Powerful, Interpretive Essays . . .

- Write to grow ideas for possible essays:
  - Read alertly, noting details and writing long off them
  - Notice details that repeat and think about patterns
  - **Note particulars, write a lot about them, and then move to big ideas**
- Use templates to draft and revise different possible theses.
  - State your idea about the text.
  - Think about what kinds of evidence will best support your idea
  - Forecast the supports in your thesis.
- Provide varied evidence to support your thesis.
  - Mini-stories
- Draft fast and furious, using tools to help you.

- *Note particulars, write a lot about them, then move to big ideas*

Supporting Reading and Writing to Think Interpretively

AS YOU PREPARE FOR TODAY'S CONFERRING AND SMALL-GROUP WORK, it will be helpful for you to keep in mind some of the big goals you have for your students—not only as writers but also as readers. After all, they'll only be able to write effective literary essays if they are reading and writing well. Because you are asking your students to write interpretive essays, you specifically will want to find ways to strengthen their abilities to read interpretively. You'll also want to support students in freewriting, ensuring they are writing in ways that help them to grow ideas about a text.

Following Interpretations across a Text

The strongest readers carry ideas with them as they move through a text. They'll read a tiny passage of text—the first few paragraphs or chapters—and generate some possible interpretations off of what they've read. Then, readers carry those ideas with them as they travel through the remainder of the text. With each new scene, they'll consider how the new information they read fits with the ideas they've grown. Then, too, when they come across information that doesn't quite fit, these readers push themselves to consider why the information doesn't fit. Perhaps it suggests an additional interpretation the reader needs to track. Or, maybe the new information upends what the reader thought was true, and the reader is left to revise or abandon her initial interpretation.

Too often, if readers pause to generate and write about an interpretation early in a text, by the time they turn the page in their notebook, the interpretation is forgotten. Or, if the reader does read on with his interpretation in mind, he reads looking only for the evidence that supports his interpretation, disregarding all evidence that goes against it.

If you find several students reading this way in your classroom, consider gathering them together in a small group, focused on strengthening their reading skills. This focus on interpretive reading skills will in turn bolster students' interpretive writing skills. You might craft a teaching point such as, "I want to remind you that to develop strong interpretations about a text, you can't just brush your first big idea off to the side and not think about it again. Instead, you've got to use your initial idea as a lens, keeping it in mind as you read on." You might bring out a chart from *Interpretation Book Clubs* (Unit 1 from Units of Study for Teaching Reading, Grade 5) to remind students of their earlier experiences with this work. You could also return to the initial interpretation of "Shells" you generated during the minilesson: people you live with, even members of your own family, can still feel like strangers to you. Explain to students that you'll need to keep this idea in mind as you read on, considering whether each part fits with or goes against your earlier thinking. Emphasize that if you find a part that goes against your idea, you might have to revise your earlier thinking.

Launch students into trying the work in their self-selected texts, and coach their work. For example, if you notice a child reading quickly through the text, not flagging any scene, you might say, "Really push yourself to study scenes closely to see if they could in any way, *possibly*, fit with your interpretation." Help the child reread a scene and think together about how it could possibly connect to her big interpretation.

MID-WORKSHOP TEACHING
Growing Ideas by Lifting Powerful Lines

"Writers, eyes up here. Your notebooks are filling up! I want to remind you of a strategy you've used before in reading that you can also use in writing. Here it is: you can lift a line from the text, jot it down on the top of a new page in your notebook, and then write long to grow ideas about that line.

"Right now, will you give this a try? Look through your text, find a line that speaks to you, one you could write a lot off of, and jot it down on the top of a new page. Then, push yourself to write long off of that line, letting your thinking grow. You'll be talking about these lines in a few minutes with other kids studying the same text as you."

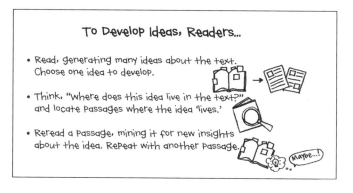

To Develop Ideas, Readers...

- Read, generating many ideas about the text. Choose one idea to develop.

- Think, "Where does this idea live in the text?" and locate passages where the idea 'lives.'

- Reread a passage, mining it for new insights about the idea. Repeat with another passage.

Maybe...!

write a lot about it, circling around potential ideas only as they write. Or, students might begin with one possible interpretation, and then, in the act of writing long, determine what it is the text is really teaching.

If you notice students writing with low volume, recording ideas briefly and then moving on, or if you see students simply recording ideas and evidence, consider gathering those students into a small group. You might begin by naming your teaching point: "Today I want to remind you that essayists linger with their thoughts. One way they do this is by using thought prompts to help them write longer and also sort of talk back to their own first ideas." Consider bringing out the chart of thought prompts your students worked with during the *Boxes and Bullets: Personal and Persuasive Essay* unit in fourth grade. If your students have worked with these prompts several times before, after reminding them of these prompts, you might coach them as they take an initial idea and use the prompts to develop it, writing long in their notebook.

Developing Freewriting Using Prompts

Student writing across the first few days of this bend will ideally resemble freewriting. That is, students might begin writing by jotting a detail they noted in the text and then

---

Josie
2/22

CROW CALL By: Lewis Lowry

When I was reading "Crow Call" by Lois Lowry, I noticed that when Liz's dad ordered 3 pieces of cherry pie, she was puzzled. "Three?" she said. It's almost like she didn't know how well her dad knew her. This made me think that one theme in this story could be: Sometimes in life, the ones who you feel don't know you very well, secretly do. In other words, there are some people who you might think you don't know very well so you think that means that they don't know you either, but that's not always the case. In this story, this theme is shown throughout the story, but this line stood out to me the most. It made me think that this could be a *theme* because Liz's expressions convinced me. For example, she was first happy to be with her dad, then confused with him, but then she changed back to happy again. She was happy to be reunited with her

---

continued...

father after war, but when he did something that showed Liz that he knew her more than she thought (buying 2 pieces of cherry pie for herself), she became confused, but just shrugged and went on. This persuaded me into thinking about that theme (sometimes in life, the people who you think don't know you very well, actually turn out to a lot,) because after she changed and changed her mind about different things, in the end, she never actually knew how much her dad actually knew her,

---

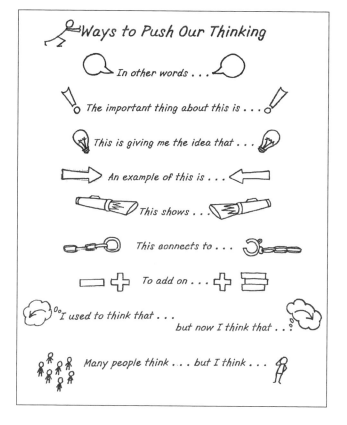

Ways to Push Our Thinking

In other words . . .

The important thing about this is . . .

This is giving me the idea that . . .

An example of this is . . .

This shows . . .

This connects to . . .

To add on . . .

I used to think that . . . but now I think that . . .

Many people think . . . but I think . . .

FIG. 6–5 Josie grows her ideas, writing long and trying out lots of different possibilities.

Talking to Grow Ideas

Call writers back to the meeting area to form same-text groups. Explain that talking and sharing ideas with colleagues is another way to generate ideas.

"Writers, as you come to the rug, will you pair up with the other kids who are studying the same text as you? I know you love the times in reading workshop when we form book clubs, and you might consider this group a book club of sorts." I helped students do this, pointing to various corners of the rug where each text group could meet. Once everyone was settled, I began again.

"One way to get more ideas for writing—to get grist for the mill, so to speak—is to talk and share your thinking with friends. You might have found a line that you're not sure amounts to much, but maybe your club can help you grow it. Or maybe you borrow an idea from a friend and expand upon it. Either way, let's talk as we do in book clubs.

"Today, you lifted lines from the text and wrote a lot about them." I added the strategy to our anchor chart. "Will you sit face-to-face in your groups and grow some thinking about those lines? Decide which of you is going to share first. Then be sure *everyone* in the club talks long about that line before moving to the next idea. Ready? Get to it!" The room erupted into conversation, and I coached into their talk, encouraging writers to take new notes as they grew more ideas.

SESSION 6 HOMEWORK

✴ LIFTING LINES AND WRITING LONG

Tonight, writers, keep growing your ideas about the text you selected. One way you might do this is by finding a line in the text that really stands out to you, maybe one that's interesting or odd or surprising, and copying it on the top of a page. You could even choose a line you talked long about with your club today. Then, you could write long about that one line. However you choose to grow your ideas, be sure that you fill at least a page in your notebook, maybe more. And as you write, work to move from the particulars of that line to some big ideas.

Analyzing How Characters Respond to Trouble

PAYING CLOSE ATTENTION to one aspect of story—in this case, character—is a powerful way for students to generate larger ideas about the text as a whole. Today, you'll remind students of this strategy and teach them to apply it to their work with literary essays. If you've worked with the fifth-grade *Units of Study for Teaching Reading*, and if you launched the year with the *Interpretation Book Club* unit, this work should feel familiar. In Session 9 in that unit, students learned that one way to grow ideas about the books they're reading is to study the challenges characters face, and they prompted themselves with two questions: What lessons does the character learn from (that problem)? Are there larger themes that the author wants to teach us through (this character)? If you started the year this way, notice ways this session draws on your earlier teaching. If you chose to launch your year differently, weave in reminders of that earlier work as relevant.

Readers have much to learn from times in their books when characters struggle. Secretly, I love it. We learn so much by studying the ways characters respond to trouble, about the characters themselves, but also about new ways of being in the world, because the ways that characters respond to problems can highlight powerful themes and help us to consider new ways of dealing with issues in our own lives.

In today's session, students will generate ideas to make interpretations about a text. The writing students do today will look a lot like freewriting in that they will be writing long to explore multiple ideas. With multiple themes in mind, students are asked to consider which are especially significant in the text and which are best supported by the evidence at hand. On many of the high-stakes assessments your fifth-graders are called to take, they are asked to do this type of analytic thinking, considering which theme or piece of evidence *best* fits with a text. Your teaching in this session helps students meet these fifth-grade expectations.

Today's share supports students in transferring their learning from Bend I, as you invite them to try out possible thesis statements for their essay. Tomorrow, you'll extend this work, coaching students to make their thesis statements more complicated.

IN THIS SESSION, you'll remind students that one way literary essayists generate ideas is to closely study the times when characters face trouble, knowing that often the character or the reader learns a lesson from those experiences.

GETTING READY

✔ Ask students to bring their short texts and sit in the meeting area with their same-text groups.

✔ Have a copy of "Shells" by Cynthia Rylant, or the touchstone text you chose for Session 6, to use for your demonstration (see Teaching).

✔ Have your writing notebook ready to jot down possible interpretations of your demonstration text (see Teaching).

✔ Be ready to add to the "To Craft Powerful, Interpretive Essays . . ." anchor chart (see Link).

✔ Display the "Template for Trying Out Possible Theses to Find the Perfect One" chart from Session 3 with the first row covered (see Share).

Analyzing How Characters Respond to Trouble

CONNECTION

Share several quotes about characters responding to struggle, and remind students about what they already know about paying attention to the way characters in stories respond to problems.

I called students down to the rug and asked them to sit in their same-text clubs. "Writers, I know today you will want to continue to grow ideas about your texts and to collect those ideas in your notebooks. So I have been thinking about how I can help you to grow ideas about those texts that are apt to be central to the texts. And I got to thinking that really, when you grow ideas about a story, you are growing ideas about the people in the story—and I remembered a quote that someone told me Walt Disney said. Listen to this quote, and think about why I am mentioning it today, when my real goal is to help you write more about your books."

You may not realize it, but a kick in the teeth may be the best thing in the world for you.

"Here is another quote by an author named Shannon Hale—it sort of says the same thing again. Will you think about how in the world this relates to you growing ideas about your characters?"

I wish stories were kinder to their characters. . . . But I guess trouble is more interesting to read about.

I gave the students time to think—a few seconds of silence—and then spoke. "Are some of you remembering a teaching point from our first reading unit this year? I hope so, because we talked about this then. We talked about how when characters respond to trouble, we learn a lot about them. What I want to remind you today is that this work can help us grow possible interpretations for our literary essays."

❖ **Name the teaching point.**

"Today I want to remind you that to grow possible interpretations from a text, it helps to study times when characters face trouble. You think, 'What does the character learn about ways to deal with this problem? What does the author teach us through the way this character learns to handle the problem?'"

By setting a context for which students listen and then pausing for a few seconds before sharing your own thoughts and reactions, you boost student engagement in the connection. Rather than passively listening to you as you share your own reflections about the quotes, students think alongside you, considering the ways in which the quotes you share could teach them to grow ideas about their characters. Weaving these small moves into your minilessons can help ensure students play a more active role.

TEACHING

Recruit students to identify the troubles the characters in your mentor text face. Demonstrate how to pinpoint specific times when the character learns a way to deal with his or her problem.

"Let's try it. You already know the troubles Michael faces in 'Shells'? Quickly turn to your partner and list the problems he faces."

I gave students a moment to brainstorm, and then called them back and named what I had heard. "Michael sure faces a ton of problems, right? He's living with his aunt, who feels pretty much like a stranger to him, his parents recently died, and he's incredibly lonely.

"Authors give problems to characters, problems they think lots of people, especially kids, share. The character usually learns a way to deal with the problem, and, in doing so, readers end up learning about ways to deal with their own problems too. For instance, the way the Panyee Football Club faced their problems taught us *all* some powerful life lessons. We learned about ways to deal with hardship, the power of teamwork, and the importance of thinking creatively to solve problems.

"So, I can take one of these problems—for instance, the problem that Michael is incredibly lonely—and think about scenes where Michael learns ways to deal with the problem. Watch me do this.

"Hmm, . . . I guess I *could* study the scene where Michael says that he's lonely, where he's talking about how much he misses his parents. But there, he's just naming the problem. He's not learning about ways to deal with it. So, maybe instead I could study that scene at the end where Michael and Aunt Esther are sitting on the couch together. I think Michael is learning something about ways to deal with his problem in this scene. Let's zoom in on that."

Model how you reread a scene closely to determine what the character learned about ways to deal with a problem, and what readers can learn as a result.

"Will you help me read the scene where Michael and Aunt Esther are sitting together on the couch? Ask yourself, 'What does the character learn about ways to deal with this problem?' and 'What does the author teach us through the way this character learns to handle the problem?'" I projected the scene and read it aloud.

> Then she flopped down on the couch beside Michael.
>
> "Oh, what would your mother think, Michael, if she could see this mess we've gotten ourselves into!"
>
> She looked at Michael with a broad smile, but it quickly disappeared. The boy's eyes were full of pain.

I paused to think aloud. "Huh? So here I'm thinking Michael's dealing with his loss by crying when his aunt reminds him of it. So that might be one way he's learning to deal with this problem. He hasn't let himself feel sad before. I'll keep reading. Will you keep thinking about what Michael learns about ways to deal with his problem?"

It's important to invite students to play a small role in your demonstration. By asking students to quickly turn and talk at the start of your teaching, you boost their engagement in the work to come, since the teaching to follow stems from the ideas they just generated.

Briefly modeling the predictable problems you expect students to have helps them envision responses when they face similar problems in their work.

"Oh, my," she whispered. "I'm sorry."

Michael turned his head away.

Aunt Esther, who had not embraced anyone in years, gently put her arm about his shoulders.

"I am so sorry, Michael. Oh, you must hate me."

Michael sensed a familiar smell then. His mother's talc.

He looked at his aunt.

"No, Aunt Esther." He shook his head solemnly. "I don't hate you."

"Okay, so it seems like Michael's dealing with the problem by crying a little and trying to hide his emotions, by turning away and then deciding to do the opposite—to look at his aunt and express his feelings." I underlined each of the relevant lines in the text as I mentioned them. "Now that I've got a sense of what's happening here, let me ask, 'What does the character learn about ways to deal with this problem?'

"See if your ideas match mine. Let's see. I think Michael's learning something here, because instead of getting all angry and yelling and saying, 'Can't you just leave me alone?' like he did at the beginning of the book, he's reacting in a quieter way. And, instead of running away from the problem, he's staying on the couch so he and Aunt Esther can talk about it. It seems like he's changing. Hmm, . . . maybe Michael's learning that when you are lonely, you can reach out to the people around you. Or, maybe he's learning that when you're sad, changing the way you're acting can really help.

"Here's the last step. I need to think, 'What does the author teach us through the way this character learns to handle the problem?' Be sure you're thinking about this too." I left some wait time so students could think alongside me. "Maybe, one theme I could write about is how when you have trouble, it helps to share your problems and unhappiness with other people instead of running from it." I quickly jotted the theme onto a page in my writing notebook. "And, I think I could write about how it's important to change when you're faced with really tough situations."

Debrief your demonstration, and restate the teaching point in transferable language.

"Did you see how one way literary essayists think interpretively is by studying scenes where their characters deal with trouble? They reread those scenes closely, asking, 'What does the character learn about ways to deal with this problem?' and 'What does the author teach us through the way this character learns to handle the problem?' Then, they can write long to develop their thinking about those themes."

ACTIVE ENGAGEMENT

Coach the same-text groups as they identify the problems in their texts and then reread scenes tied to the problems, noting the lessons learned or themes.

"Ready to try it? Work with your same-text group. Brainstorm a few problems your characters are facing."

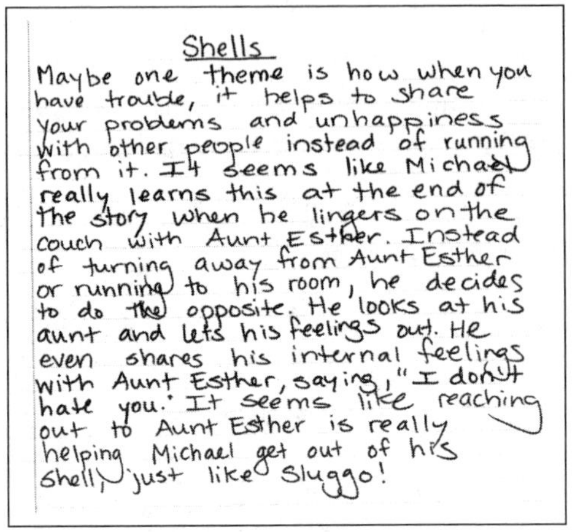

Shells

Maybe one theme is how when you have trouble, it helps to share your problems and unhappiness with other people instead of running from it. It seems like Michael really learns this at the end of the story when he lingers on the couch with Aunt Esther. Instead of turning away from Aunt Esther or running to his room, he decides to do the opposite. He looks at his aunt and lets his feelings out. He even shares his internal feelings with Aunt Esther, saying, "I don't hate you." It seems like reaching out to Aunt Esther is really helping Michael get out of his shell, just like Sluggo!

FIG. 7–1   A teacher models the start of a notebook entry for her students.

Today, you are teaching students another strategy they can use to grow ideas about their texts. The writing students do today should look more like freewriting, with students trying out different ideas, rejecting ideas when they are proved invalid or are unsubstantiated, and using more tentative language such as "Maybe . . . ," "Could it be . . . ?" and "Perhaps. . . ." Students' writing today should not resemble a published literary essay. Showing a quick example of your writing is one way to ensure students have a vision of what their notebook entries could look like.

A minute later, I voiced over. "Now, find a scene where the character deals with one of those problems. Then, reread it closely, thinking, 'What does the character learn about ways to deal with this problem?' and 'What does the author teach us through the way this character learns to handle the problem?'"

I gave students a few minutes to work, while I moved from club to club, coaching their work. I noticed one club was flipping through the text, having trouble choosing a scene to study, so I paused to give the students a tip. "Scenes where this work really pays off are often where the character realizes something related to the problem or where the problem gets resolved. See if you can find one of those kinds of scenes to study in your text."

When most students had finished re-reading the scene, I voiced over, saying, "Now, try writing-in-the-air to grow your thinking, to determine some possible interpretations."

Highlight the work of one club to give all students a vision for how to lift the level of their work.

I called the students back and gestured to Zoey and Mohammed to share what they had discovered. Zoey started. "We're reading *One Green Apple*. We thought one problem for Farah is that it's hard for her to talk to her classmates because most of them speak English, and she doesn't know much English. And, she's kinda lonely and homesick."

Mohammed continued. "So we decided to look at the part with the apple press. The one where she gets to help the other kids make the apple press work. We thought this was important, 'cause after that she was more a part of things with her classmates."

Zoey jumped in. "We thought maybe Farah learned that one way to deal with feeling lonely and left out is to jump in and just try things out. She could have just stood back, like when she was the last one to drop her apple in. But instead, the other kids are asking her to be part of things, and she's trying them out."

LINK

Situate the work students just did in the broader context of the bend, and encourage writers to try any generating-ideas strategies they now know, especially the strategy from today's session.

"With this new strategy, you've now got five strategies literary essayists use to grow ideas for possible essays. Remember that essayists often study times when their characters face trouble, since regularly there are lessons or themes to be learned from their responses." I gestured toward our anchor chart, touching the place where I'd just added our new strategy for growing ideas.

Across the minilesson, you are regularly repeating the teaching point. This repetition, using similar language each time, helps ensure students leave the minilesson knowing what was taught. You might also choose to post the questions posed by today's teaching point on a chart or a whiteboard, so students can refer to them as they work independently.

Today's link supports students in drawing on a repertoire of strategies. You invite students to choose from any of the strategies they know for growing possible ideas. Celebrate that students are taking different, self-selected paths to the same goal.

To Craft Powerful, Interpretive Essays...

| Write to Grow Ideas | Use templates to draft and revise different possible theses | Provide varied evidence to support your thesis |

- Read alertly, noting details and writing long off *them*

- State your idea about the text

- Mini-stories

- Notice details that repeat and think about patterns

- Think about what kinds of evidence will best support your idea

- Note particulars, write a lot about them, then move to big ideas

- Forecast the supports in your thesis

- Lift a line and write off of it

Draft fast and furious, using tools to help

- Study times when characters face trouble, thinking about themes

• **Study times when characters face trouble, thinking about themes**

"Will you scan the list of strategies and give me a thumbs up when you know how you'll grow your ideas today?" I waited until most students had a thumb up. "Tell your partner what your plan is."

Emphasize that by the end of the workshop, students will begin crafting a thesis that captures a central interpretation of their text and developing supports for that thesis.

"At the end of writing today, you'll be developing some possible thesis statements and supports for ideas about the lessons or themes that seem central to the text you're reading. Today, as you're freewriting and growing ideas, be on the lookout for when your interpretations repeat or start to sound similar. This might be a signal that you're circling around an interpretation that is central to the text. If you find one like that, you might write long off of it to get ready to choose your thesis and supports later today. Or, you might start developing a thesis statement about it, trying on different ways your thesis could go. Off you go!"

Adding the new strategy to the anchor chart in front of students makes sure the chart is a living, breathing document for students, rather than just serving as wallpaper hanging up in the room. To make your charts more useful for students, consider grouping all your writing charts together in one spot in the room so students know where to look to get ideas for their writing pieces. Also, regularly retire charts that are no longer in use by students. Some teachers photograph their charts before taking them down and add the photographs to an ongoing Charts Binder, organized by genre. Students can access the binder when they need to refer to an earlier chart.

Supporting a Range of Writing and Thinking

TODAY YOU WILL WANT TO GET RIGHT TO WORK conferring individually and pulling small groups. You might use some time to meet with students who interpret the minilesson literally and to support students who are already thinking interpretively and are ready to think symbolically about the texts they are reading. Students will probably also benefit from one-on-one conferences to help them develop their thesis statements.

If Writers Interpret the Minilesson Literally

You may find writers who apply today's teaching point in a very literal manner. For instance, you might find students who are paying attention to and writing about the character's problems, instead of pushing their jotting to lessons and themes, or who jotted lessons the characters learn that are limited to a very specific situation the characters faced. After complimenting the work the children are doing paying attention to the character's problems, you'll want to state your teaching point. "I want to remind you that when you are growing interpretive ideas, it helps to use very general language at first, and then you can get more specific as you are trying to support that claim." You might share an example from the "Panyee Football Club" video. You could say, "I *could* say that the soccer team's problem is they have no field and they learn that if you have no soccer field you should build your own, but that idea is *so* specific that very few people in the world could learn from it." Then, emphasize that you could instead share more transferable thinking: *The Panyee Football Club's problem is they have no field, and they learn that when you have a big problem in life you don't just give up, you work together with others to solve it.* Coach your writers as they work to make their themes transferable to broader situations. You might even encourage them to jot a few possible ways to word their theme. This will set them up to craft thesis statements that include broader themes. Then, remind them to write long, growing their thinking off of those ideas.

Pushing Writers to Consider Objects and Titles as Symbols

If your students experienced the unit *Interpretation Book Clubs* unit from Units of Study for Teaching Reading, you may find that some will be writing interpretively. They'll be jotting ideas about lessons and themes their text teaches, and they'll be ready to continue transferring what they know about interpretation into their literary essay work.

You'll want to remind writers about something they learned in that previous unit—that often authors include objects in stories that carry greater meaning, and that these objects often relate to the major themes or lessons in a text. You might demonstrate to

---

MID-WORKSHOP TEACHING
Freewriting Toward a Thesis Statement

"Writers, let me pause you for a moment. Shake your hands out and stretch your fingers! The reason I'm asking you to do this is because you are coming around the home stretch of growing ideas, and it's time to think about a strong idea that you can craft into a thesis about a lesson or theme your text teaches. To get ready for this, it will help to freewrite to grow your thinking. And I want to remind you of some things you know about good freewriting.

"You know that strong freewriting is when you let all your thoughts out onto the page without stopping or crossing things out, right? I want to remind you that another part of good freewriting is that a writer stays with one idea for a long time, writing about it over and over again in different ways, as if trying to get it just right.

"Will you, right now, scan your notebook and star a theme or two that your text teaches? Then, push yourself to write long about that theme, without stopping. Use everything you know about freewriting and using thought prompts to keep you going. In several minutes I'll call us back together for the Share, and you'll begin developing a thesis statement and supports for the text you're writing about."

---

a small group how you think through the meaning of the hermit crab shell in "Shells" by writing to develop possible ideas. You might model writing quickly in the air to grow your ideas: "The hermit crab shell kinda seems to be a symbol of Michael's feelings, like he is keeping them inside a shell. How could all this connect to a theme? Maybe it's all about how it's best to allow people to 'come out of their shells' when they are ready." Then ask writers to think about any objects that reappear in their texts and channel them to ask, "What might this object seem to stand for or be a symbol of? How does this connect to the theme of this text?" Students can write long to develop their ideas about symbols in the text.

You might gather another group of students to discuss how titles can be symbolic. To start, name for the students why you've gathered them together: "Today I want to teach you that titles often have significance beyond their literal meaning. Readers consider what the title of their book might mean on a deeper, more symbolic level." Explain that sometimes readers do this work at the end of a story, and other times they encounter a line or scene along the way that seems to relate directly back to the title. Students could consider why the title of the text is "Shells" and not "Hermit Crabs." You might encourage them to think, "The author could have titled the book _____ but instead she titled it _____. Why might she have done this?" Then, they can write long about their ideas.

Keep a special eye on your coaching as you support students. You'll want to resist the urge to say, "That's right! That *is* what that symbol means," when students suggest a possible meaning. Instead, you might say, "That's interesting. What makes you think that symbol might carry that meaning?" or "Out of all the possible meanings you've generated, which one is *best* supported in the text?" In this way, you'll strengthen your students' analytic reading skills, helping them to consider multiple possible meanings for symbols and then to rank those symbols to determine which might be best.

For students who wrote about symbols, you might consider channeling them toward thesis statements that take the symbolism of their texts into account. For example, students could write about how a particular theme is shown through three symbols, writing, "The text teaches . . . through Symbol A, Symbol B, and, most of all, through Symbol C."

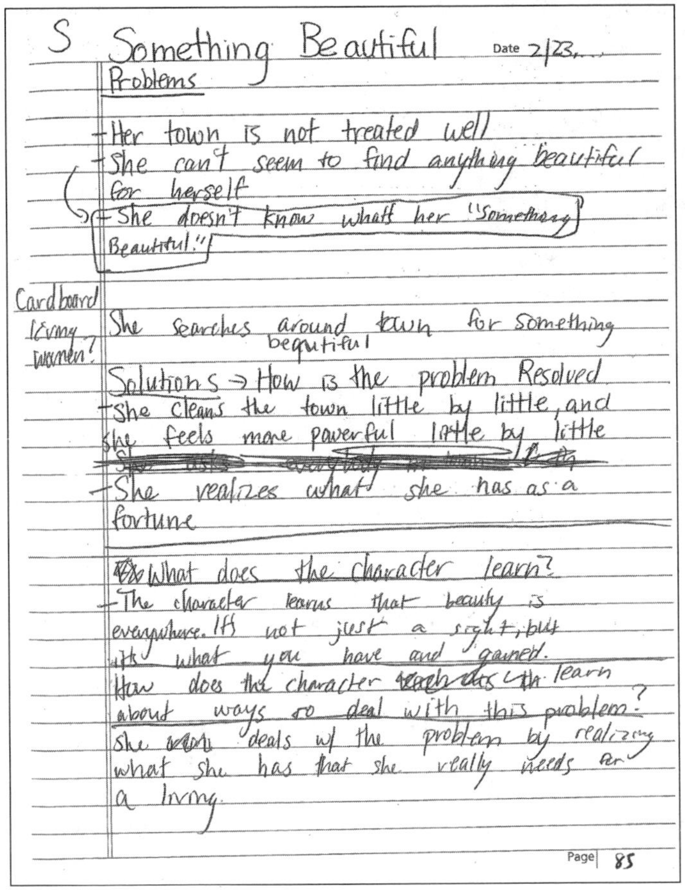

FIG. 7–2   Sana writes about the problems in "Something Beautiful," then considers what the character learns from dealing with those problems.

Getting Going on a Thesis Statement

Remind students that a thesis requires a powerful idea and strong supports to back it up. Channel students to use familiar thesis templates to generate multiple possible thesis statements.

"Wow, writers! You must be proud of the hard work you're doing. Your notebooks are filling up with a ton of big ideas about themes in your texts, and you're grounding your thinking in small, specific details. And you know that once writers have spent time exploring a text, they often pause to consider what they really want to say to readers about a text. They can jot those ideas as possible thesis statements.

"You've done this before," I reminded them, gesturing toward the "Template for Trying Out Possible Theses to Find the Perfect One" chart they'd used to generate thesis statements in Session 3. I had covered up the section that read "The character is . . ." since I was channeling students toward essays about themes.

"Quick, turn and remind your partner about how you use this chart." I listened while students turned and talked, and then pulled them back together to name out the steps I heard.

"I heard you saying that literary essayists start by thinking about what they really want to say about a text, and they can use those sentence starters to help them get some ideas down. And then, when they've got some ideas, they back them up. They try out all different kinds of ways to support their thesis.

"Well, what are you waiting for?" I joked, gesturing toward the students. "Get to it!"

After a few minutes, I voiced over, "Oh, and writers, don't forget to try out a few different supports for your thesis. For each try, make sure your supports match each other, that they're all ways or all times when or all reasons. Whisper about it with your club if you get stuck or want a second opinion." I coached students as they tried supporting their thesis with parts, ways, or reasons.

Template for Trying Out Possible Theses to Find the Perfect One	
1) First state one idea about the text.	2) Then forecast the essay's structure.
• The character learns...	• (The character) shows this through (one part of the text), (another part of the text), and most of all, (another part of the text). • (The character) shows this through (one way), (another way), and most of all, (another way). • (This is the claim) because (one reason), because (another reason), and most of all, because (a third reason).
• The text teaches (or is really about)...	• (The text) shows this through (one part of the text), (another part of the text), and most of all, (another part of the text). • (The text) shows this through (one way), (another way), and most of all, (another way). • (This is the claim) because (one reason), because (another reason), and most of all, because (a third reason).

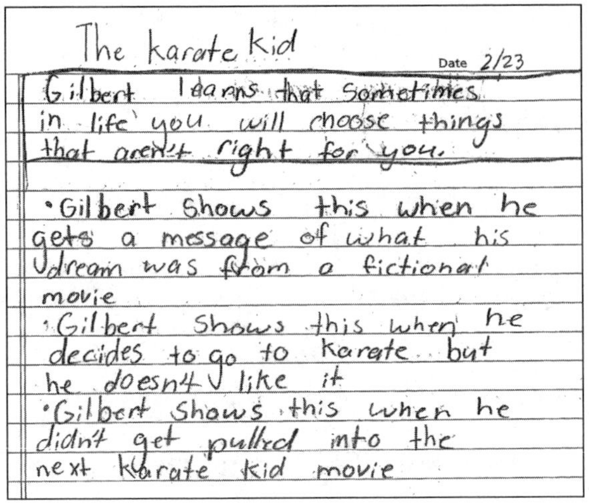

The Karate Kid

Date 2/23

Gilbert learns that sometimes in life you will choose things that aren't right for you.

- Gilbert shows this when he gets a message of what his dream was from a fictional movie
- Gilbert shows this when he decides to go to Karate but he doesn't ✓ like it
- Gilbert shows this when he didn't get pulled into the next Karate Kid movie

FIG. 7–3 Alexandra develops her initial thesis statement with three specific times from her text.

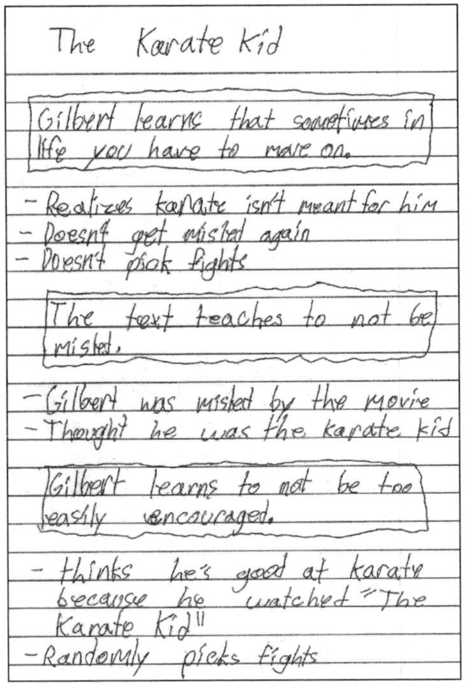

The Karate Kid

Gilbert learns that sometimes in life you have to move on.

- Realizes karate isn't meant for him
- Doesn't get misled again
- Doesn't pick fights

The text teaches to not be misled.

- Gilbert was misled by the movie
- Thought he was the karate kid

Gilbert learns to not be too easily encouraged.

- thinks he's good at karate because he watched "The Karate Kid"
- Randomly picks fights

FIG. 7–4 Liam tries out multiple versions of a thesis statement.

❧ TESTING THESIS STATEMENTS

Tonight, instead of doing a lot of writing, do a bit more reading to test your thesis statements. You want to make sure each thesis can be well supported by the text. Take the text you have been reading and growing ideas from, and this time, reread it closely with the boxes and bullets you created today as a lens.

As you reread, test each thesis statement to be sure it's strong. You can ask yourself:

- Is there evidence to support my claim?
- Is there enough evidence to support my claim?
- Is there different evidence for each bullet?

Develop a system to mark your strongest thesis statements. If your thesis statement isn't strong, see if there's a way you can revise it to make it even stronger.

Developing Stronger Thesis Statements

AT SOME POINT IN MY YOUTH, my parents decided I was old enough to make my own bed. I remember my first attempts, tossing one end of the sheets into the air while holding onto the corners of the other end, watching the sheets fall slowly, like a parachute descending. It took many tries to get the sheets to fall just right. Once the sheets were properly aligned, I tucked them in. This involved walking around the ends of my bed, smoothing, pulling and tucking, over and over, until the sheets fit snugly around the mattress. Pull too hard, and the other end comes untucked. Don't pull hard enough, and the sheets tuck unevenly, which can unmake a bed quite quickly.

All this is to say that many things in life—like changing the bedsheets—involve an iterative, recursive process. Each time you go through the process, it isn't exactly the same, but the repetitive nature helps you hone your work and gets you closer to your goal.

The same is true for writing a strong thesis. You have to start by tossing out your thesis, and seeing how it lands, how it holds against the text. If it doesn't land across the entire text you might need to revise to make sure your thesis is the right fit. Then you need to "smooth, pull, and tuck," that is, you need to smooth out the wording of the thesis and supports to make sure they are parallel and categorized. Throughout this process, you almost write your entire essay in your mind to make sure the thesis statement you're considering holds true. Paul Deane from Educational Testing Service says this work of rehearsing how an essay could go is essential to help writers write and rewrite their thesis statements.

Today you'll introduce students to the iterative nature of crafting a powerful thesis and supports. You'll coach them through finessing a thesis statement, first using one from your class demonstration text, "Shells," and then working with one of the thesis statements they generated during the share of Session 7. Students will test, rethink, and revise their thesis and supports, and then repeat the process until they've settled on what they want to say about the text. By the share of today's session, you'll coach them as they develop systems to organize their evidence.

IN THIS SESSION, you'll teach students that essayists develop stronger thesis statements by checking their initial theses against the text, rereading parts of the text to test whether that draft of a thesis actually holds true.

GETTING READY

✔ On chart paper, write the thesis statement students will work with: "The text teaches that people can change" (see Teaching and Active Engagement).

✔ Be ready to read a few scenes from "Shells" to test your thesis statement against (see Teaching and Active Engagement).

✔ Students need their copies of "Shells" (see Teaching and Active Engagement).

✔ Students need their writing notebooks and texts to test out their own thesis statements against their texts (see Teaching and Active Engagement).

✔ Create a chart titled "Kinds of Supports Literary Essayists Use" (see Link).

✔ For each student, prepare three booklets containing three pieces of lined paper stapled together. Students will use them to collect evidence for their thesis statement. You might also choose to make available blank paper if students want to create folders to collect evidence (see Share).

✔ Record your final thesis statement and supports about "Shells" across pages in booklets, and be ready to share it with students (see Share).

Developing Stronger Thesis Statements

CONNECTION

Share a social example to illustrate how people get an initial idea and then test it out to make sure it works. Connect this to the work essayists do.

"Writers, will you imagine this with me for a minute? You're getting dressed for an important occasion, and you find a fabulous scarf or tie to wear. You hold it up, and it seems perfect! You just love it. It's got brilliant colors, and it makes you feel snappy. You're pretty sure it's exactly what you want to wear today.

"Then you put on the rest of your outfit. Are you all set then, ready to head out the door?" I looked around the room, pausing dramatically. "I'm pretty sure that there's not a one of you who would just throw on the rest of the outfit and head out the door. No way. And you know why? Because you need to make sure that snappy tie or scarf *goes with* the rest of your outfit. Am I right?" Heads nodded.

"Here is my point. When you get dressed to do something important, you've got to test your tie or your scarf to make sure it works with the rest of your outfit. It might be a great splashy tie or scarf on its own, but it might look *awful* against your plaid shirt. This process of hypothesizing that a particular tie or scarf will work—and then double-checking your hunch—is a process that essayists know very well."

❖ **Name the teaching point.**

"Writers, today I want to teach you that essayists don't just settle with their first rough draft of a thesis; they revise that thesis statement over and over to make it stronger. One way for you to revise your thesis is to check it against the evidence."

TEACHING AND ACTIVE ENGAGEMENT

Explain that writers develop thesis statements by holding an initial idea against the text and reading and rereading to determine whether their claim fits with the text.

"Remember that when you check whether your tie or scarf works with your whole outfit, you take a step back and look at the tie, the scarf, and at the whole outfit, and you ask yourself, 'Do these fit together? Do they go?'

◆ COACHING

In Bend I, when you first asked students to write thesis statements, you used a similar metaphor about a shopper trying on clothes. Your connection today harkens back to that earlier instruction and helps kids see that the more sophisticated thesis work is not just finding a thesis that could fit a text. It's finding a thesis that perfectly fits a text and matches what you want to say.

"That's just what writers do. Of course, you may have a bunch of possible thesis statements (some kids I know call them PTSs—Possible Thesis Statements). Choose one. Then hold it up against the text, asking 'Does what I have claimed about this book actually go with the text? Does it actually ring true?'

"To check this out, it's important to actually reread parts of the text, thinking 'Does *this* part of the text go with what I'm claiming about the book? Does *this* part?'"

Guide students as they reread a text with a shared thesis statement in mind, considering whether scenes precisely fit their thesis or whether their thesis has to be revised in light of their rereadings.

"Ready to try it? Let's take one of our possible thesis statements about 'Shells' and test out whether it holds true when we go back to reread the story, thinking more carefully about whether what we are saying about 'Shells' is really truly true *and* is the important thing we want to say about the story."

I pointed to the chart paper on which I'd written one of the thesis statements we'd generated:

The text teaches that people can change.

"Let's reread a few scenes in 'Shells' and test out whether this thesis holds true for those scenes. Let's see . . ." I drew my finger down the page of the short story, illustrating that the first step is to skim for a relevant section. "Let's start with the scene we studied yesterday, the one where Michael and Aunt Esther are on the couch talking. And as you reread, ask yourself, 'Now that I'm checking with the actual details of the story, does the story *really* match my claim, my thesis? Is this the truest and most important thing I can say?'" I projected the relevant section of text. "Let's reread and check."

> Then she flopped down on the couch beside Michael.
>
> "Oh, what would your mother think, Michael, if she could see this mess we've gotten ourselves into!"
>
> She looked at Michael with a broad smile, but it quickly disappeared. The boy's eyes were full of pain.
>
> "Oh, my," she whispered. "I'm sorry."
>
> Michael turned his head away.
>
> Aunt Esther, who had not embraced anyone in years, gently put her arm about his shoulders.
>
> "I am so sorry, Michael. Oh, you must hate me."
>
> Michael sensed a familiar smell then. His mother's talc.
>
> He looked at his aunt.
>
> "No, Aunt Esther." He shook his head solemnly. "I don't hate you."

"Well, what do you think, writers? Does this part of the text go with what we're claiming about the text? Look at the actual details of the story to make sure they really match our thesis. Turn and study this part with your partner."

This is challenging work. One way you're weaving in extra support for students during today's lesson is by asking them to work with a familiar section of the text, such as the one you used in the minilesson yesterday.

Coach partnerships as they reread, pushing them to see more nuances in the text. Demonstrate for students how you discuss the way lines from the text fit with a claim.

I knelt down next to Walden and Kiara. "I guess part of it fits," Walden said. "That part where it says, 'Aunt Esther, who had not embraced anyone in years, gently put her arm about his shoulders.' That's showing she's changing."

I listened to another partnership and noticed they were also restating lines from the text without really explaining them, so I voiced over the hum of voices, speaking to the whole class. "I notice that many of you are choosing particular lines in the passage that provide evidence that yes, your claim, your thesis, is supported in the text. Thumbs up if you have isolated a line or two that make your point." Many signaled that they'd done this; other thumbs were rocked back and forth, suggesting not yet, perhaps, sort of.

"Great. Now the key thing to remember is that you can't just point to a line in the text and say, 'See, that supports my point.' You actually need to spell out *how* the line fits with the claim, to discuss the way the line goes with your claim. So if the claim is that the short story teaches that people can change, and you have shown Aunt Esther not talking on the phone, you need to say something like this (listen carefully to how I *discuss* the line I have chosen from the text)."

> Aunt Esther usually never has time for Michael. She is usually too busy talking on the phone. (See, I basically just repeat what happens in the line.) It might not seem like a big thing that she isn't on the phone now but this is a change and *her* change makes a big difference because now she and Michael end up talking about that crab, and that becomes a big part of the story. It shows that people can change because she changes. (Now I talk about why this line is a big deal and how it fits with the claim that she is changing.)

"Keep working, this time not just finding lines that support your thesis, but also discussing them." I gave students another minute to talk.

Debrief, naming the transferable work that students did, and discuss ways to extend the work further.

"Writers, this process is just getting started, but I think you're already seeing how it works. You start with your PTS, your Possible Thesis Statement, and then you hold it up against the text, rereading parts and asking, 'Does *this* part of the text go with what I'm claiming about the text? Does *this* part?' When lines fit, you discuss them, explaining *how* the line fits the claim. And, when you find lines that don't fit, that will usually lead you to revise your thesis."

Rally writers to try this again in their own texts. Channel them to reread parts of a story with a Possible Thesis Statement in mind, and to test those parts against the claim. Coach into their work.

"Are you ready to try this with your text? Choose one of the Possible Thesis Statements you tested last night for your text, maybe the one you ranked as strongest. Once you've got that in mind, will you start rereading? Read just a passage with your PTS—your claim—in mind, thinking, 'Does *this* part of the text go with what I'm claiming about the text?' Remember, it's not enough to name what fits. You also have to be able to explain *how* it fits. And be ready to discover

Not only will you want to coach writers by challenging them directly to be sure their thesis matches the supports and vice versa, you'll also want to coach partners to push each other to make sure that their claim fits with their supports, that their supports go with the claim. We want to support students to be strong partners to one another, to listen closely, and to hold one another's ideas accountable to what is stated in a text.

When students need additional support, it helps to have a model ready to share how the work could go. We've used a different scene from "Shells" here so as not to do the work for students.

parts that *don't* fit. If you find one of those, you might need to revise your thesis. Get started, writers!" I coached students as they got started.

After a few minutes, I voiced over with a reminder. "Be sure to check more than one part of the text to make sure your PTS holds true. Holding your thesis statement up to a few parts of the text will help you check to see if it really holds true across the text and if it's the *most important thing* you want to say about the text."

I gave students another minute to work, and then called for their attention. "Share what you found with your partner. Does what you've claimed about the book actually hold true across the text? Don't just say, 'Yeah, it does.' Instead, point to *specific lines* in the text that hold true and talk about how they fit (or don't fit) with your PTS."

LINK

Emphasize the iterative nature of this process. Set students up to reread, rethink, and revise their thesis statements. Explain that students might also consider crafting their supports as they reread.

"Writers, this is work you can do often, whether you're trying to make sure your scarf or tie matches just right with your outfit, or whether you're working to develop a thesis statement that more precisely captures what the text is *really* about. Essayists carry possible thesis statements with them to a text, reading and rereading passages from the text with that thesis in mind, seeing what fits and revising when parts of the text don't quite fit.

"This is a cycle. You start with a thesis, then you reread—and what you reread leads you to revise; you get a new thesis, and then you reread with that new thesis in mind, and so on.

"Can I give you one more tip before you head off? Here's the thing: to write a thesis, you've got to think about what your boxes and bullets will be. As you test out Possible Thesis Statements today, will you also be alert to how your supports could go? You've done this for one literary essay already, so you're getting to be experts at this. What kinds of supports will you use? Will you back up your thesis statement with times? reasons? kinds? characters? Or, will you back your claim with a problem and a solution?" I revealed a one-day chart that captured the kinds of supports literary essayists often use.

Kinds of Supports Literary Essayists Use

- Different parts of the story
- Ways
- Reasons
- Kinds
- Different characters from the story
- Problem and solution

"You've got a busy day of rereading and rethinking and revising in front of you writers. Get to it!"

While students are testing their Possible Thesis Statements, be on the lookout for students who could benefit from additional support. Instead of coaching individual students, consider voicing over tips to the entire class, so that everyone benefits from the suggestions. For example, you might voice over a tip about how to reread a scene closely to make sure each detail fits. Or, you might remind students to hold their thesis against multiple parts of the text to make sure it's true.

Notice that in this link, we not only repeat the teaching point, but also harken back to the clothes analogy we used in the connection and in Session 3. Repeating your teaching point and your references across a unit creates a narrative thread that can help students make connections between your teaching and their learning.

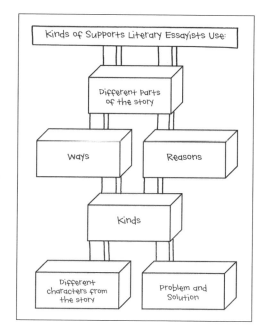

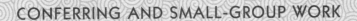

Lifting the Level of Thesis Statements

TODAY, you'll want to focus your conferring and small-group work on supporting students with strengthening their thesis statements. If you notice students who are exhibiting some of the predictable problems with their thesis statements, look back to the conferring and small-group work section in Session 3 for ideas of how to support students. There you'll find suggestions for how to support students who are writing thesis statements with supports that are overlapping, supports that are too specific, and supports that are not parallel, among others.

Revise thesis statements to make them more precise.

For students who have solid thesis statements already backed up by logical supports, you'll want to think about ways to support them in making their thesis statements even stronger. One way is to teach them to make their thesis statements more precise, to find the perfect wording to capture what they're trying to say.

To address this need, you might gather a small group of students. You could start by naming your teaching point, saying, "Writers, literary essayists search for the precisely right words to capture their ideas about a text. One way they do this is by reaching for the precise phrase, metaphor, or image to capture what they're trying to say about the text." Then, you could model for students how you try this work using a shared text, either "Shells," the "Panyee Football Club" video, or "Little Red Riding Hood." For instance, you might lay out a simple but accurate thesis statement and show students how you revise the thesis to make it more precise. You could show students how you

---

MID-WORKSHOP TEACHING   Rethinking by Studying Parts that Don't Fit

Students were confidently choosing parts that fit their claim, so I gave another push. "Writers, readers, are you ready for another challenge? Sometimes—often, even—the really thoughtful reader will find parts of your text that *don't* fit your thesis, that even make you think your first draft thesis wasn't exactly, perfectly accurate. When that happens, try to pay close attention to ways that your thesis (like your tie, your scarf) doesn't exactly *go with* your text, and get ready to change your thesis. Often you don't throw the thesis out, you just tweak it a little. This is the hardest part of essay writing, and it is crucially important. Try doing some of that hard work now. Jump to a scene you think doesn't quite fit, or reread a scene with parts that don't fit that you might have skipped over." I gave students a few minutes to reread a scene while I circulated around the room.

"Talk with your partner. What parts don't quite fit? How might you tweak your thesis so it also fits those parts?" I coached kids while they talked.

Rafael and Imani were talking about *The Stranded Whale*. Rafael said, "My thesis was '*The Stranded Whale* teaches that sometimes things don't go the way you planned.' But I can't think of a part that doesn't fit."

"Look back at the text. Scan through the different scenes on the lookout for one that might not fit," I coached.

Imani looked at her text for a minute and then said, "What about at the end when Mom is angry? The kids knew she'd be angry. They said it in the first line. So, I think that doesn't quite fit because that's the way the kids planned she'd act." I encouraged them to reread the scene and then moved on to coach another partnership.

"Writers, by today's Share, you should settle on what, precisely, you want to say about your text. Back to work!"

---

move from "'Shells' teaches that people can change over time" to "'Shells' teaches that people can come out of their shells over time." Then, you can rally students to try this work with their thesis statements while you coach.

Be ready to coach student with tips as they work. You might coach one student to try out different wordings, searching for six or seven different ways of saying something before studying them and choosing the best one. You might coach another student to reread, looking to see if there's a precise phrase, metaphor, or image already used in the text that she could use in her thesis. You might coach a third student to reread the text with his revised thesis in mind, checking to see if it is precisely right.

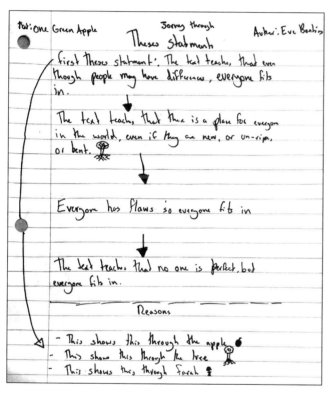

FIG. 8–1 Emmy experiments with a few ways her thesis statement could be worded to find the best possible wording.

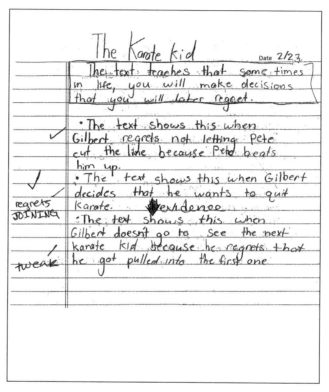

FIG. 8–2 Alexandra tests each of her supports to determine which hold true to the text and which she should tweak.

Setting Up for Collecting Evidence

Celebrate your students' work with thesis statements, and remind them that they need to set up a system for collecting and sorting the evidence they'll gather to support their thesis statements.

"Your thesis statements have changed in major ways today. They're getting so much stronger! Quick, share with your partner your original thesis statement from today. Then share your new thesis statement with your supports, the one you worked really hard to revise." I gave students a minute to share.

Walden was reading "Last Kiss." He said, "I think my thesis will be 'The text teaches that things can change in an instant. The text teaches this through the dad, and it teaches this through the mom.'"

Julia shared her thesis for *The Stranded Whale*. She said, "I decided on 'Sally learns that you can't solve every problem. The text shows this through the rescue workers, through the kids trying to save the whale, and, most of all, through the whale dying.'"

"Now that you've got solid thesis statements, you'll need a system to help you collect and sort through all your evidence. During our last bend, many of you collected your examples and mini-stories on booklets of paper stapled together, and some of you developed your own systems. If you have a system that works well for you, you can certainly use that one here. But because writing literary essays is especially intense work, I'm recommending that you all use booklets again for this next round of essay writing."

Share your own example to remind students of how booklets can be used as a system to collect and organize writing.

"Let me remind you how booklets work." I showed children my first booklet for collecting and organizing my writing about "Shells." "On the top of each booklet, you'll recall, there is a box, and inside that box I write my thesis and one support—one bullet. Then I leave a few pages behind that support so I have room to add in my evidence." I read it aloud.

> *"Shells"* teaches that things get better if you change.
>
> - This is true for Sluggo.

"Now let me show you support two." I showed the class that, again, on the top of the booklet, there was the stem of my thesis and my second bullet. I read it aloud.

> *"Shells" teaches that things get better if you change.*
>
> - This is true for Aunt Esther.

Then, I showed the class the blank pages after that support page that would be reserved for different kinds of evidence. After that, I picked up my third booklet and again read it aloud.

> *"Shells" teaches that things get better if you change.*
>
> - Most of all, this is true for Michael.

"Writers, each of these additional pages allows me to gather information that will help me write a strong draft. It's easy to add more pages or take away a page. I simply rip out a page, or I remove the staple to add a page and restaple the booklet again. This makes it easy for me to revise even as I'm collecting information. So, take these booklets I've prepared for you, and, after you receive yours, begin right away setting up your booklets with your boxes and bullets. You'll need one booklet for each support. You'll recall during the last bend you only had a page or two for each support, but this time around, I imagine you'll collect *lots* more evidence, and so I'm encouraging you to use one booklet for each support.

"Of course, if you have another system that works well for you, you can use that instead. Tonight you'll begin gathering the evidence for each bullet or subsection of your essay, and you'll continue that work tomorrow."

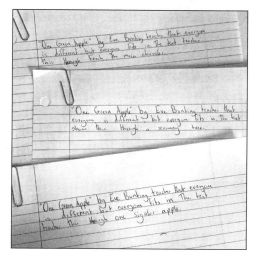

FIG. 8–3 Saul creates booklets to collect evidence for each of his supports.

✤ SETTING UP FOR COLLECTING QUOTES

Instead of doing a lot of writing tonight, do a bit more reading instead. Take the text you have been reading and growing ideas from, and this time, reread it closely with the boxes and bullets you created today as a lens. Take a highlighter or a pen, and mark up the places in your text that *really show* evidence of your bullets, the supports for your claim. You might highlight a paragraph, a couple of lines, and/or some dialogue from the text. You'll be using this evidence for your work tomorrow.

Choosing and Setting Up Quotes

IN THIS SESSION, you'll teach writers that literary essayists select quotes from a text to support their ideas, choosing the best quotes and writing around the quotes to show how cited material supports an essayists' ideas.

GETTING READY

✔ Prepare a chart with the headings "What Essayists Quote" and "How Essayists Quote," leaving space for bullet points beneath each heading (see Connection).

✔ Highlight the quotes used in one paragraph of "Eleven" by Adam (see Connection).

✔ Add to the "To Craft Powerful, Interpretive Essays . . ." anchor chart (see Connection).

✔ Be prepared to display your booklet containing thesis statement and supports for "Shells" (see Teaching).

✔ Select a few quotes from "Shells" that fit with one of your supports, and be ready to display them to students (see Teaching).

✔ Prepare a "Tips for Quoting a Text" chart (see Active Engagement and Mid-Workshop Teaching).

✔ Be sure students have copies of "Shells" (see Active Engagement).

✔ Project the last two pages of "Shells" (see Active Engagement).

✔ Display the "To Craft an Angled Mini-Story" chart from Session 4 (see Link and Conferring and Small-Group Work).

✔ Create a "Ways Writers Unpack Quotes" chart (see Share).

✔ Be sure students have a copy of the Grade 5 Opinion Writing Checklist (see Homework).

QUOTES ARE POWERFUL. A strong quote has the power to stay in the hearts and minds of an audience for generations. A strong quote has the power to move people to action. Just consider the potential of some of these famous quotes:

You miss 100% of the shots you don't take. —Wayne Gretzky

You must do the things you think you cannot do. —Eleanor Roosevelt

If you want to lift yourself up, lift up someone else. —Booker T. Washington

Nothing is impossible, the word itself says, "I'm possible!" —Audrey Hepburn

Words matter. And quotes matter too, especially to a literary essayist. Quoting a text is essential to the work of writing a literary essay. Without it, an essay is reduced to talking around and about a text, rather than thinking alongside and through a text.

In this session, you'll teach your students that to write a literary essay well, writers select quotes from a text that fit their claim and, at least in their minds, they rank those quotes to consider which does the work they need done. Then, you'll explain that it's not enough to simply plop a quote into their essays—the quote usually needs context to make sense. The context that the essayists write to set up the quote helps to make the cited passage fit tongue-and-groove into the essay. The biggest message you'll convey to students today is that literary essayists insert quotes from the original text (the short story, poem, novel, and so on) to make their case.

Tonight's homework is important. You'll channel students to flash-draft their essays, writing a bare-bones version of a literary essay that they'll spend the remainder of the bend revising and strengthening. If you are concerned about sending this work home with students, you might choose to insert an additional session into the unit, reserving tomorrow's writing workshop as a time for students to flash-draft their essays. Students will need drafts of their essays for Session 10.

Choosing and Setting Up Quotes

CONNECTION

Conduct a mini-inquiry with the mentor essay you used in Session 1: "Eleven," written by Adam. This time, channel writers to name the kinds of quotes they notice Adam using.

"Friends, remember the first day of this unit when you conducted your inquiry on what makes a good essay? So many of you said that to write a literary essay, you have to use *text evidence*, and you pointed out different types of text evidence in the essays, including quotes.

"Today I'd like to follow up on that investigation with another quick inquiry. You talked earlier in this unit about how Adam included quotes from 'Eleven' in the essay you analyzed. To do the same thing, it seems like we need to do an inquiry, asking how literary essayists like Adam decide which lines to quote. What *kinds* of quotes do they use?"

I revealed a blank chart titled "What Essayists Quote" and "How Essayists Quote" and placed a passage from Adam's essay, "Eleven," under the document camera. On the passage, I had already highlighted a few of the quotations Adam included in his essay, drawing attention to them. "Turn and quickly study the quotes I've marked with your partner. Ask, 'What kinds of things does Adam quote? How does he seem to decide on parts to quote?'" I leaned in to listen, and then jotted what students noticed on the chart.

In return for Mrs. Price mistreating Rachel, Rachel then goes on to mistreat her classmates. Rachel thinks of her classmates in a derogatory way. <u>An example of this is when Rachel commented, "Maybe because I am skinny, maybe because she doesn't like me, that stupid Sylvia Saldivar says, '. . . I think it belongs to Rachel!'"</u> Then, later on, Rachel comments, "But the worst part is right before the bell rings for lunch that stupid Phyllis Lopez, who is even dumber than Sylvia Saldivar, says she remembers the red sweater is hers!" In both these examples, Rachel is calling her classmates dumb and stupid. She's doing this in her mind, but her feelings probably affect her actions too. <u>Sandra Cisneros also shows Rachel mistreating her classmates when Rachel describes the sweater as smelling like "cottage cheese" and ". . . all itchy and full of germs that aren't even mine."</u> This shows that Rachel is disgusted with wearing her classmate's clothes. The sweater, it turns out, belongs to Phyllis, and she must feel awful seeing Rachel cry over the fact that Rachel needs to wear her sweater.

Today's connection is unusual: We pack in a tiny inquiry. To keep the rest of your minilesson around the 10-minute mark, you'll want to keep the pace brisk (but not rushed).

Recalling the inquiry that students did earlier in this unit demonstrates to them that the skills they learn are always important. It reminds them that reading and writing are inextricably linked and that skills they have learned across any unit could always be used.

Reconvene the class and gather their observations onto chart paper. Reiterate the importance of quoting from sources as a way to give evidence for a claim.

After a minute, I reconvened the class and debriefed what I had heard, referring briefly to the chart I had made while kids talked. "Writers, you noticed a couple kinds of quotes literary essayists use. Roland saw that you can quote what characters say aloud in a story. Imani mentioned that you can quote powerful parts. Saul noticed that you don't even have to quote a whole sentence from a text. Right here Adam quotes just the important words and phrases from the story. All these different kinds of quotes helped Adam provide strong evidence for his claim."

This connection is meant to be brief, just a few minutes in length. If you're worried about the inquiry running long, you might choose to write the chart in advance. You could reveal just the inquiry question before the inquiry, and then reveal the remainder of the chart as you name what students noticed.

What Essayists Quote

- Juicy parts that are colorful, different, surprising (the sweater smelled "like cottage cheese")
- Parts where the character's exact words show his/her personality ("that stupid Phyllis Lopez who is even dumber than Sylvia Saldivar")

How Essayists Quote

- Sometimes they quote whole sentences or even two.
- Sometimes they quote just fragments, phrases.

❖ **Name the teaching point.**

"Today I want to remind you that quotes add voice and power and life to an essay. Because quotes are a big deal, writers are careful to choose quotes carefully. Writers want the parts they quote to do important work for the essay."

I revealed the new bullet on our chart.

ANCHOR CHART

To Craft Powerful, Interpretive Essays . . .

- Write to Grow Ideas
  - Read alertly, noting details and writing long off them
  - Notice details that repeat and think about patterns
  - Note particulars, write a lot about them, and then move to big ideas
  - Lift a line and write off of it
  - Study times when characters face trouble, thinking about themes
- Use templates to draft and revise different possible theses
  - State your idea about the text
  - Think about what kinds of evidence will best support your idea
  - Forecast the supports in your thesis
- Provide varied evidence to support your thesis
  - Mini-stories
  - **Quotes**
- Draft fast and furious, using tools to help

- Quotes

TEACHING

Demonstrate for students the process of selecting quotes. Show how you first choose an idea from your essay that you want to support, and then go back to the text to find quotes that fit.

"Let's think about how we can carefully choose quotes for our essay on 'Shells.'" I displayed my first booklet, containing my thesis statement and supports for "Shells," under the document camera.

> *"Shells" teaches that things get better if you change.*
>
> - This is true for Sluggo.

"The first thing we need to do is to reread the story, just marking parts that maybe, possibly, could be quoted. To speed up our work today, I already reread the story and I marked these parts as possible quotes." I displayed this list on the document camera.

> ### Possible Quotes: Essay on "Shells teaches that things get better if you change."
>
> Esther surprised him. She picked up the shell and poked the long, shiny nail of her little finger at the crab's claws.
>
> "Well, for heaven's sake, come out of there!" she said to the crab, and she turned the shell upside down and shook it.
>
> The crab, finished with the old home that no longer fit, was coming out of his shell.

Demonstrate how to rank quotes based on what best supports the claim.

"Okay, we chose the idea we want to find quotes for, and we have already selected some possible quotes. Our next step is to decide which of these quotes *best* fits our support that things get better for Sluggo when he changes. To do that we need to sort and rank the quotes. Will you help me do this? You'll be trying this with a partner in this text in a couple minutes."

I read the first two quotes aloud. "All right, the first two quotes are okay. They both show things not going very well for Sluggo. But these first two quotes don't really show any *change* in Sluggo, do they?" Students shook their heads no.

"I agree. Let me check the next one." I read the third quote aloud. "Hmm, . . . what do you think? How would you rank this quote? Tell your partner."

I gave kids a minute to talk and then continued. "Well, I agree, this quote is quite nice. Sluggo is coming out of his shell! It *shows* him changing, doesn't it?"

Focus your demonstration on the parts you anticipate will be newest and trickiest for students. Here, we speed through selecting possible quotes, and instead emphasize ranking and transitioning into quotes.

High-stakes assessments often require fifth-graders to rank information, considering which details best fit or which theme is mostly true. Your teaching here supports this work.

Show writers how you add a quote into your booklet by writing a clear, brief summary of that part of the text, and then demonstrate how you transition into the quote.

"Let me give you a tip: You always need to be thinking about your reader, even in the early stages of your writing. If I'm trying to convince my readers that Sluggo is one character who learns this lesson that *things get better if you change*, then I can't just plop this quote into my booklet without explaining why it fits. So, it helps readers if you first write a quick summary of what is going on in the part of the story you quoted, and then introduce the quote. Watch me do this." I opened my booklet and wrote under the document camera.

> At the very end of "Shells," readers see things getting better for Sluggo as he changes and grows. Aunt Esther and Michael have just shared a tender moment, and then they decide to check on Sluggo to see how he is doing. When they look down, they see Sluggo changing. The text says, "The crab, finished with the old home that no longer fit, was coming out of his shell."

"Did you notice, writers, that I quoted a whole sentence from the text, which is one of the ways you noticed an essayist can quote a text?"

Debrief what you demonstrated to reiterate that writers first find quotes, then sort them, and then contextualize them for later use.

"Writers, this is one process essayists use to find and collect quotes. They choose a support that needs evidence, and then they reread the text looking for possible quotes. If they find several quotes that could fit, essayists may rank them to see which is the best fit. Finally, they record the quote, sometimes introducing it with a brief, clear summary of the text, so readers understand how the quote fits the support."

ACTIVE ENGAGEMENT

Channel writers to go through the quote-selecting process with their partner, this time to find evidence for your second support. Coach partners as they work.

"Are you ready to try this? Will you find a good quote for our second support, our second bullet?" I displayed the second booklet.

> "Shells" teaches that things get better if you change.
> - This is true for Aunt Esther.

"Go through this quote-selecting process step-by-step with your partner. The first step is done for you, but you and your partner will need to find quotes to go with the idea, and then continue down this list of tips." I gestured toward a new chart, "Tips for Quoting a Text."

While you always want to keep in mind the overall goal of a minilesson—the teaching point—it is also wise to tuck little tips into your teaching. In this case, you are tucking in the tip of how to introduce a quote. The trick is to make sure these little tips don't cloud or distract from the overall message—that they don't bog down the clarity and brevity of your minilesson delivery.

You could, if you wanted, streamline this process even further by highlighting a few quotes that you already think will work. If you chose to go this route, you would channel students to sort and rank the quotes you preselected, and then coach students as they wrote-in-the-air brief summaries that would weave the quote into the mentor literary essay. This decision depends on what skills you'd like your students to practice, and how much time you have remaining to teach a ten-minutes-or-less minilesson.

Tips for Quoting a Text

- Find an idea that needs a quote.
- Find several quotes that could go with that idea.
- Rank the quotes to see which best match the claim.
- Introduce the quote into your essay:
  - Give a brief, clear text summary to set up the quote. "In this part . . ."

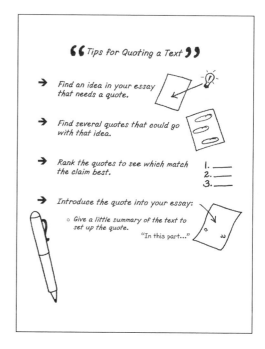

"Work with your partner to find a few quotes, see which fits best, and write-in-the-air how you would introduce the strongest quote with a little summary. Go for it." I projected the last two pages from "Shells," pages I knew would support the bullet—especially the scene where Aunt Esther embraces Michael—and then knelt to coach students at work.

I listened to Rafael and Julia as they talked. "There are two good quotes here. I can't decide on the best one. Maybe the part where Aunt Esther says, 'I am so sorry' shows a huge change in her," Rafael said.

"But then there's the part where she puts her arm around Michael. That quote seems super important because it literally says she had not done anything like that 'in years,'" Julia said.

"So I guess the question is this: which seems to *best* match the claim that things get better if you change?" I asked.

Rafael thought for a minute. "I guess the second one. Because after she hugs him, Michael smells his mom on Aunt Esther, and then he says he doesn't hate her." Julia nodded.

"Sounds like you ranked them and found the best quote. Take a moment to write a little summary in the air together, introducing the quote." I moved on to coach other partnerships.

LINK

Rally writers to the important work of supporting their claims with evidence. Remind writers to draw on a repertoire of strategies as they try this work.

"Writers, providing evidence for a support is important and tricky work. The stronger the evidence you find, the more likely it is that your readers will agree with your claim. Finding strong quotes that back up a support is a particularly powerful way writers convince their readers of their ideas.

"As you head off to write today, you'll probably want to spend some time finding quotes that go with your claim, sorting and ranking those quotes, and then introducing those quotes with mini-summaries. But remember, you know a variety of ways of providing evidence. From the first part of our unit, you know that you can also use mini-stories, so you'll want to collect a variety of supports today." I gestured toward the "To Craft an Angled Mini-Story . . ." chart from Session 4 to remind students of this work.

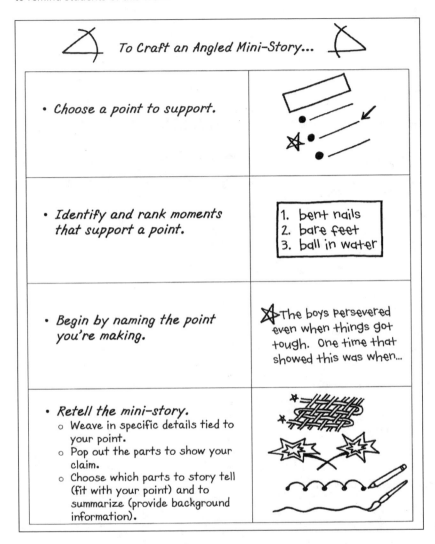

"What are you going to do to provide evidence for your supports today? Turn and plan with your partner."

*Notice the ways in which, throughout the unit, we use the Link as a moment to remind students of the repertoire of strategies they know and can use in their writing. Notice that today (and most days) we don't assign the minilesson. This is intentional. According to John Hattie, in his now-famous books on the science of learning—*Visible Learning *(2008) and* Visible Learning for Teachers *(2011)—students who are able to self-assign are more likely to be independent, self-regulated learners who can transfer their learning to other days and other times. Too many teacher-made assignments can make students overly dependent on teachers, which is often the cause of the I'm-Done-What-Do-I-Do-Next-Syndrome you may see in some writers. Ultimately, not only are we teaching students how to write; we're also teaching them how to learn.*

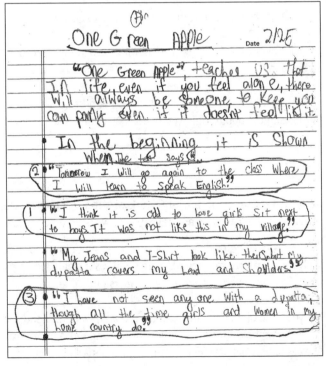

FIG. 9–1 Alain developed his own system for collecting and sorting quotes.

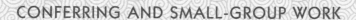

Strengthening Students' Use of Evidence

AS STUDENTS WRITE TODAY, you'll want to pay special attention to the evidence your writers are collecting to support their claims. Some of your emphasis will be on supporting students as they transfer their learning from Bend I to this new essay, so you'll want to be sure students are including powerful mini-stories that match their theses. The rest of the time, you'll want to teach your students strategies to select quotes that best support their claims and to quote accurately.

Remind students to transfer their learning from Bend I.

In Bend I of this unit, you taught your students that they could support their claims by including mini-stories. In today's Link, you encouraged your students to draw on this powerful strategy as one possible way to support a claim. As you confer with students today, look for students not only to be including mini-stories, but also to be angling those mini-stories to support their claim. If you see students simply retelling events from the text or telling every detail from an event without making decisions about which details to include and which to omit, you'll want to remind those students of the work you did in Session 4. Reference the "To Craft an Angled Mini-Story . . ." chart, and coach students as they move through the steps on the chart. If you find students need additional support, you might pull out the mini-story you modeled in Session 4, and remind students of how you created your angled mini-story.

Students locate quotes, but those quotes don't exactly fit their claim and supports.

Some of your students may be rereading through their texts and finding many quotes, but the quotes don't quite fit their claim. If students are unable to locate quotes that provide evidence for their supports, first congratulate them on their initial attempt, and then suggest that they may need to consider revising their claim and supports. When conferring with one such student, you might say, "Finding a good quote is tricky work, and it looks like you've found lots of them! The next part is to ask yourself, 'Does this quote fit my support?' If it doesn't, you might need to hunt for even more quotes that might fit your support. If, after hunting for quotes, you still don't find a quote to fit,

you might have to revise your claim and supports, or cut something out." Then, coach the writer as he studies and revises his supports to be sure he can find evidence for each one.

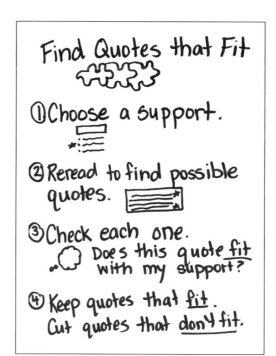

FIG. 9–2   A teacher created a chart to support a small group.

"Writers, can I pause you? I want to remind you that you *already know* ways to introduce quotes into your essay. Remember these strategies from fourth grade?" I revealed the bottom of the "Tips for Quoting a Text" chart, where I had added a few familiar strategies from the fourth-grade unit, *The Literary Essay: Writing About Fiction*, from Units of Study in Opinion/Argument, Information, and Narrative Writing.

"To practice using this chart, quickly put your finger on a quote you might include in your essay. It can be in the book or in your booklet. Right now, plan how you will share this quote with your partner, using one of these ways to introduce the quote."

I gave students a minute to rehearse silently, and then said, "Try it out with your partner. Write-in-the-air to show how you'll introduce your quote."

Tony was reading *Something Beautiful*. "I've got a quote about how even the smallest things can still be beautiful."

"Great! Now, choose how you'll introduce it into your essay." I gestured toward our chart.

Tony continued. "I guess I could try the third one. I could say, 'Aunt Carolyn from *Something Beautiful* thinks about something tiny that is beautiful in her life. She says 'My baby's laugh is something beautiful.'"

After a few minutes, I said, "Back to collecting evidence, writers! And make sure you jot down the introduction to your quote that you and your partner wrote-in-the-air."

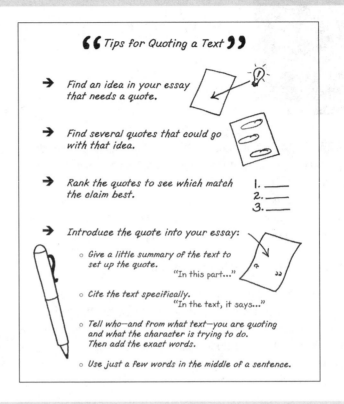

❝ *Tips for Quoting a Text* ❞

→ Find an idea in your essay that needs a quote.

→ Find several quotes that could go with that idea.

→ Rank the quotes to see which match the claim best.
1. ___
2. ___
3. ___

→ Introduce the quote into your essay:
   ○ Give a little summary of the text to set up the quote.
     "In this part..."
   ○ Cite the text specifically.
     "In the text, it says..."
   ○ Tell who—and from what text—you are quoting and what the character is trying to do. Then add the exact words.
   ○ Use just a few words in the middle of a sentence.

Students misquote the text.

Sometimes a student will have taken a quote out of context, suggesting it supports the claim when in fact the student missed some of the true meaning of the text and has essentially misused a quote. When you notice this, remember that a learner needs to approximate, to do things partially right and partially wrong, en route to mastery. If the writer has made a good effort to locate a quote that supports his or her claim, celebrate that effort. You could also say, "Although I am thrilled that you have found a line to quote and inserted it into your essay, I think that in this instance the line you have quoted doesn't actually mean what you are suggesting it means. I've read this story about a hundred times, and I don't expect you to necessarily see what I see in it, but if you are willing to take on a challenge, could you reread not just the quote but the story around the quote and see if you can figure out why I'm saying that actually there is a bit of a problem to even this great work you have done?" You might end by delivering a bit of encouragement, saying to the child, "Mostly, though, keep doing more of what you have done as you quote. You are on your way!"

Unpacking Quotes

Remind writers that essayists not only introduce quotes, they also unpack quotes. Share a few common prompts for unpacking quotes. Channel writers to try a few in their own writing.

"Writers, your reader should never be left wondering, 'Why is this here?' To prevent this, you'll want to unpack—or explain—your quotes a little bit after you've quoted them.

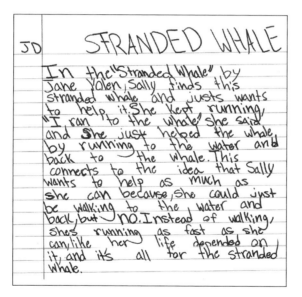

FIG. 9–3 Adam introduces and unpacks a quote.

FIG. 9–4 JD writes long to explain how his quote fits with his support.

"I want to remind you of a few ways writers unpack quotes." I unveiled a new chart.

Ways Writers Unpack Quotes

- What this means is . . .
- This shows . . .
- This connects to the idea . . .
- This is important/significant because . . .
- This supports . . .

"Will you take a moment to find a quote in your booklet and then try to unpack it using one of these prompts? Explain it so that your readers understand precisely *how* that quote fits with your claim."

After a few minutes, I said, "Writers, get with your partner. Share one of the quotes you unpacked. Partners, listen carefully. Do you understand how, precisely, the quote fits your partner's claim? Give each other feedback."

Ways Writers Unpack Quotes

- What this means is...
- This shows...
- This connects to the idea...
- This is important/significant because...
- This supports...

✷ FLASH-DRAFTING YOUR LITERARY ESSAY

Writers, remember when you flash-drafted your essay on the "Panyee Football Club" video? You used the "What Makes a Literary Essay?" chart as a checklist as you drafted to help you remember all the parts of the essay. Tonight, you'll do something similar, this time using the Opinion Writing Checklist to help you draft. You'll transfer everything you learned about flash-drafting a literary essay to this new essay you'll draft. If you notice one of your bullets doesn't have a lot of evidence, look for more evidence you can include in your draft. Then, you'll let your pen fly down the page without pausing too much or too often until you have a whole draft, ready to bring to tomorrow's workshop. Be sure to use the writing checklist in your writing folder to help you. Ready? On your mark, get set, go!

Supporting a Claim with an Analysis of Craft

AUTHORS WRITE WITH INTENTION. Every choice an author makes, from a character's name to a book's title, is deliberate. Think for a moment about the writerly decisions Katherine Applegate makes in her book *Home of the Brave*. Some readers might wonder how she came to name the cow "Gol," which means *family*. Other readers might wonder about the symbolism of the soft blue-and-yellow cloth Kek keeps in his pocket. For an essayist, thinking more deeply about an author's deliberate choices can help reveal the deeper meanings in the text and can help the writer to more strongly support a claim.

Your students come to this session having grown ideas about what their texts are *really* about and having crafted interpretive thesis statements that capture the central themes in those texts. Today you'll teach students that the work they've already done to support their thesis statements with mini-stories and quotes is just the start. You'll teach them that they can also support their thesis statements by rereading a text closely, noting the ways an author uses specific craft moves to develop themes, and then incorporating that evidence into their own essays.

This session might extend your students' earlier work studying author's craft. If you taught the *Interpretation Book Clubs* unit from Units of Study for Teaching Reading, your students learned they could consider the choices an author *did not* make to help them better understand the choices an author *did* make. In that unit, you will have introduced students to the Narrative Goals and Techniques cards, and channeled them to note the goals authors aimed toward, as well as the techniques those authors used to achieve their goals. If your students did not have this instruction, you might choose to extend the Connection of this lesson, using that time to introduce students to the Narrative Goals and Techniques cards provided in the online resources that accompany this unit. You might distribute the cards, and ask students to look across the cards with a partner, teaching each other what each card means. In this way, students will be ready to use the cards during the teaching and active engagement.

IN THIS SESSION, you'll teach students that literary essayists analyze author's craft, writing about the ways an author's goals and techniques might support students' claims.

GETTING READY

✔ If students do not have Narrative Goals and Techniques cards from *Interpretation Book Clubs*, prior to class you may want to make sets of these cards by printing the charts "Narrative Writers Aim toward Goals Such As . . ." and "Narrative Writers Use Techniques Such As . . ." (each on a different-colored paper), cutting them apart, and placing a set of both in a baggie for every student (see Connection and Teaching).

✔ Have a copy of the Narrative Goals and Techniques card sheets ready to project (see Connection and Teaching and Active Engagement).

✔ Be ready to project a portion of your flash-draft to show students how you revise your draft to include an analysis of author's craft (see Teaching).

✔ Add to the "To Craft Powerful, Interpretive Essays . . ." chart (see Link).

✔ Share the "Ways Writers Acknowledge Authors" chart to help students refer to the author in their essays (see Conferring and Small-Group Work).

✔ Be ready to revise the "Ways Writers Unpack Quotes" chart from Session 9 (see Mid-Workshop Teaching).

✔ Be ready to read aloud a section of "The Marble Champ" by Judah that students studied in Session 1 (see Share).

✔ Copy the Grades 5 and 6 Opinion Writing Checklist to send home with students (see Homework).

The analytic reading expectations for your fifth-graders are challenging. Fifth-graders are first expected to notice the goals authors aim toward and the different techniques authors use to achieve their goals, and then students are expected to name those techniques using literary language. After that, students are expected to discuss those goals at length, considering ways their texts would have been different had the author made different choices. This is work that's particularly valued on the high-stakes assessments your fifth-graders take. Your teaching today supports students in meeting and exceeding these expectations. And from the work we've seen in fifth-grade classrooms across the globe, we know your students are capable of rising above these expectations with tons of success.

"Thinking more deeply about an author's deliberate choices can help reveal the deeper meanings in the text."

In today's share, you'll remind students of another way literary essayists support their claims: by creating parallel lists that follow a predictable, repetitive structure. Parallel lists are a regularly used rhetorical device in political speeches, such as Martin Luther King's "I Have a Dream" speech. If your students experienced *Boxes and Bullets: Personal and Persuasive Essays* and *The Literary Essay: Writing about Fiction* in Grade 4, then they learned to create parallel lists by choosing a point they wanted to make and then repeating some of the key words from their support several times. We recommend bringing that teaching into today's share as a reminder, rather than making it the work of a minilesson.

Supporting a Claim with an Analysis of Craft

CONNECTION

Remind students of their earlier work with the Narrative Goals and Techniques cards. Ask students to reacquaint themselves with the tool.

"Writers, do you remember these?" I held up the Narrative Goals and Techniques cards. Most kids nodded. "I hope you do, 'cause you did a *ton* of work with them earlier in the year in reading. Do all of you remember studying powerful

FIG. 10–1   Narrative Goals cards

FIG. 10–2   Narrative Techniques cards

◆ COACHING

Here, you reference teaching from Interpretation Book Clubs: Analyzing Themes, *the first fifth-grade unit in* Units of Study for Teaching Reading. *In Session 18 of that unit, students learned they could study the choices an author did not make to better understand the choices the author did make. In Session 19, students learned they could name an author's goals and techniques more precisely by using literary language. If your students did not receive this prior instruction, you'll want to alter your teaching here accordingly.*

You might, for instance, introduce students briefly to each set of cards. For example, you could distribute the Narrative Technique cards and say, "Here's a list of a few techniques narrative writers use as they write. Look at them briefly. Which are familiar to you? Touch each card that seems familiar, and tell your partner what it means. Which cards mention a technique that is new for you?" You could also decide to limit the number of cards you give to your entire class or to groups within your class. You might give students only the cards you have already taught in your previous minilessons and read-alouds.

scenes in your book club books, noting what goals an author seemed to be aiming toward (goals like 'show character motivation') and thinking also about what techniques that author used to achieve those goals (thinking, for example, that the author writes a character's inner thinking to support the goal of showing character motivation)? I'm remembering that when you did this work earlier this year, some of you discovered techniques that authors use that aren't even in our set of Goals and Technique cards. Remember how you added 'word choice' and 'repeated lines' to our set of cards?"

"Will you take a minute to reacquaint yourself with these cards? Partner 1, put out the goals cards, and Partner 2, will you put out the techniques cards? Talk about what any tricky cards, any tricky words, might mean." I gave the students a minute to talk while I listened, and then redirected the class's attention back to me.

"Writers, there is a special way literary essayists use the Goals and Techniques cards that will help you write stronger interpretive essays."

❧ **Name the teaching point.**

"Today I want to teach you that it is not just the plot and the characters in a story that carry messages to readers. The way an author writes—*the author's craft moves*—also help to carry messages to readers. Literary essayists can support a claim by naming those craft moves and explaining how they fit with a claim."

TEACHING AND ACTIVE ENGAGEMENT

Recruit students to research you as reread part of your essay and consider the craft techniques the author used.

"Writers, I need your help to teach you how to do this. I can see the way an author's craft supports the message in a text and write about it in a literary essay, but I am terrible at figuring out how to help kids do this work! Would you be researchers and watch what I do really closely, whispering with your partner, or jotting as you see me doing something, so you find a way to put into words whatever you see me doing? Then in a jiffy, you'll have a chance to try.

"I am going to try this with our second support. Let's work on this part of the essay. I did a little work on it last night," I said, displaying the section of my essay addressing the second support under the document camera.

"To start, I usually reread a section of my essay on the lookout for parts where I might be able to mention the author's craft." I turned to address the class directly. "You know some powerful literary techniques to be on the lookout for as I reread 'Shells.'" I displayed the "Narrative Writers Use Techniques Such As . . ." chart. "I've got to reread my essay, thinking, 'Where in my essay could I refer to the techniques the author Cynthia Rylant used?' Will you think about what techniques I could name too?" I reread the section of my essay aloud, emphasizing the parts of it (marked in bold on the following page) where I could refer to the various techniques Rylant used.

Resist the urge today to explain to students what every card means. You'll want to avoid walking them through each card, one by one. If you worry that students will not be familiar with a majority of the cards, you might introduce them during your read-aloud period, or you might limit the number of cards you distribute, perhaps handing out only eight goals and eight techniques—those cards with which you believe students will be most familiar.

Notice the ways you set students up to take on active roles across this lesson. First, you invite students to watch you as researchers, note the moves you make, and name them out so that they can try those same moves later. Then, you ask students to note the craft moves the author used and to write about craft moves in the air. These small moves help keep students active across your demonstration.

Another way the text teaches that things can get better if you change is through Aunt Esther. At first, Aunt Esther is closed off from Michael. **She yells at him, saying, "Don't yell at me!" She also spends her afternoons talking with her friends on the phone instead of talking to Michael.** Later, though, Aunt Esther allows herself to be vulnerable in front of Michael. She does this first in small ways when she takes interest in Sluggo and takes Michael to the store to buy more hermit crabs. But then Aunt Esther changes in big ways at the end of the story when she accidentally hurts Michael's feelings by talking carelessly about his parents. **She whispers an apology to him, saying, "I am so sorry, Michael." Then she embraces him, and touches his arm.** This shows in a big way that Aunt Esther is allowing herself to change. In this case, Aunt Esther changes when she allows herself to be vulnerable.

Coach partnerships as they discuss which techniques the author uses in the scene you selected, and then name for the entire class the techniques you hope they noted.

"I know my point will be the strongest if I make it using academic language. Look at your Techniques cards, and see if you can name a few of Cynthia Rylant's techniques that I am already using as evidence for my essay." I listened as students quickly turned and talked, and soon I reconvened the class.

"How many of you noticed I wrote about Cynthia Rylant's *dialogue*? That line 'I'm so sorry, Michael,' jumped out because the dialogue shows change." I underlined the lines as I talked. "And, did you notice that I wrote about Cynthia Rylant's *revealing actions*? Those are actions that let us readers know something about the character. Cynthia Rylant wrote that Esther *whispered* and *embraced him*. Those seem like pretty descriptive words."

Quickly demonstrate how you revise your draft to support a claim using an analysis of author's craft. Recruit students to finish writing the paragraph in the air.

"Keep watching me. I've got to revise my draft to include an analysis of the author's craft moves you just noted." I projected the relevant paragraph from my draft. "I've already written a bit about this scene here when I wrote 'She whispers an apology to him, saying, "I am so sorry, Michael." Then she embraces him and touches his arm.' Now, I've got to name Cynthia Rylant's technique and say a bit about it. Here goes." I demonstrated for the students how I revised the piece, adding a few lines of writing to describe the craft technique that was used.

Another way the text teaches that things can get better if you change is through Aunt Esther. At first, Aunt Esther is closed off from Michael. She yells at him, saying, "Don't yell at me!" She also spends her afternoons talking with her friends on the phone instead of talking to Michael. Later, though, Aunt Esther allows herself to be vulnerable in front of Michael. She does this first in small ways when she takes interest in Sluggo and takes Michael to the store to buy more hermit crabs. But then Aunt Esther changes in big ways at the end of the story when she accidentally hurts Michael's feelings by talking carelessly about his parents. She whispers an apology to him, saying, "I am so sorry, Michael." Then she embraces him, and touches his arm.

One of the benefits of the Goals and Techniques cards is that they help hand academic language over to students. As you coach partnerships, remind them to use the literary language on the cards as they're discussing the moves the writer made.

To model this revision, you could show students how you draw an arrow and add revisions into the margin.

Cynthia Rylant uses specific revealing actions to show that Aunt Esther is changing. First, she has Aunt Esther <u>whisper</u>. That's a revealing action because it shows a big change from when she <u>yelled</u> at the start of the story. And then Cynthia Rylant . . . This shows in a big way that Aunt Esther is allowing herself to change. In this case, Aunt Esther changes when she allows herself to be vulnerable.

"Writers, will you pick up from here? You might tell about other revealing actions or about the dialogue she's using. Start with: 'And then Cynthia Rylant . . .'" I knelt to listen to partnerships as they wrote-in-the-air about the author's craft moves.

Julia was writing-in-the-air with her partner: "And then there's dialogue. Aunt Esther said, 'I'm sorry.' That shows a change."

"Remember to give specific examples of places where the author used that technique," I coached.

Julia nodded and continued, "That shows change too, because earlier she yells, 'Don't you yell at me!'"

Cull from students their observations of your process, naming out the steps you went through as you demonstrated.

"Researchers, I know you've been watching and jotting. Talk together and list what you noticed me doing as a writer that you could also try." I listened, coaching students to be specific and name the steps in the process. After a minute, I reconvened the class.

"Let me say back what I heard. Give a thumbs up if you said one of these steps. First, I chose a support, and then I reread my essay, noting the author's techniques I could write about, but had not unpacked or named in a clear way. I considered a bunch of techniques the author used, not just one, and then I named them precisely, using the Goals and Techniques cards. Next, I found places in my writing where I could revise and insert a description of author's craft. Finally, I wrote to connect the author's craft move to my claim."

LINK

Send students off to revise, encouraging them to draw on the revision strategies you've taught in this bend, as well as the strategies you've taught in the previous bend.

"Whenever you're developing your essays, remember that one powerful kind of evidence you can use is an analysis of author's craft. Specifically, you can look at how an author's craft moves relate to and help show the big points you're trying to make. You'll probably want to try this out today. Keep your Narrative Goals and Techniques cards handy. And don't just throw in any old evidence. Be critical. If you notice your author uses several techniques, ask yourself, 'Which one of these *best* supports my claim?' The stronger your evidence, the more convincing your essay will be to your readers.

"And remember, there are other techniques you'll want to draw upon today." I referenced our "To Craft Powerful, Interpretive Essays . . ." chart, where I had added the day's new sticky note, "Author's Craft." "Look over your flash-draft and think about what kinds of evidence you'll need to add in to strengthen your piece today, and give me a thumbs up when you've got a plan." When most students had their thumbs up, I sent them off to revise.

In today's link (as in yesterday's), you'll notice we ask kids to self-assign the work they are going to be doing on their own literary essay. According to Grant Wiggins, one of the ways we help learners successfully transfer learning to other situations is to encourage learners to practice judgment, not just a skill. When we ask kids to make a plan for their day's work (instead of assigning a specific skill), we challenge students to reflect—to think critically about their own learning and what they need to do to make their writing even better.

To Craft Powerful, Interpretive Essays...

Write to Grow Ideas
- Read alertly, noting details and writing long off them
- Notice details that repeat and think about patterns
- Note particulars, write a lot about them, then move to big ideas
- Lift a line and write off of it
- Study times when characters face trouble, thinking about themes

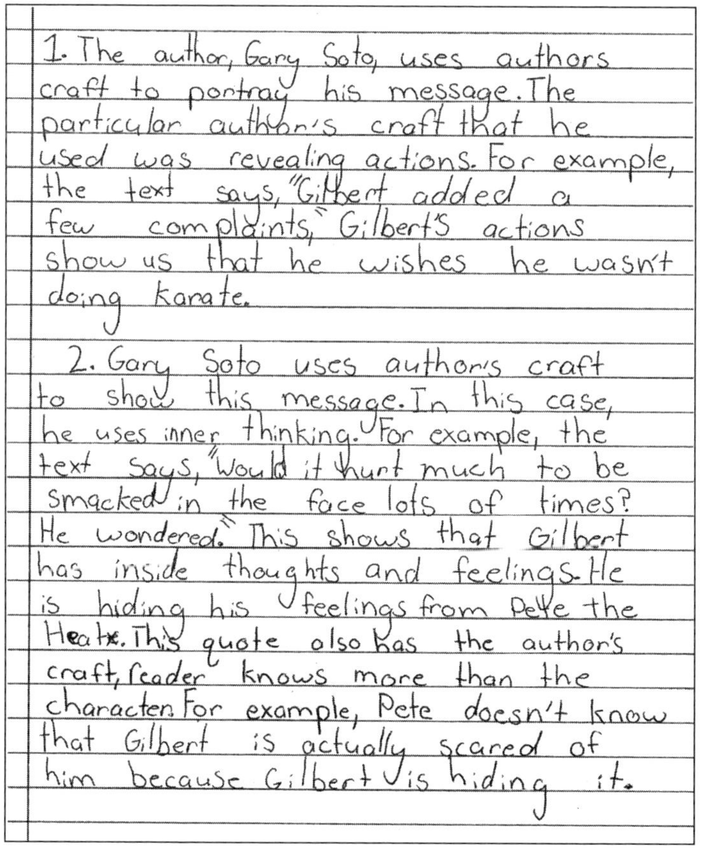

Use templates to draft and revise different possible theses
- State your idea about the text
- Think about what kinds of evidence will best support your idea
- Forecast the supports in your thesis

Provide varied evidence to support your thesis
- Mini-stories
- Quotes
- Author's craft

Draft fast and furious, using tools to help

1. The author, Gary Soto, uses authors craft to portray his message. The particular author's craft that he used was revealing actions. For example, the text says, "Gilbert added a few complaints." Gilbert's actions show us that he wishes he wasn't doing karate.

2. Gary Soto uses author's craft to show this message. In this case, he uses inner thinking. For example, the text says, "Would it hurt much to be smacked in the face lots of times? He wondered." This shows that Gilbert has inside thoughts and feelings. He is hiding his feelings from Pete the Heat. This quote also has the author's craft, reader knows more than the character. For example, Pete doesn't know that Gilbert is actually scared of him because Gilbert is hiding it.

FIG. 10–3 Alexandra makes revisions to include an analysis of author's craft in her essay.

Strengthening Evidence with an Emphasis on Craft

TODAY, you can expect that your students are deep into the work of developing evidence to support the claims in their essays. To do that well, they'll need to draw on all that you have taught them so far in this unit (and all they've learned prior to this unit as well). The challenge when writing essays is to create cohesion between claims and evidence, and to write with as much precision and clarity as possible. To do that, it helps for writers to truly embrace the fact that everything is open to revision. Of course, in addition to continuing to support all of that work, you'll also want to help writers apply the teaching that you did today. For example, chances are good that it is new for them to think about how the text they're analyzing was written, and about ways the author's decisions about craft advance a life lesson, a theme.

Coach writers to rank evidence that best supports a claim.

Fifth-graders are often asked to sort and rank their answers on standardized assessments. The questions they might see on such tests tend to look like these: *Which of these themes best captures the text? Which detail most likely explains why the character acts this way?* These questions require students to think analytically, to look across a set of possible answers, and to weigh those to determine which best answers the question.

To teach a student how to rank evidence, do a little preparation prior to the conference. It helps to prepare a claim with several samples of evidence that appear across a text. For example, you might prepare several samples of evidence that show your theme is true for Michael. Be sure your evidence is varied—some quotes, mini-stories, lists, and analysis of author's craft. Then, show a student how you quickly look across this evidence and ask, "Which evidence *best* supports this point?" and rank the evidence in front of you from *best supports* to *least supports*. Think aloud about how you could revise your essay as a result of your ranking. Coach the student as he tries the teaching you just demonstrated in his own writing. Coach the student to look across his evidence and make decisions about which evidence will best convince his reader. At the

MID-WORKSHOP TEACHING
Transitioning between Evidence and Analysis

"Yesterday, you learned about transitions that help writers unpack their quotes. Well, I'm thinking that these transitions can actually help you anytime you want to unpack evidence, whether you want to unpack quotes, or mini-stories, or an analysis of author's craft." I revised the title of our earlier chart, removing *Quotes* and replacing it with *Evidence*. "These transitions words and phrases help readers understand the link between evidence and analysis."

"Before our workshop ends today, check your essay thoroughly. Reread it, asking yourself, 'Is *all* the evidence in my essay unpacked?' If you find you're missing analysis, you'll definitely want to insert it into your essay, so your readers understand why your evidence is there and how it fits with your supports. Get back to revising!"

Ways Writers Unpack Evidence

- What this means is...
- This shows...
- This connects to the idea...
- This is important/significant because...
- This supports...
- All this demonstrates...
- This provides further proof for...
- What's significant about this is...

end of the conference, you might leave the student with a Post-it® artifact, on which you jotted him a reminder of what he just learned.

Help students incorporate observations about craft into their essays.

Some students might notice an author's goals and techniques but might have trouble framing what they noticed with clarity. You might gather these students together and give them some sentence frames that will help them describe an author's goals and techniques. Then, coach students to rehearse these frames orally before coaching them to revise the frames into their writing.

> The author used _____ to_____. For example, _____. This shows readers _____.
>
> One technique that kept repeating is _____. In each instance, the author did this because _____.
>
> The author's goal was _____, and he or she did this by _____. For instance, _____.
>
> The author could have _____, but instead the author _____. This shows _____.

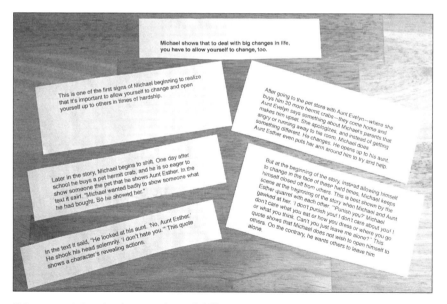

FIG. 10–4   A teacher lays out lots of different evidence for a small group to sort and rank to determine which evidence best supports the claim.

Teach students to consider words and their shades of meaning.

Other students might have it easy identifying the most obvious craft techniques—dialogue, internal thoughts, first-person narrator—but might have difficulty identifying less obvious techniques—mood, tone, or symbolism. You could gather these students to help them consider words that have different shades of meaning. You might say, "Authors choose their language intentionally. Readers need to notice the language an author uses and ask, 'Why might she have chosen this word, this phrase?'"

Briefly remind students that they've already done this work with "Shells," and draw their attention to the passage at the beginning of the text when Michael refers to Aunt Esther as *the woman*. Then you might think aloud about how the author may be using that specific word to establish the mood in the piece—one of tension between family members—a division between people whom readers would otherwise presume to share a close relationship. Then rally students to carefully reread short passages of text that tie in to their claim, to note the author's specific word choice, and ask, "Why might the author have chosen this word, this phrase?" Encourage students to try out multiple possible answers as you coach their work by saying, "Maybe. . . . Could it be. . . ? Perhaps. . . ." Students can then write long to develop their thinking.

Teach students to refer to the author across their essays.

You might find a group of students who write about author's craft and lift lines from the text but who do not reference the author. Consider gathering these students to teach them they can lift the level of their writing by directly citing an author when they quote a text or when they discuss an author's craft moves. You could display a mini-chart of phrases that writers can use to acknowledge the author. You might share a few instances of how this could go, using your literary essay on "Shells" as an example.

Ways Writers Acknowledge Authors

- At first, the author . . .
- Then, the author . . .
- Later, the author . . .
- The author shows/describes/explains/develops . . .
- According to the author, . . .

Then, coach writers as they revise their body paragraphs to include direct references to the author. Encourage writers to reread their revisions after inserting a new phrase to be sure their writing still makes sense.

Developing Parallel Lists

Remind students of their prior learning around parallel lists. Reference a familiar example to show how a student used a parallel list to develop his point.

"Writers, you've been busy filling your essays with powerful evidence and unpacking that evidence so your readers totally get what you claim. I want to remind you of one more way you can give evidence for your supports. Remember last year when you learned to use parallel lists to develop your ideas? A parallel list can give your essay the rhythm it needs to make your supports memorable and convincing. You might have noticed that Judah did this in his essay on 'The Marble Champ' that we studied earlier. Let me read a bit to you. Will you notice how Judah repeats a list of examples to really drive home his point that the main character, Lupe, overcame her difficulties because she believed in herself?" I read one portion of the literary essay aloud, stressing its repetition of parallel lists.

"Here goes: '*Lupe believed in herself* to try and win the academic awards. *Lupe believed in herself* to work and try to become good. *Lupe believed in herself* to go to the games and try to win.'

"Writers, did you hear how Judah repeated that phrase, *she believed in herself*? The repetition of that parallel list not only drives home Judah's point, but it also makes it a little more memorable and convincing."

Set students up to create a parallel list to provide evidence for one of their supports. Then, channel them to share their lists with partners, listening for how the lists sound.

"Right now, will you flip through your booklet to choose a support you could develop to include a parallel list? Maybe you choose the support that has the least evidence, or maybe you choose the support you think really needs a parallel list to help drive home your point. Once you've chosen that support, try building a list to go with it. Remember, it helps to look for specific examples from the text that provide evidence for whatever it is you want to say."

I gave students a few minutes to work on their own as I offered tips to various students. "Think about which part is most important to repeat. . . . Look for another tiny example to back up that idea. . . . Remember to keep repeating the same part at the start of each line.

"Writers, will you pause for a moment? Not only do parallel lists have to *look right*, they also have to *sound right*. You want your parallel lists to have their own rhythm. When you practice saying your parallel lists aloud, you can get a feel

> Mrs. Markham ignores Willie when he asked about the beggar, Mrs. Markham ignores Willie when he tells her about the fish with no eyes, Mrs. Markham ignores Willie whe he asks too many questions.

FIG. 10–5 Mica creates a parallel list by repeating a powerful phrase from the text.

> Story "One Green Apple"   Author: "Eve Bunting"
>
> Farah gets extra attention on the hay wagon by a girl named Anna. Farah gets extra attention when the class is picking apples by the teacher. Farah gets extra attention by the apple cider machine by a boy & Anna.

FIG. 10–6 Emmy repeats part of her support to create a parallel list.

for *how* they sound—and *if* they sound convincing. Will you take a moment with your partner to rehearse your parallel lists in the air? Turn and rehearse!" Partnerships jumped into action.

Kiara was sharing her parallel list about "The Stranded Whale" with Amira. "They took care of the whale with their sweaters, their words, and their actions," she said.

"You found three things you could say about the text," I complimented. "To say them in a parallel list, it helps to choose a part to repeat. Remember, Judah started each line with 'She believed in herself.' How could your lines start?"

Kiara thought for a minute and then said, "Maybe it could go 'The children cared for the whale with their sweaters. The children cared for the whale with their words. The children cared for the whale with their actions.'" I moved on to coach other partnerships.

SESSION 10 HOMEWORK

 ## PAUSING TO REFLECT AND SET GOALS

Writers, you've got two more days to work on this essay. Tonight, instead of doing more revisions, will you take time to study your essay, noting what you're doing well and what you still need to do to make your essay even stronger? Use the Grade 5 and 6 Opinion Writing Checklist to help you. Mark the boxes on the checklist to show what you're doing. Be honest with yourself as you do! You wouldn't want to mark *Yes!* for transitions if you've only used transitions *two times* in your essay. Develop your own system to help you mark the boxes for each item on the checklist and to find the evidence of each item in your essay. You might jot Post-it notes, write little labels in the margins, or use different colored pencils to show what you've done.

Then, look at the items you checked as *Not Yet* and *Starting To*, and set some goals. What do you need to do to make your piece stronger? Jot a to-do list for yourself. You'll have time to revise toward these goals tomorrow.

Writing "To Do," list Alexandra   2/29
• I need to use more phrases that help the reader follow what I am saying, such as "Another reason," and "The most important reason."
• I need to pull my reader in so that they will want to keep reading my essay and they will be hooked on.
• I need to use words like "specifically" and "In particular" to be more precise.
• I need to explain why my evidence supports my claim and I need to present my evidence in a sensible order.

FIG. 10–8   Alexandra jots goals based on her piece's particular needs.

Name: Sivan   Date: 3/29

Opinion Writing Checklist

	Grade 5	NOT YET	STARTING TO	YES!	Grade 6	NOT YET	STARTING TO	YES!
	Structure				**Structure**			
Overall	I made a claim or thesis on a topic or text, supported it with reasons, and provided a variety of evidence for each reason. overall = Red	☐	☐	☑	I not only staked a position that could be supported by a variety of trustworthy sources, but also built my argument and led to a conclusion in each part of my text. overall = Dark Blue	☐	☐	☑
Lead	I wrote an introduction that led to a claim or thesis and got my readers to care about my opinion. I got my readers to care by not only including a cool fact or jazzy question, but also figuring out was significant in or around the topic and giving readers information about what was significant about the topic. lead = Green	☐	☐	☑	I wrote an introduction that helped readers to understand and care about the topic or text. I thought backwards between the piece and the introduction to make sure that the introduction fit with the whole. light blue = lead Grade 6	☐	☑	☐
	I worked to find the precise words to state my claim; I let readers know the reasons I would develop later.	☐	☑	☑	I not only clearly stated my claim, but also named the reasons I would develop later. I also told my readers how my text would unfold. Gr. 6	☐	☑	☐
Transitions	I used transition words and phrases to connect evidence back to my reasons using phrases such as *this shows that* . . . . Transitions = Pink	☐	☐	☑	I used transitional phrases to help readers understand how the different parts of my piece fit together to support my argument. Gr.6	☑	☐	☐
	I helped readers follow my thinking with phrases such as *another reason* and *the most important reason*. I used phrases such as *consequently* and *because of* to show what happened.	☐	☐	☑	Dark Green = Transitions			
	I used words such as *specifically* and *in particular* in order to be more precise.	☑	☐	☐				

FIG. 10–7   Sivan color-coded his checklist, then underlined evidence he found for each checklist descriptor in the corresponding color, which helped him determine what he was already doing, and what goals he needed to set.

Beginnings and Endings

ear Teachers,

You'll notice that this letter breaks from the traditional format in this book. That's because today, we turn the workshop over to you. Instead of detailing precisely how the minilesson, mid-workshop teaching, and share could go, we give you some suggestions and encourage you to design your own workshop based on the needs of your class. Before the bend draws to a close tomorrow, you'll want to plan and teach a minilesson that will help your students put the finishing touches on their literary essays. To do this, you'll want to draw on the methods and techniques you've been using across the unit.

To prepare for this session, you might want to collect students' writing folders and read the most current drafts of your students' essays. As you read them, pay particular attention to the organization of your students' writing, especially their beginnings and endings. Take note of issues you'll want to address to the whole class, as well as needs that are best addressed one-on-one or in small groups.

As you read their writing, you might notice, for example, that many students begin their essays by simply stating a claim, and then moving quickly to elaborating upon their first support. Other students might attempt to hook their readers, but might do so in ways that do not directly relate to their claim. Or, you might notice students who end their essays by restating their claim with the exact same words they used to introduce the claim.

If any of the above scenarios are true for your writers, you'll want to read this session carefully. It outlines possible ways to teach beginnings and endings for literary essays. If your analysis of students' essays revealed different needs than the ones we describe above, you may want to modify today's teaching accordingly. You might, for example, choose to teach students ways to use transitions to move between different parts of an essay. Or, you could teach students ways to elaborate upon their evidence and support students to explain in varied ways how their evidence fits with their claim.

MINILESSON

For the connection of today's minilesson, you might reference the homework from the previous session. Ask students to bring their homework with them to the meeting area, and channel partners to give each other a tour of their writing. Each student can take turns sharing the work they did to study their writing to notice strengths and determine goals. Give students a few minutes to do this, and to also share their plans for revision. Then, you might explain that today, students will be able to work toward their goals, and that you'll teach them one more way to strengthen an essay.

Next, you'll want to name your teaching point. You might say, "Today I want to teach you that when literary essayists craft introductions, they work to help readers understand what's significant about their text. One way they do this is by beginning with a universal statement before introducing the text and their claim."

During your teaching, you might use the explanation with an example teaching method. That is, you might talk students through the process you use to generate several introductions for an essay. As part of the homework for the previous session, students studied the writing checklist, so you might begin by explaining how you first got ideas for an introduction by looking across the Grade 5 and 6 expectations for Leads on the Opinion Writing Checklist. Project the relevant sections of the checklist as you talk about them, or ask students to reread those sections on their copies of the checklist. Consider underlining and discussing a few key phrases from the checklist as you read it aloud. For example, while reading the Grade 5 expectations for Leads, you might underline the words *figuring out was significant* and then think aloud that what is important about a text is often the essayist's thesis.

Next, you might choose to share a few sample introductions that are based on the criteria of the Leads strand of the Grades 5 and 6 Opinion Writing Checklist. You might choose to project and read aloud several possible leads, pausing from time to time to draw students' attention to the ways you introduce a big idea or write a brief summary of the text. Consider highlighting or underlining the ways you begin each introduction, as students can emulate your techniques as they write their own leads. Below are some sample leads you might show if you're writing about the short story "Shells."

Opinion Writing Checklist

	Grade 5	NOT YET	STARTING TO	YES!	Grade 6	NOT YET	STARTING TO	YES!
	Structure				**Structure**			
Overall	I made a claim or thesis on a topic or text, supported it with reasons, and provided a variety of evidence for each reason.	☐	☐	☐	I not only staked a position that could be supported by a variety of trustworthy sources, but also built my argument and led to a conclusion in each part of my text.	☐	☐	☐
Lead	I wrote an introduction that led to a claim or thesis and got my readers to care about my opinion. I got my readers to care by not only including a cool fact or jazzy question, but also figuring out what was significant in or around the topic and giving readers information about what was significant about the topic.	☐	☐	☐	I wrote an introduction that helped readers to understand and care about the topic or text. I thought backwards between the piece and the introduction to make sure that the introduction fit with the whole.	☐	☐	☐
	I worked to find the precise words to state my claim; I let readers know the reasons I would develop later.				I not only clearly stated my claim, but also named the reasons I would develop later. I also told my readers how my text would unfold.			
Transitions	I used transition words and phrases to connect evidence back to my reasons using phrases such as *this shows that . . . .*	☐	☐	☐	I used transitional phrases to help readers understand how the different parts of my piece fit together to support my argument.	☐	☐	☐
	I helped readers follow my thinking with phrases such as *another reason* and *the most important reason.* I used phrases such as *consequently* and *because of* to show what happened.	☐	☐	☐				
	I used words such as *specifically* and *in particular* in order to be more precise.	☐	☐	☐				

Possible Introductions

- The world can be a tough place for someone who has faced a major loss, especially if that someone is a kid. In the story "Shells" by Cynthia Rylant, Michael loses his parents and moves in with his Aunt Esther, who at first seems not to care about his needs. Luckily, things don't stay that way forever. "Shells" teaches that things can get better if you change. This is true for Sluggo, for Aunt Esther, and, most of all, for Michael.

- <u>In life</u>, everyone faces hard times. Some people face hard times in school, and some people face hard times at home. How you deal with those hard times is what makes all the difference. In the short story "Shells" by Cynthia Rylant, Michael has hard times because his parents recently died and he has to move in with his Aunt Esther, who doesn't seem to care about him at first. "Shells" teaches that things can get better if you change. This is true for Sluggo, for Aunt Esther, and, most of all, for Michael.
- <u>In literature, authors write a lot about</u> characters who face particularly tough times. What's fascinating to see is that characters respond to these problems in different ways. "Shells" by Cynthia Rylant is filled with characters who change gradually when they encounter problems. "Shells" teaches that things can get better if you change. This is true for Sluggo, for Aunt Esther, and, most of all, for Michael.

To give students a more active role in the teaching portion of your minilesson, you might invite them to notice how you start each introduction with a big idea—something you're *really* trying to say about the text. Then, you say a little bit about the problem in "Shells." Finally, you end the lead with your claim. Ask students to consider which of your leads best fits with what you're trying to say about the text. Then, you could model how you choose which introduction best fits with your essay, based on students' feedback.

For the active engagement, you might channel students to move their essays through the same lead-generating process. You could set students up to first reread their claims to consider what they really want to say about the text. Then, you might ask students to work with a partner to try writing a sample introduction in the air. Encourage them to begin with phrases similar to those you highlighted in your mentor introductions: *The world can be . . . , In literature, authors write a lot about . . . , In life, you should always/never . . . .* Or, students can develop their own ways to begin an introduction.

Coach students as they work with their partners. Remind them to include their claim and supports, to connect their universal idea to the big problem in the text, and to write a brief summary of the text.

In your link, you'll want to restate the teaching point and add it to your anchor chart. Then, be sure to emphasize to students that today—and every day—they should draw from the repertoire of strategies they have learned across the unit. Remind them of the revision plans they jotted for homework last night—the same plans they shared with their partners in the connection. Students should be working toward those plans *and* considering ways to strengthen their introductions as they head off to write independently today.

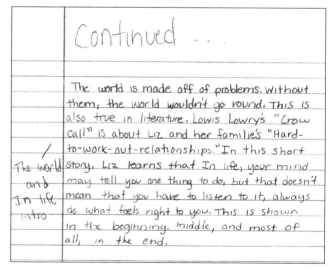

FIG. 11–1 Josie tries different introductions to her literary essay.

CONFERRING AND SMALL-GROUP WORK

You might choose to split your conferring and small-group work time today so you support students with strengthening their introductions and with working toward their self-identified goals.

First, you might focus your attention on students' introductions. For example, you might notice some students are including lengthy retellings of the text in their introductions. You might gather those students and recruit them to study the retellings in your sample introductions, noting their length. Then, you could coach students as they revise their retellings to be more concise.

You might find another group of students who are writing brief retellings, but who aren't tying their retellings to their claims. You could call these students together and teach them that their essays will have more impact if the details they include in their retellings fit with their claim. Then, channel students to revise their introductions while you coach their work.

Whenever students work toward self-selected goals, it can be powerful to honor and support those goals. To do this, you might pull next to a writer and ask him what he is working on. After he shares his plan, you might ask, "What's feeling tricky? What could you use help with?" Then, you can teach the writer a strategy to tackle that difficulty.

Mid–Workshop Teaching

For your mid-workshop teaching, you might choose to explain that literary essayists use literary language as they write. Literary language helps essayists to be taken seriously and be trusted by their readers. You might introduce a list of literary terms and then show writers how you might use them in your own literary essay. You might say, "For example, instead of just writing 'Michael is upset,' I might write: 'Michael, the main character, is upset,' or 'Michael, the protagonist of "Shells," is upset.'" Encourage students to incorporate literary words into their essays as they reread and revise.

SHARE

For today's share, consider teaching students how to craft powerful conclusions that connect to a claim. You might begin by telling a brief analogy about how beginnings and endings matter. For example, you could explain how runners, when running a race, have to start strong and finish strong to beat their personal best time. Relate the analogy to the work students are doing with their essays. Next, you might introduce a chart with a few strategies that can help writers develop powerful conclusions. Explain that while a few of these are familiar strategies from fourth grade, a few are also new strategies.

You could share a sample conclusion with students, one that you had prepared prior to the day's session. Ask students to name with their partner what strategies you used in your conclusion.

As you can see, the characters in "Shells" undergo major changes across the story. They go from being closed off and more isolated from one another to being more open. From now on, I will be kind to the people around me and sensitive to their needs. You never know what people are going through. They might just need a little kindness and a little time to help them come out of their shells.

Then, you could add the strategy to the anchor chart and explain that students will have opportunities to work on their conclusions tonight for homework.

Warm regards,
Katie & Mike

Homework

Today, you taught students strategies to develop strong conclusions. Tonight, you could invite students to craft strong conclusions. To start, students will benefit from rereading their entire piece to get a sense of what it's really about. Then, they should try out several possible conclusions, using the strategies they learned in school today and any others they invent. You might want to send them home with a copy of the "To Craft Powerful Conclusions, You Can . . . ." chart.

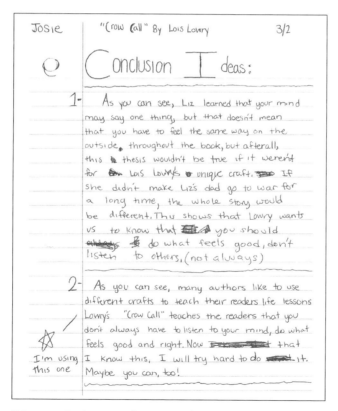

FIG. 11–2   For homework, Josie tried out multiple conclusions before choosing the best fit with her entire essay.

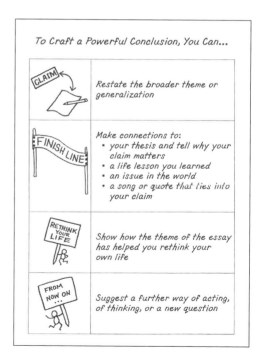

Editing Seminar Stations

IN THIS SESSION, you'll teach students that essayists get their writing ready for publication by editing, specifically by paying careful attention to grammar and convention rules to make their essays clear and effective.

GETTING READY

✔ Prepare several editing seminar stations around the room. Each station should have a folder with a station card containing a grammar or convention rule. There are several you can print from the online resources; you may choose to make others based on the needs of your students (see Teaching and Active Engagement and Conferring and Small-Group Work). 👆

✔ Be ready to project the "Using Punctuation to Cite Sources" station card, or be ready to display a different station card you select for students to work with across the minilesson (see Teaching and Active Engagement). 👆

✔ Students should have their essays with them in the meeting space (see Teaching and Active Engagement).

✔ Ensure students have copies of the Grades 5 and 6 Opinion Writing Checklist (see Mid-Workshop Teaching and Share). 👆

TODAY YOU'LL PROVIDE STUDENTS with deep and lasting help with editing for grammar and conventions. The tricky part of this work is that writers can only edit for conventions they have already mastered. How often have we seen kids using an editing checklist, happily checking off "Yes!" next to "fixing run-on sentences," only to look over their shoulder and wonder whose writing they were looking at? When Ray Pecheone of the Stanford Center for Assessment, Learning and Equity (SCALE) worked with us on writing checklists, he reminded us that checklists are a reminder for the writer; they are not instructional.

You will need to *teach* students the grammar and conventions you want them to use, but you don't have to teach each grammatical structure separately as an explicit whole-group lesson. For some writers, your instruction will serve mostly as a reminder. But other students will need to ponder, and even once they grasp the concept, they may not immediately see where this work applies in their own writing. Remember that your students will be in stages of approximation; they are young, come from many different linguistic backgrounds, and often compose in digital codes quite different than academic ones.

We've found that centers are tremendously helpful with grammar and conventions instruction. The time that each student spends at a center can be flexible. You can direct them quietly to one or another center, and they can return to them later if needed. Centers help you structure your class so that all children are learning and practicing grammar and conventions, while meeting the needs of children with different stages of language growth.

The centers are set up to include an instructional piece, examples, and invitations for students to apply their learning to the editing of their own work. Research as students are learning, so that you can study the relationship between reminders of familiar conventions and independent transfer, and the relationship between the introduction to new, tricky grammar and independent transfer. Jump in as needed, and help students see the places in their own writing where what they are learning will apply.

You will find several centers in the online resources, but if students need help with other conventions, create your own centers based on those rules. For more resources on supporting writers in learning grammar and conventions, we encourage you to consult *The Power of Grammar: Unconventional Approaches to the Conventions of Language* by Mary Ehrenworth and Vicki Vinton and *Practical Punctuation: Lessons on Rule Making and Rule Breaking in Elementary Writing* by Dan Feigelson.

> *"Academic English will not only help students excel in school, but it will also help give them access to more kinds of jobs and careers."*

You'll also see that we emphasize code-switching throughout this session, and in general when talking about academic English. There are rich linguistic traditions that students emerge from, and they will participate in other digital ones with more fluency than we do. Academic English will not only help students excel in school, but it will also give them access to certain jobs in this country and around the globe—such as jobs in science, aviation, or in the economic markets. If you're clear that you are coaching students not because you think "fixing their writing" is the goal, but because "becoming powerful" is the goal, they will dive into this work with zeal.

By the end of today's session, students will have made final edits to their literary essays. You will ask students to publish them for tonight's homework so that everyone is ready for a celebration in Session 13. Look ahead to Session 13 for ideas about how you might organize a celebration that allows students to share their literary essays with a broader, authentic audience.

Editing Seminar Stations

CONNECTION

Tell students that they already know how to speak and write in different language varieties. Explain that people speak and write in different ways for different audiences.

"Writers, did you know that all of you can speak and write in different languages?" A few students nodded, but most looked surprised or doubtful.

"It's true! How many of you talk the *exact same way* to your friends as you talk to your family or a teacher? How many of you speak the *exact same way* in this classroom as you do on the playground?" A few lightbulbs went off in students' heads and they nodded.

"I could go on. How many of you text? When you text a friend, do you type the same words you might write in an essay?" I started speaking in a stuffy, proper manner as I pretended I was texting on a cellphone. "'I would like to go to the park. I would like to go to the park for many reasons. The first reason I would like to go to the park is . . .'" The class broke into a smattering of laughter. "How many of you write an essay the same way you type a text? Probably not many of you. You probably don't write an essay like this: '*OMG*, that ook is *gr8* and *btw* it just made me and my *bff lol*!'" The class erupted into laughter, and I joined them for a moment before returning to my point.

"My point is this: we all speak and write in different ways for different audiences. The fancy word for this is *code-switching*, and we all do it. None of the languages you and I use are 'better' or more 'right' than any other, but you do have to use these languages well, and each of these languages gives you power in different situations.

"The writing you do on your cellphone is called *texting*. The writing you do for academic essays also has a name. It's called *academic English*. It's not always the language you use on your cellphone, or with friends on the playground, or with family at the dinner table (though sometimes it is). But it's the language of academic essay writing, and it matters.

"This fancy, formal kind of writing is about more than just making your writing look spiffy. It's also about being clear, powerful, and effective. If a reader isn't clear what you are trying to say, or if a reader sees that your essay isn't following the fancy, formal rules of academic writing, then that reader might not understand your writing. Worse, that reader

The trick in this connection is to strike a balance between honoring and respecting kids' home languages and digital fluencies, while revving them up to become powerful at academic English as well.

might make assumptions about your writing in te same way that a friend might wonder what's going on with you if you started texting a literary essay on a cellphone. You catch my drift, right?"

Name the teaching point.

"Today I want to teach you that writers often study grammar and conventions to make their writing more clear, compelling, and impressive. One way they do this is to study examples of effective writing, think about the conventions or rules of this writing, and then try to apply those rules to their own writing."

TEACHING and ACTIVE ENGAGEMENT

Ask students to think of something they are trying to get better at. Explain to writers that when you are trying to get good at something, one way to do so is to take a little seminar on it.

"Writers, take a moment to think about your life outside of school. What is something—maybe a hobby, maybe a sport or a skill—you are trying to get better at?" I paused for mere seconds. "Now, let me ask you another question: *how* do you try to get better at this thing? What do you do to get better?" I let the class break into momentary conversation.

"All right, some of you watch people who are good at the thing you are trying to get better at, some of you read about that thing. Some of you also said that you listen to others who are experts on that thing, right? When an expert gives a little talk about that thing, you learn from it, right?" Students nodded.

"Writers, today you're going to have a chance to study some rules of grammar, by giving yourself little seminars. A seminar is the name for a little class given by an expert."

Take writers through the process of how to o through a seminar station by first reading about the language convention and then studying examples and nonexamples of that language convention.

"Let's do this together. I'll start by choosing a seminar folder and by reading the rule. We'll read the rule and then look at examples and nonexamples of the rule." I grabbed a folder from a stack of folders containing different seminar station activities. "Okay, this folder is titled 'Using Punctuation to Cite Sources.' Let's see what's inside." I pulled out the station card that listed the rule and placed it under the document camera. "Will you read this with your partner?" I gave partners a minute to read.

"Wow, this stuff sure sounds fancy, right? With all these rules, I *know* it's going to make your writing clearer and easier to read. Before you apply these rules, you have to make sure you really get what they mean. Take some time with your partner to talk about each rule. Try and figure out what's wrong with the 'Avoid This' sentences and what's better about the 'Instead, Do This' sentences." I leaned in to listen and support their conversations.

Teachers, you could swap this convention for another if there's a convention that might be a more pressing need to teach your students. Consider this minilesson as a guide for how you might introduce one grammar or convention rule. If you do choose another convention for the minilesson, you will find other printable seminar stations in the online resources.

Roland and Annie were studying the section about using commas to introduce quotations into a sentence. "I'm not sure why the first one's wrong, 'cause I see a comma in it, right after *in the text*," Roland said.

"Comparing the 'Avoid This' example to the 'Instead, Do This' example can help to show what's wrong with the first example," I coached. Annie and Roland started reading the second example.

"I guess the second one's different because it's got another comma. And it's right before the quote. So maybe the comma has to be right before the quote to be right," Annie said.

Channel writers to apply the convention to their own writing.

"The next step in this process is to take what you learned and what you noticed and transfer the rule to your own writing. Work with your partner. Look for places where you quoted the text. Check to see if you are following these rules. If you are already doing what one part of the rule calls for, see if you can push each other to try some of the other rules and apply them to your writing. Turn and edit!"

I knelt to continue coaching partnerships. To some partnerships, I helped them find places where they quoted a text to see if they followed the convention. For others, I helped them see that if they didn't quite have a quote yet, now would be a good time to find one. Still other writers were using one of the first two pointers of the rule, but could be pushed to try quoting partial sentences from texts. After a couple minutes, I called the class back together.

LINK

Send students off to the seminar stations to learn more about how they can use grammar and convention rules to make their writing clearer and more effective.

"Writers, today you'll spend some time at different virtual seminar stations. There are half a dozen stations around the room. With your club, spend less than ten minutes at each one. Remember to first read the rule. Then, study the examples and nonexamples of the rule. Talk about them to make sure you understand them. Finally, you might take your own notes on the rule to make a plan for your edits, or get to work editing your writing right away. Regardless of what station you visit and what edits you make to your literary essay, remember that one way you can get better at something (like making your writing fancier) is to attend a little seminar on it. Clubs, off you go."

Using Punctuation to Cite Sources

What does it mean to cite sources?

Citing sources means that you show, within the body or your writing, that you took words, phrases, or sentences from another place, usually another text or another person.

What are some rules about citing sources?

There are many rules about citing sources, but here are a few important ones:

- Place a quotation mark at the beginning and end of the words cited from a text.
- If the sentence ends with a quotation, the end mark goes inside the final quotation mark.
- To introduce a quotation in a sentence, use a comma (unless you use the word *that*).
- If you only quote part of a sentence, use a lowercase letter at the start (unless the quote starts a sentence).

Can you give me examples?

Yes! See the examples for each rule below.

Place a quotation mark at the beginning and end of the words cited from a text.

AVOID THIS: Little Red Riding Hood's mother warned her, saying, Behave yourself on the way, and do not leave the path.

INSTEAD DO THIS: Little Red Riding Hood's mother warned her, saying, "Behave yourself on the way, and do not leave the path."

If the sentence ends with a quotation, the end mark goes inside the final quotation mark.

AVOID THIS: Her mother said, "Mind your manners".

INSTEAD DO THIS: Her mother said, "Mind your manners."

To introduce a quotation in a sentence, use a comma (unless you use the word *that*).

AVOID THIS: In the text, it said "The wolf ran straight to Grandma's house and knocked on the door."

INSTEAD DO THIS: In the text, it said, "The wolf ran straight to Grandma's house and knocked on the door."

FIG. 12–1   Using Punctuation to Cite Sources card

Supporting Editing

CONSIDER YOUR ROLE for the first several minutes of workshop to be that of a carnival barker. You'll want to exhort and cajole clubs to different seminar stations, talking up the stations to make them seem wildly exciting. You might say things like, "Ooh, 'Using Verb Tense Correctly.' This one is about making your writing sound really fancy and ensuring it makes *a lot* of sense." Or you might say, "Do you ever have a friend who goes on and on and on and has a hard time stopping talking? Well, this seminar station will keep you from sounding like that person. It's 'Fixing Run-On Sentences Using a Variety of Punctuation.'" You could of course assign clubs to particular seminar stations based on their needs or interests, and simply rotate clubs around the room every ten minutes. But you may find that students will be more engaged if they have choice in where they prefer to direct their own learning.

To help students be successful at this work, you might channel certain students to specific seminar stations where you know they will have the highest chance of doing well. You might also set students up for success by providing seminar stations that address the major grammar and conventions needs in your class. If you have a large number of children who need extra support with the basic rules of capitalization and punctuation, then you will want to provide folders for stations that support that work. Then, too, you might have students who need support with more advanced work, such as maintaining a consistency in style and tone, and you'll want to provide material for those learners as well.

If Students Have a Hard Time Understanding the Rules of the Convention

Some students might have a tough time wrapping their heads around what the convention rule is trying to convey. If this is the case, you might channel kids to do a close read of the rule, pushing them to reread it and ask, "What do I notice? What do I see? What words pop out at me?" Then channel students to talk about what the rule seems to be teaching. In some cases, you might want students to look at the examples and nonexamples first. You can channel students to ask the same questions, naming what they notice and what they see first, and then read the rule.

If Students Find It Challenging to Transfer the Convention into Their Own Writing

You might find that some students can understand and articulate a particular convention rule, but have difficulty applying that rule in their own literary essay. If this is the case, you might pull alongside those students with your own writing notebook to do a little demonstration of the rule. If you are teaching students how to vary sentence patterns, then you might take a short passage of your own writing that has a series of short, choppy sentences.

You might say, "I want to teach you that you can not only edit for how your essay *looks*, but you can also edit for how it *sounds*." Then model rereading your passage, noting how all your sentences seem to start the same way and are about the same length. After that, show students how to edit for sound, varying your sentence length and the way you begin your sentences. You might demonstration how to combine two short sentences into a compound sentence, or you might demonstrate how to begin a sentence with an introductory clause or phrase instead of the subject. After you demonstrate, coach students as they try similar work in their own writing.

Alternately, you might use the guided practice teaching method. To do this, you could set up a group of students to apply a grammar rule to their own writing. Once all students are working, you act as coach, whispering tips to individual students and voicing over tips you think everyone in the group might benefit from. If you are supporting a small group with using the correct verb tense, you might voice over by saying, "Make a decision about what verb tense you're writing this part in . . . Look at that verb. What tense is it in? Does that make sense? . . . Reread this part aloud and look for verbs in the wrong tense . . ." and so on. This ongoing coaching will help lift the level of students' work.

"Writers, pause your seminar learning for a moment. Inside your writing folders, you each have a copy of the Opinion Writing Checklist. Take a moment to pull out that checklist and look at the 'Language Conventions' section. Right now, will you take some time to reread your literary essay and edit for the language conventions listed on your checklist? You'll also want to apply the edits from the information you learned at the seminar stations. If there was something important you learned, you could add that convention to your checklist! Ready? Get to it!"

Opinion Writing Checklist (continued)

	Grade 5	NOT YET	STARTING TO	YES!	Grade 6	NOT YET	STARTING TO	YES!
Craft	I made deliberate word choices to had an effect on my readers.	☐	☐	☐	I chose words deliberately to be clear and to have an effect on my readers.	☐	☐	☐
	I reached for the precise phrase, metaphor, or image that would convey my ideas.	☐	☐	☐	I reached for precise phrases, metaphors, analogies, or images that would help to convey my ideas and strengthen my argument.	☐	☐	☐
	I made choices about how to angle my evidence to support my points.	☐	☐	☐	I chose *how* to present evidence and explained why and how the evidence supported my claim.	☐	☐	☐
	When it seemed right to do so, I tried to use a scholarly voice and varied my sentences to create the pace and tone of the different sections of my piece.	☐	☐	☐	I used shifts in my tone to help my readers follow my argument; I made my piece sound serious.	☐	☐	☐
	Language Conventions				**Language Conventions**			
Spelling	I used what I knew about word patterns to spell correctly and I used references to help me spell words when needed. I made sure to correctly spell words that were important to my topic.	☐	☐	☐	I used resources to be sure the words in my writing were spelled correctly, including returning to sources to check spelling.	☐	☐	☐
Punctuation	I used commas to set off introductory parts of sentences, for example, *At this time in history,* and *it was common to . . . .*	☐	☐	☐	I used punctuation such as dashes, colons, parentheses, and semicolons to help me include or connect extra information in some of my sentences.	☐	☐	☐
	I used a variety of punctuation to fix any run-on sentences.	☐	☐	☐				
	I used punctuation to cite my sources.	☐	☐	☐				

FIG. 12–2

If Students Show a Particular Expertise for One of the Conventions

Some of your students might be strong in a particular convention, and if that is the case, you might consider setting up those writers to lead seminar stations. You can channel these writers to explain the rule in their own words, to show their peers where the convention appears in their own writing, and to provide feedback to the other students at the seminar station. Research by John Hattie in his book *Visible Learning for Teachers* (2011) has indicated that students get most of their feedback for learning not from us teachers, but from their peers. What better way to harness that fact than to channel peers to lead seminar stations to provide feedback to their fellow writers?

To a group of writers at a station, you might say, "Each of us has expertise in something, and when we know something well, we teach it to others. Roland here has shown he is kind of a pro at using commas to separate items in a series. I was wondering if he could show you a little about what he knows?" In this way, you can set up writing experts at each station who can lead the conventions seminars.

Editing in Preparation for Publishing

Channel writers to make a to-do list to support them as they finish their essays, using the Opinion Writing Checklist as a guide.

"Writers, will you take this time to make a little to-do list for yourself, one that is based off the Opinion Writing Check-list? That way, you'll be all set up for your homework this evening, when you make the final edits to your published essay. What do you need to do tonight to make sure your essay is ready to celebrate toorrow?" I circulated the room and coached writers as they got to work making their checklists and continued their final edits.

SESSION 12 HOMEWORK

 ### FINALIZING YOUR ESSAY FOR PUBLICATION

Writers, take the evening to look at the to-do list you made at the end of writing workshop today. Check off each item on your to-do list as you polish your literary essay and make the final edits or changes your piece might need. Tomorrow, we will celebrate our literary essays together, and so you will want to get your piece ready to share with our learning community.

Celebration

**ear Teachers,**

Today marks the end of Bend II. Across this bend, you've helped your students dramatically lift the level of their essay writing. Your students are now adept at reading texts analytically and writing to grow their ideas off those texts. They know how to develop strong, interpretive claims and how to back up those claims with varied evidence: mini-stories, quotes, parallel lists, and an analysis of the author's craft. You've taught them how to lift the level of their introductions and conclusions, and you've supported students as they edited their work to make it audience-ready.

As you make decisions about how students will publish their essays and design your celebration, think too, about how you can help students understand the value of literary essays, especially their value in school settings and other academic venues. The way you structure student publication and class celebration can help students see their work as part of a broader tradition of academic thinking and writing about texts. It is powerful to help students understand that writing a literary essay actually helps them to think about texts—and about life—in more complex ways. Writing a literary essay well requires students to think deeply and to engage closely with a text, and through that process of reading, rereading, and revising, students come to see more in the texts they are reading.

THE CELEBRATION

You'll want to consider different ways to ask students to publish their work that reflect the ways literary scholars often publish their writing. Here, we'll share some of the tried-and-true celebrations our pilot classrooms loved. We encourage you and your students to innovate and design your own ways of celebrating. Regardless of what you decide, it's essential that your students have an audience to share their final work with.

For this celebration, you might consider publishing your students' essays online. Goodreads.com is one such platform where students might share their work. Goodreads is a site that allows readers to catalog the books they want to read, post their own reviews of books, and rate books they have read. While many of the reviews posted on the site are more persuasive in nature, others are literary, and the literary ones explore themes and characters in texts. As of the publication date of this book, there are 58 reviews posted for Cynthia Rylant's short story collection *Every Living Thing*, which includes "Shells," the touchstone text for this bend. How exciting would it be for your students to add their voices to this conversation!

You might create a class account, and then invite students to log on to Goodreads.com to post their literary essays alongside corresponding texts. Then, to extend the work, you could invite students to add comments and compliments to each other's posts. We encourage you to also invite families as well as other students in the school to visit Goodreads to also read students' uploaded essays and to post comments that add to the celebration.

In the same vein, you might set up students to upload their work to Amazon.com, BarnesandNoble.com, or on the website for your local community bookstore. Prioritize the websites your students most frequent. If you decide to publish this way, keep in mind that writing posted on GoodReads.com, Amazon.com, and other sites is public, so you'll want to make sure that you acquire permission from families. A sample permission slip is available in the online resources.

Alternately, you might decide to encourage students to share their literary essays locally. For instance, you could share students' literary essays with the school library, or with other classes in the school. One way kids could share their work is through the use of QR (quick response) codes. Kids could record themselves reading their literary essays aloud and save the files online to a site such as DropBox. Using simple software like Qrafter, kids could create QR codes that link to their recordings online. They could then print the QR codes and add their names, then tape the QR codes to the covers of the texts that they wrote about. Anyone who wants to listen to an essay could scan the code with a cellphone or computer camera and gain instant access to the audio recording of a student's literary essay on that one text. This could equip readers with information to make more thoughtful decisions about what they read. You could send copies of the QR codes to the library and to other classes around the school to broaden the audience for students' literary essays.

FIG. 13–1   This QR code links directly to heinemann.com.

Or, you might rally students to publish their essays in anthologies. For instance, you might encourage students to organize their essays by text, so that there's one anthology containing all the students' essays about *The Stranded Whale* and another containing essays about *One Green Apple*, and so on. Inside each anthology, readers could find a variety of essays that explore different angles of the text. You might even channel clubs who have been studying a shared text to work together to craft introductions to their anthology, so readers gain insight into the kinds of themes that will be explored across the anthology. These anthologies could be gifted to the school library and other classrooms around the school. Of course, you'd also want to proudly display copies in your classroom library.

Regardless of what you decide, consider ways you can make the celebration feel festive and important. You might play celebratory music while you distribute the anthologies of essays to students with a lot of fanfare. You could follow that with a special reading period for kids to curl up and read essays by their classmates or to dive in and read their classmates' postings on Goodreads and leave feedback. Or, you might invite kids to each wrap up an anthology to give as a gift to someone who would really benefit from it. You could encourage students to create stationery to write note cards to include with their anthologies. Then, they could deliver their anthologies to the intended recipients.

You could also set up students to engage in conversations about the themes they wrote about in their essays. If your school has several fifth-grade classes, you might reserve the gym for a period and set aside

The Stranded Whale By: Meera

The world can be a place where you can't have the things you want in life. The world can be a place where you can feel emotions, you don't want to feel. In the text the Stranded Whale, the protagonist Sally shows just that. Sometimes in life things don't go the way you want them to go you can feel powerless, no matter how hard you try. Sally feels this in the beginning, middle and End of the story. When she despite all other effort thought she didn't do anything to help in the beginning of the passage. When she got Mad at everything in the middle of the passage. Most significantly when she didn't appreciate her medal at the end of ~~the~~ story.

In the beginning of the text, Sally learns that Sometimes in life, things don't go the way you want them to go, you can feel powerless, no matter how hard you try. An Authors technique that is repeated multiple times is tone. Tone effects on how the Character is feeling. For example when the Animal rescue man said proudly "Good Job kids", his tone is happy. But as the story goes on sallys actions and thoughts immediately change to a different tone. After the Animal rescue said that, Sally thought she did nothing. This conveys a negative, almost guilty tone. But in reality she did do alot. Specifically when she tried to dampen the whale, and using back breaking teamwork to help get the whale back into the moving tide. "We had a whole ocean of water, but I worried it wouldn't be enough". An image that can clearly be identified is the tide going back every time they tried to help the whale, even though old leviathan was really heavy and large. This shows that Sally learns that, Sometimes in life things don't go the way you want them to go you can feel powerless... no matter how hard you try, in the beggining of the passage.

In the middle of the story, Sally learns that, Sometimes in life things don't go the way you want them to go you can feel powerless no matter how hard you try. After all the teamwork and Effort, Sally had a breakdown. She got mad at everything as a result of Leviathan dying. She was mad at the unforgiving Ocean as the tide went farther away. Their short arms compared to the whales large body. And most importantly how they didn't have the right equipment, particularly a boat, to have succeeding at saving the whale. Seeing that whale flopping joyusly out into his home in the deep blue marine world. This should show how Sally learns that, Sometimes in life things don't go the way you want them to go, you can feel powerless... no matter how hard you try.

In the end of the story the protagonist Sally learns, Sometimes in life things don't go the way you want them to go, you can feel powerless, no matter how hard you try. To add on when she recieved the medal and she consequently didn't appreiciate it. As I'm saying this I'm realizing that the medal is the last thing sally wanted due to her action and tone. Furthermore it as a slight connection to her grandpas death. As a result of her medal, she put ~~the medal~~ her medal into her drawer never to be seen again. This is important because the medal should have been given ~~with pr~~ or taken with pride and honor not dissapointed and unthankfulness. Right then and there as the medal touched her hand she felt ~~of~~ a spark of shameful guilty ~~feel in~~ going threw her body. She really didn't want the medal, She wanted to see old Leviathan again. One peice of evidence is the text says "I would have given that old medal back in a portland instant just to see old Leviathan again, Swimming joyusly out to sea. If you look at the key words, Such as old which shows a nostalgic feeling or portland instant which is a metaphor for a desire or producing a setence thats conveying a not happy setence. This should show how Sally learns that Sometimes in life things don't go the way you want them to go, you can feel powerless... no matter how hard you try.

In many points in your life you can feel powerless like you didn't get what you wanted which causes you to look back at your efforts inferring and thinking that they are useless and unhelpfull. To conclude, Sometimes in life things don't go the way you want them to go, you can feel powerless, no matter how hard you try. In the text The Strand Whale the protagonist Sally learns this in the beginning, middle and end of the story.

FIG. 13–2 Meera's published literary essay about "The Stranded Whale."

sections in the gym as a special place for each text students wrote about. Invite students who studied one text to gather in one section with their texts and literary essays in hand to discuss the central themes of the text. To make the event feel more festive, you might call it a *literary salon*, play classical music, and offer students juice to drink during their discussions. The event could culminate with students receiving an anthology of literary essays, written by all the other fifth-graders who wrote about the same book.

AFTER THE CELEBRATION

Finally, to wrap up the bend, you may want to ask students to take out the Opinion checklist and to reflect on their writing. Channel them to ask themselves, "How does my writing now meet Grade 5 expectations?" Be sure writers celebrate the ways in which their writing has grown stronger. Much of the work of the next bend asks writers to transfer what they learned in Bends I and II into Bend III. Channel writers, then, to reflect on the strategies that worked best for them. Then too, you could rally writers to set goals for the next bend of the unit, to identify a few high-priority areas in which they'd like to strengthen their skills. You might display these goals proudly inside or outside the classroom, so the work students are doing is visible to the entire learning community.

Happy celebrating!
Katie and Mike

The Karate Kid Essay
By: Ga-In

In literature authors tend to write stories with happy endings and character's having dreams, that come true. In the short story **The Karate Kid,** by Gary Soto, the main character Gilbert Sanchez has a dream of becoming the karate kid. Gary Soto chose to twist the story up a bit. Instead of Gilbert's dream coming true, Gilbert realizes karate wasn't for him. The text teaches that sometimes in life you may dream of something but it may not come true, because karate wasn't helping Gilbert, two karate was boring, lastly karate was hard.

One reason why, sometimes in life dreams may not always come true is because karate wasn't helping him. This is important because, he wanted to face his own challenges. One example is, before Gilbert's second battle with the Heat, Gary Soto says, "nothing can save him but the U.S Army." I would expect someone who takes karate would at least doge one punch or kick. This proves that, Gilbert's karate lesson's weren't helping.To add on to that during his fight he wasn't using his karate skills. An example is that, "The blow sent Gilbert the ground, where he stayed with his eyes closed until recess was over." He was to afraid to get back up. The technique Gary Soto uses is, revealing actions. This is important because, karate wasn't even helping him be braver. It may be true that, he was brave to tell the Heat to go to the back of the line but, that courage was coming from the movie not karate. I can't blame him that he can't fight because his instructor is one of the problems. Mr.Lopez didn't care to help them become better students. One example is, the instructor would, "gaze out the window" or he would "ignore him and the other boys" This is important because, nobody was encouraging Gilbert to follow his dreams. Neither are they trying to help him accomplish it. But still gilbert was a motivated character.

Another reason why, sometimes in life dreams might not come true is because, karate was boring. In other words, he didn't enjoy it. One example is, that "The next week was pretty much the same thing." You might had thought after that week something was different but, "By the end of the month Gilbert was bored to tears." In other words everyday they did the same thing. Another example is, Gilbert was so bored doing karate that,"During dinner that night a smiling and a very happy Gilbert told his mom that the studio was closing" The technique Gary Soto uses is tone to show the characters feelings. This proves karate was boring.

The last reason why, sometimes in life dreams may not go as planned, is because karate was hard for him. Gilbert expected karate not to be so hard but he made a horrible assumption.One example is,"But when it was time to do a basic drill he was at a loss." This shows that Gilbert had a long way to go. Not only was it hard, he was confused. "He looked out the corner of his eye and saw the other kids moving their arms in different patterns ." Another example why karate was hard was because, "His shoulder was sore." Not only that but "the bottom of his feet were blistered" This prove karate wasn't really for Gilbert.

Gary Soto wanted to write a unique story. Most authors write stories with happy endings. For example maybe of a girl who dreams to become a princess and in the end does. One of the messages Gary Soto is trying to give is even when you try hard to accomplish a dream, it may not. The main character Gilbert was a very motivated character, but his dream did not come true. I learned to think before you dream that was the mistake he made. In life, even when you put a lot of effort into your dream there is a chance it may not come true, one karate didn't help him, two it was boring, three it was hard. Gilbert learned that he was mislead by the movie.

FIG. 13–4   Ga-In's published literary essay about "The Karate Kid".

Writing for Transfer: Carrying What You Know about Literary Essay across Your Day, Your Reading, Your Life

Transferring What You Know to Any Opinion Text

IN THIS SESSION, you'll teach students that writers can transfer the tools and strategies they've developed for writing literary essays to help them write a host of different kinds of opinion pieces.

GETTING READY

✔ Be ready to update the "What Makes a Literary Essay?" chart (see Teaching and Active Engagement).

✔ Select an accessible text to use for today's inquiry and make one enlarged copy for each group of four students. We recommend "Maureen's Speech to the Graduating Fifth-Grade Class," which students will also use in upcoming sessions (see Teaching and Active Engagement).

✔ Prepare labels for students to affix to opinion texts to annotate places where they show the same characteristics as literary essays. You might print them on sticker paper, or you might cut apart the labels and put them in a baggie. You'll need one set for each group of four students, plus additional sets for each student (see Teaching and Active Engagement and Link).

✔ Prepare a small packet of opinion texts for each student to study. We've included a few texts you can use in the online resources for this unit. Be sure to include "A Letter to the National Museum" and "A Persuasive Letter on Peer Pressure" as these texts will be used again across the bend. You might also include the "Extended Response about Rats," "Petition to the Principal about Recess," and the "Editorial about Video Games" (see Link).

✔ Keep a copy of "Maureen's Speech to the Graduating Fifth-Grade Class" on hand to use as you coach students (see Share).

A S EXPECTATIONS FOR KIDS skyrocket and the world becomes more and more complex, do you ever get that sinking feeling that you'll never teach your kids enough? This session, and indeed this bend, is designed to address that sinking feeling. The big purpose of your upcoming writing workshop will be to move heaven and earth to teach kids that in the end, school sets them up to move forward with the skills they need to learn on their own—but that's all school can do. School will never teach them all they need to know. In the end, they'll be required to jerry-rig, to improvise, to invent. And that will require them to draw on their knowledge to do work that has no explicit step-by-step directions, nor one right template to follow.

In this bend, you'll be helping kids transfer all they have learned about writing literary essays and about interpretation of fiction texts so that they are ready to respond with flexibility to the high-stakes academic challenges that will come their way in the future. You'll help kids transfer what they have learned to real-world situations. Perhaps they read a newspaper article and want to write a letter to the editor, taking issue with what they have read. Perhaps they have a cause that they want to advance, and need to rely on evidence to persuade others to join that cause. Perhaps on a high-stakes assessment, they encounter a prompt that asks them to write an essay not on a fiction text but on literary nonfiction, or comparing two texts. In this bend, you'll help your students be ready to draw on what they know with flexibility so they can handle *any* challenge that comes their way.

Today, you'll set the stage for the bend by inviting students to revisit work they did at the start of the unit. You'll invite them to again study other writers' work, this time studying opinion writing of all different kinds. They will consider essays, editorials, letters to the editor, answers to standardized test questions, and they will notice both how these other instances of opinion writing are like literary essays and how they differ. Students will also determine what parts these texts include and how those parts are connected. During today's session, students will conduct an inquiry; they will first examine a speech, and then examine other kinds of argument writing, doing all this with the "What Makes a Literary Essay?" chart at their side, noticing similarities and differences. This is powerful work. Opinion writing, whether it be a speech, literary essay, or petition, has many recurring features. Your students will come to discover this through their inquiry today.

"Students can use the skills they've developed as literary essayists to help them plan and draft any opinion piece."

Today's inquiry sets the stage for upcoming work in the bend. In the next two sessions, you'll teach students that they can use the skills they've developed as literary essayists to help them plan and draft any opinion piece. To do this, you'll provide a series of scenarios that invite students to plan and draft petitions, speeches, editorials, and other kinds of opinion writing. As students plan and draft, you'll remind them to draw evidence from across a variety of texts to support their thinking, including drawing on both fiction and nonfiction texts when that is required. Once students experiment with a few scenarios, you'll invite them to choose one piece of writing and spend a few days taking it through the writing process. Along the way, you'll teach them to be their own job captains and to make plans for what their piece really needs. Several of the texts for today's session, especially "Maureen's Speech to the Graduating Fifth-Grade Class," "A Letter to the National Museum," and "A Persuasive Letter on Peer Pressure," resurface repeatedly across this bend, so make sure students have opportunities to work with those texts today.

Transferring What You Know to Any Opinion Text

CONNECTION

◆ COACHING

Explain to students that they'll be starting a new bend where they'll be transferring everything they know about writing literary essays to help them write any kind of opinion writing well.

"Last night after school, I brought all your literary essays home, and I curled up on the couch to read them. I'd seen bits and pieces of them along the way, but it was enthralling to see your final accomplishments. Before I knew it, my stomach was growling, and I glanced at the clock only to see that, to my surprise, hours had passed! I'm really struck by how much stronger you've gotten at writing literary essays.

"Here's the thing though, writers. This whole time, you've been thinking you were becoming stronger and stronger as literary essayists, and you were actually developing your skills as opinion writers in general. *Literary* essays are, after all, essays, and essays are a kind of opinion writing. And the cool thing is that what you have learned about literary essays will also be true for a lot of writing, especially writing that fits under the larger umbrella of 'opinion' or 'argument' writing.

"Today, you start a new bend in the road in this unit. And I thought you could start this upcoming part of the unit the same way you started the whole unit—by studying other writers' work. Remember how we did this at the beginning of the unit when we studied those sample literary essays? Only today, instead of studying *literary* essays, I thought it would be useful if you studied all different kinds of opinion pieces. Some of these will be essays, and some will be editorials or letters to the editor or answers to standardized test questions. I thought you could study these kinds of texts, thinking about how they are like literary essays and how they are different."

❖ **Name the teaching point.**

"Today I want to teach you that when you know how to write literary essays, you have the tools and strategies you need to write all kinds of essays—and lots of other writing too. You have the tools and strategies you need to make pieces of writing that aren't *exactly* essays, but are similar."

The launch of a new bend is an exciting time for you and your students. After all, it signals that there's new work ahead, often new work that involves increased sophistication or calls students to apply all that they know with more independence. Look for ways to launch a new bend in any writing unit with a little fanfare, celebrating all that students have accomplished in the past and setting the stage for the work to come.

TEACHING AND ACTIVE ENGAGEMENT

Remind students of a familiar chart you created together in Session 1. Channel students to reread the chart and take note of anything they've learned recently that should be added.

"Remember working with this chart earlier in the unit?" I gestured toward the "What Makes a Literary Essay?" chart from Session 1. "Before you get started studying other kinds of opinion pieces, will you take a minute to reread this chart with your partner? Remind each other of the kinds of things that make a literary essay, and see if there's anything you've learned that should be added to the chart."

I listened while students talked and quickly added two sticky notes to the chart.

In his book Choice Words: How Our Language Affects Children's Learning, *Peter Johnston writes about how one way to support transfer is by reminding students that they can begin a new activity by taking stock of what they already know, by activating their prior knowledge. He outlines several benefits of this work, writing, "First, it reduces the magnitude of the problem to be solved. Second, it puts the new problem in the context of old, already-solved problems. Third, it opens the possibility of more connections among the new knowledge and what is already known" (45).*

> **ANCHOR CHART**
>
> ### What Makes a Literary Essay?
>
> - Starts with an introduction
>   - Hooks the reader **and explains what's significant**
>   - Names the author and text
>   - States a claim and some supports
> - Has body paragraphs
>   - States the claim and one support
>   - Gives evidence that shows the support is true
>   - Includes explanations of evidence
>   - Uses transitions to move between parts
> - Ends with a conclusion
>   - Restates the claim and supports
>   - Makes the reader think
>   - **Ties the whole essay together**

Rally students to work in teams to study one piece of opinion writing—a speech—and to take note of similarities between that piece and a literary essay. Encourage them to annotate the text.

"Now that you're super clear on what makes a literary essay, will you see which of those same parts show up in other kinds of opinion or argument writing? I found this speech that a fifth-grader wrote and she stood on stage last year at her graduation and delivered to all her classmates. It's about all the things that could make her classmates strong leaders in middle school. You're going to graduate soon, so I thought this one might be neat to study." I projected the speech.

"This speech was written by a student named Maureen. I'm going to put a few enlarged copies of it around the rug. Will you gather in groups of four around each enlarged copy of the speech? You'll have about five minutes to read it and mark it up together, asking, 'What moves have I learned as a literary essayist that I also see other writers using in other kinds of opinion writing?' I'm giving you some label stickers that say each part of the 'What Makes a Literary Essay?' chart. You can affix them to the paper to mark what you notice right on the speech." I quickly distributed label stickers and copies of the speech around the rug.

Dear Graduating Fifth-Graders,

I first want to congratulate everyone in the fifth-grade class at Kennedy Elementary. All of us have worked hard at school. All of us have had fun at school. And now, all of us are getting ready to move up to middle school. It's a little scary, right? After all, we're about to move to different schools and meet different people. We will face pressure and stress like we never have before. To do our best in middle school and beyond takes leadership. We all need to be leaders. What are the qualities of being a leader? To me, a good leader has to have clear goals, strong communication skills, and a positive attitude.

One quality that leaders have is crystal-clear goals. To be a leader in middle school and beyond, we need to know exactly where we are and where we are going. We need to say to ourselves: what is it we *really* want to get out of middle school? And then we need to work toward that goal. Some of us might want to get good grades. Some of us might want to make new friends. Some of us might want to make the school a better place for everyone. Whatever that goal is, we first need to name it and then make a plan. Albert Einstein once said, "If you want to live a happy life, tie it to a goal." I believe that setting goals will not only make us happy, like Einstein said, but it will also make us better leaders.

To be a leader in middle school and beyond also takes strong communication skills. We have to be able to communicate well with so many people. Just think of all the different audiences we have to talk to! We have to be able to communicate with our families for later bedtimes and more freedom. We have to communicate to teachers when the material is too hard or too easy for us. We have to communicate with the principal about ways to make the school even better. Not to mention all the ways we have to communicate well with each other: talking, texting, writing notes. All of these need to be done well for us to be leaders and to succeed in middle school and beyond.

And last, but certainly not least, to be leaders in middle school we have to have a positive attitude. We have to believe that we can achieve our goals. We have to believe that the world can be a better place. I know this is true from experience. One day our teacher asked us to conduct an experiment. She challenged us to spend an entire day acting as though we were sad and bored. When we saw other students in the hallway, we looked away. When someone said hello, we said

We made the decision to get students more active in the minilesson by asking them to work in teams to annotate the text. If you feel your students need more support, you might read aloud the text to them, pausing along the way to get students talking about what they notice. Or, you might choose to gather a small group of students near you and read aloud the text to them if you feel the reading level of the text would be too challenging.

nothing. When we all talked in class, we all talked about how miserable we felt going through life with a negative attitude. Then, the next day, our teacher gave us another challenge: to spend the entire day smiling and saying hello to everyone. I remember walking down the hallway and saying good morning to a group of first-graders. At first they looked nervous, but then they all smiled back and said good morning to me! Now, whenever I see those first-graders in the school, I always stop to talk with them and ask them how they are doing. This story shows that others are drawn to people with positive attitudes. If we are to be leaders in middle school and beyond, we have to have positive attitudes, too.

There are many ways to succeed in life. One way to succeed is to become a leader. Leaders don't have to be the most outgoing or the most intelligent. You can "lead by example," as they say. To be a strong leader, you have to have a vision. You have to be able to share that vision. And you have to be able to share it in a positive way. Congratulations again to all the graduating fifth-graders, and I hope you have a great summer!

Encourage teams to discuss similarities between the speech and a literary essay, as well as to study the differences.

After most teams had finished reading the speech, I voiced over and said, "Writers, are you thinking about our big question: What moves have you learned as a literary essayist that you see this writer using in her speech? Share what you're noticing with the rest of your team." I coached teams as they turned and talked.

"Well, it has an introduction," Julia said to her team.

"Yeah, but it's kinda different from a literary essay. There's no author or title. Maybe 'cause it's not about a book," Marco responded.

"But I think it does tell what's significant about the topic. Like where it says 'To do our best in middle school and beyond takes leadership. We all need to be leaders,'" Walden added.

"Be sure to label that," I coached. "Be specific, and add arrows or symbols to show where specifically in the speech the writer did that work."

I paused the class to share a tip. "Writers, as you're noticing and annotating what's the same about this speech and the literary essays you've been writing, will you also pay attention to what's different? What makes a speech distinct? How is it different from a literary essay? Keep annotating!"

Tony shared an observation. He said, "I found something kinda like a mini-story, where she talked about acting sad and bored one day and then happy for a day and how they felt different."

It is not crucial for kids to finish this work. They'll get the gist of the activity easily.

In Choice Words: How Our Language Affects Children's Learning, *Peter Johnston writes, "Connections are at the heart of comprehension or understanding. They provide anchors and retrieval routes. The more connections, the more flexibly something can be accessed" (46). A literary essay and a speech are dissimilar enough that your students may not naturally think about how all the skills they've gained in crafting literary essays can translate over to the work of writing a speech. Johnston writes that one way to increase transfer is to encourage children to think about ways in which one thing is like another thing. He writes, "We want children to ask themselves not only 'What do I know about this?' but 'What do I know that is like this?'" (46). You'll want to support this kind of transfer today as you coach students. This coaching will help students build connections so they can access their knowledge more flexibly across this bend and in future situations.*

"Hmm, . . . that's one kind of evidence that we see Maureen using. What other kinds of evidence does she use that literary essayists also use? What kinds of evidence doesn't she use? Point to examples in the piece." Students talked, noting that she used mini-stories, quotes, and parallel lists, but that she had not mentioned the author's craft.

LINK

Set writers up to go off and study other opinion writing, noting moves those writers make that are similar to the moves that literary essayists make.

After teams had several annotations on their speech, I said, "Writers, here's what I'm thinking. You're already noticing that this one opinion piece, this speech, has a bunch of the same moves that literary essayists use. I think you need to figure out which of *your* literary essay moves, which of *your* tools and strategies, apply to other opinion pieces."

"I've copied a little packet of pieces you can use to try out this work of reading and annotating the moves you see." I got kids passing out the packets while I talked. "There's a letter to a museum about a poorly made exhibit, a persuasive letter about peer pressure, an editorial about video games, an extended response about rats, even a petition to a principal about recess. I'm also passing out sets of labels you can affix to places where you see the parts of a literary essay within each of the pieces you study. You'll try this work on your own, to

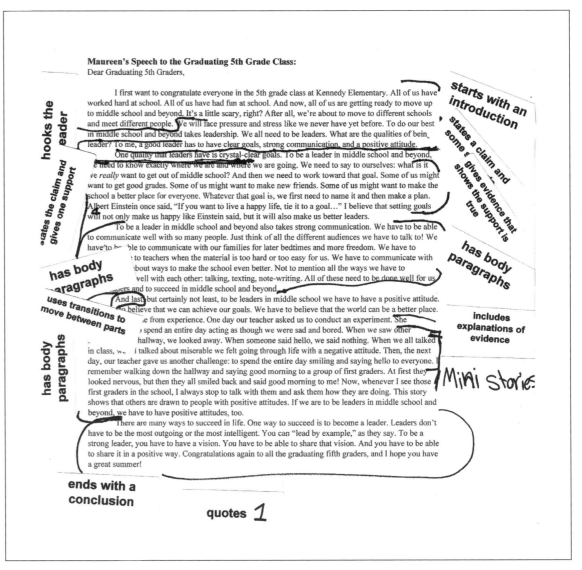

FIG. 14–1   A team annotates Maureen's speech.

The order in which we recommend sequencing the texts is deliberate. The first two texts, "A Letter to the National Museum" and "Persuasive Letter on Peer Pressure," discuss leadership skills, and they will be used across the upcoming sessions in the unit. It's important that students get a chance to work with those texts today.

start, but will you and your partner choose one of the early pieces you both want to start with? Later, you'll have time to compare what you're noticing, and that will give you a lot to talk about."

I gave students a minute to flip through their packet and quickly plan what they would read. Then I said, "As soon as you've got a plan, head off! You've got important work ahead of you: to notice how what you've learned about writing literary essays can help you with any kind of opinion writing you encounter."

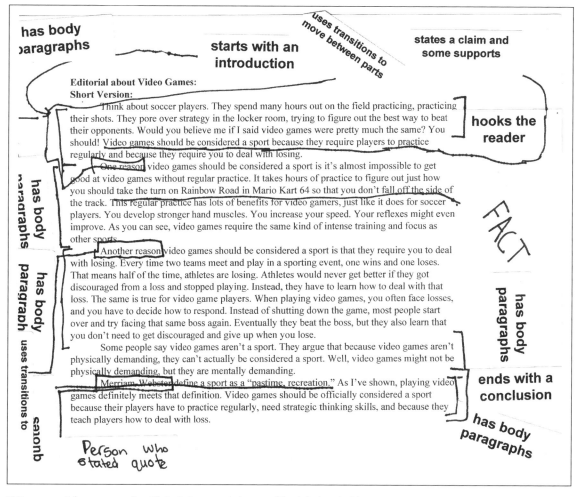

FIG. 14–2   Adam uses sets of labels to annotate an editorial about video games.

Table Conferences to Support Annotation and Transfer

WOULDN'T IT BE NICE TO BE ON ROLLER SKATES TODAY? You could move effort-lessly from student to student, offering a bit of quick coaching to lift the level of work one student is doing before skating away to the next child. While it may not be possible (or practical) to break out the roller skates, there are techniques that can help you reach as many students as possible today. One way to reach more students is to extend the teaching you've done with one child into table conferences. Table confer-ences are particularly effective when you can anticipate that a third (or even half) of your students will need hands-on help applying your teaching to their new work. They are typically used during the start of a new unit of study, and they can also be effective when writers are taking on new and different work within a unit.

To lead a table conference, you might begin by coaching one writer while he studies a text and annotates what he notices. Imagine you share a tip with that writer: "You're noticing ways the text you're studying and your literary essays are similar. Be on the lookout, also, for ways in which the texts are different. You might create your own labels to mark up what's different." Next, spend a minute or two coaching the writer while he tries the work.

Then, you could transition to a table conference. To do this, you might pause all the writers at the table, saying, "Writers, can I have your attention for a minute?" Then, you'll want to transfer the teaching that you did in your individual conference to the rest of the table. You could say, "Writers, let me share with you something that Saul is trying that I think all of you could benefit from. He's found a ton of ways his opinion piece is similar to a literary essay. Now, he's paying attention to ways his opinion piece is actually *different* from a literary essay. For example, he noticed . . ." After highlight-ing a bit of what one writer tried, you could rally all the writers at the table to try that work, saying, "Will you give this a try right this moment? As you read through, notice what's the same *and* what's different about your piece and the literary essays you've written." Then, you could spend a minute or two coaching students as they try applying the work to their own text analysis.

Here are some specific areas you might pay attention to while leading quick coaching conferences and table conferences:

◆ **Discussing connections between literary essays and opinion pieces:** It's critical that students note the ways in which the opinion pieces they are studying today are similar to their literary essays. If you see students reading their new pieces without pausing, you might coach, saying, "Be on the lookout for what's the same as you read. Pause and flag similarities as you find them."

◆ **Analyzing connections among different opinion pieces:** Just as there are similarities between literary essays and other opinion pieces, there are also similarities among the opinion pieces within students' packets. If students are ready for an extension, you could encourage them to lay two opinion pieces side by side. For example, they could study an editorial next to a petition, noting the ways the two texts are similar and different.

◆ **Noting differences, as well as similarities:** You tucked this work into your minilesson today, but you can anticipate students will need more support in this area. If students are confidently noticing ways the new text is similar to a literary essay, you might say, "What's different?" If students feel like most parts are similar, you could say, "Let's look more closely. What, exactly, is the same about this writer's introduction and a literary essay? Are there any ways it's different from a literary essay?" You could even pull out a familiar literary essay, perhaps Adam's essay on "Eleven" from Session 1, and get students to study that essay next to their new text.

◆ **Highlighting thesis statements that forecast the text's structure:** A thesis statement provides a solid foundation for an essay, and you've devoted significant time to helping students craft thesis statements that forecast the text's structure. Many of the pieces students are working with today have thesis statements that forecast the structure of the piece, but some do not. You might

"Writers, most of you have annotated that first piece you chose to study." I held up Jada's piece for the class to see. "Take Jada, for example. She's been studying that petition to the principal about bringing back recess time, and she found a parallel list where the writer said, 'Recess can teach kids how to share . . . Recess can teach kids how to play games . . . Recess can teach kids how to express themselves . . .' That's just one of the parts she annotated.

"Will you get with your partner and spend a few minutes comparing what you already found in that first text you selected? Share what you notice in those pieces of opinion writing, their parts and how they go together, and talk about how those parts compare to what makes a literary essay. And, as you do, be sure you're pushing your partner to give you evidence. Don't just let your partner say, 'He gives evidence,' and then move on. Instead, you might say, 'Can you give an example? Where do you see proof of that?'" I gave students a few minutes to compare their findings, and then channeled them to continue reading through the different pieces and jotting their observations.

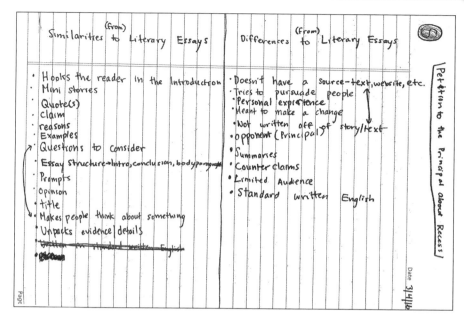

FIG. 14–3   Sana jots notes to capture ways the "Petition to the Principal about Recess" is similar to and different from literary essays.

draw students' attention to the thesis statement, saying, "In your literary essays, your thesis statement told readers what was to come in your essay. Let's study this piece. Where's the thesis statement? Does it do the same work here?" Then, you could coach students while they study the thesis statement and the ways in which it plays out across the test.

◆ **Giving a nod to test preparation:** One of the pieces your students are working with today is a sample answer to a standardized test question. If your students are required to take high-stakes standardized assessments, you might pay particular attention to this piece while you coach students. Encourage students to notice all the ways the "Extended Response about Rats" is similar to their literary essays. Also encourage them to note the differences. For example, they might notice how the thesis statement differs from that of their literary essays.

Analyzing a Piece to Determine the Writer's Process

Explain that once writers know how to write a literary essay, they can draw on that knowledge to write other texts.

"Writers, can I share a new tip with you? The important thing about today's work is this: to realize that an editorial is similar to a literary essay, and to realize that an essay on a reading test is similar to a literary essay, and a speech is similar to a literary essay—I could go on and on—but the important thing is that once you know how to write literary essays, you can write a whole world of other texts as well."

Challenge partners to study one of their opinion texts closely to note how it was constructed. Coach them as they speculate on the process the writer followed to write his or her text.

"In a moment I'm going to ask you to take the piece of writing you studied today and think of it as a finished cake—and your job will be to work with your partner and with another partnership to figure out the recipe. I know, that sounds strange, right? These pieces don't have recipes that you'd find in cookbooks. But stick with me: It's not easy to look at a cake and to figure out that the chef added eggs and baking powder and a dash of vanilla together . . . and it definitely won't be easy to figure out what your writer did to write whatever it is you are studying . . . but the best things in life *aren't* easy. And learning that you can study a finished piece of writing and make a good guess about the author's process for making something similar—that's a big deal.

"So right now, get with another partnership, and make a decision about what text you want to study. You might choose the kind of text *you* most want to write, so you can learn how to make it yourself. Once you've got a piece in mind, study it closely to figure out the recipe, the process the writer went through to make it."

As students started, I checked in with a group of students I knew could use extra support figuring out the process the writer used. I brought "Maureen's Speech to the Graduating Fifth-Grade Class" with me so I could give a quick example.

"Let me show you what I mean when I say 'figure out the process the writer used.' Look at this first paragraph from Maureen's speech, for example. I know the author used an introduction, but I want to figure out her process. Hmm, . . . *how* did she write that introduction? Maybe I could say she starts by giving a little background about what happened in the past, and then she introduces a problem: that middle school is scary. Finally, she tells one way kids can solve their problem: by being good leaders."

USING WHAT YOU KNOW TO WRITE *ANY* OPINION PIECE

Today, you learned that you can use what you know about writing literary essays to write any kind of opinion piece. You studied six distinctly different opinion pieces, noticing how each is made of the same parts that literary essays are made up of. And then you studied one of those pieces carefully to figure out its "recipe," or how those parts came together to make the whole piece of writing.

Tonight, try your hand at writing one of those different kinds of opinion pieces: a petition, an editorial, a speech, an opinion article on a book, or even a sample test answer. Choose the kind of piece you want to write, choose a topic, and then get started. For instance, you might write a petition arguing that kids should be able to have cellphones at school, or you might write an opinion piece analyzing a song you love. The possibilities are endless! Jot your response in your notebook, writing at least a page and a half.

> Alexandra
>
> Dear Editor,
>
> I enjoyed reading your article about animal abuse, ("Stop Animal Abuse!") it was very entertaining and it hooked me in. However, you forgot to address some important things, here they are. Most animals are misunderstood, and that is why they are abused, some people abuse animals to get money, and finally, people don't understand how cruel it is to treat animals harshly. These three things are very important components to animal abuse that you forgot.
>
> The first thing that you forgot to address in your article against animal abuse was, Most animals are misunderstood, and that is why they are abused. This means that people don't understand animals enough to know their reasoning, and that is why animals are abused. Take our friend the fox for an example, farmers used to be

FIG. 14–4 Alexandra crafts a letter to the editor in response to an article on animal abuse that she felt was missing critical information.

Tackling Any Challenges
that Come Your Way

IN THIS SESSION, you'll teach students that writers prepare for any opinion writing situation they encounter by transferring what they know about writing literary essays to a new situation.

GETTING READY

✔ Be sure students have read the articles on leadership prior to today's minilesson: "Maureen's Speech to the Graduating Fifth-Grade Class," "Persuasive Letter on Peer Pressure," and "A Letter to the National Museum." Students should have copies of all the articles (see Teaching and Active Engagement).

✔ Print out the Leadership Scenarios and put them in a hat or other container that students can draw them out of (see Teaching and Active Engagement and Link).

✔ Be sure the "What Makes a Literary Essay?" chart is visible (see Teaching and Active Engagement).

✔ Prepare an "Outline for a Speech to the School Board" (see Teaching and Active Engagement).

✔ Create a "Transfer What You Know about Writing to New Situations" chart (see Teaching and Active Engagement).

✔ Have a student's annotated text from Bend II ready to show students (see Teaching and Active Engagement).

TODAY YOU LET STUDENTS IN ON AN IMPORTANT TRUTH: that teachers can't prepare students for every possible scenario, challenge, or task they'll confront. What we *can* do is set them up to recognize when they can apply information and strategies they have learned in one area to another. Specifically, today you'll remind students that much of what they've come to understand about the art of literary essay writing is transferable to the art of *any kind of opinion writing*. Whether they set out to write an editorial, a persuasive letter, or a debate, students can draw on this knowledge to construct a powerful piece of opinion writing.

Of course, there are larger implications for today's instruction. While students may focus their attention on essay writing, they are in fact acquiring something larger: the ability to *transfer*. They are practicing how to take the skills and strategies associated with *anything* they try to accomplish—not just opinion writing, but geometry, drama, physics, a soccer game—and apply these to new situations. This is increasingly important in a world that is growing increasingly complex, especially the technological world. For instance, the first computers were often the size of a small building. Today, the smart phone in your pocket is tiny in comparison and much more powerful. In the face of changes like these, we must be ready to adjust quickly and seamlessly to changing information, transferring what we already know to reimagine and reinvent that knowledge into a brand-new context, often with a new set of rules. And, of course, this will be especially important for children, who will perhaps see more large-scale changes in their lifetimes than we may see in ours.

In today's Connection, you set the stage for this work by listing the numerous forms that opinion writing can take in the world and explaining that you can't teach kids how to tackle each and every one of those different forms. During the combined Teaching and Active Engagement, you'll give students the opportunity to apply their literary writing skills to a new context, this time to a specific real-life scenario they will examine as a class. Together, they'll think about how they might outline an opinion piece that addresses the scenario.

When they go off to write, partnerships will each choose a new scenario to tackle together. This work will feel like a game to students—after all, they'll be drawing scenarios out of a hat—but you'll know students are strengthening their opinion writing skills as they write toward the different scenarios. Students will spend the next few days writing in response to different scenarios. Then, you'll channel them to choose one of the pieces of writing they will have generated and develop that writing through two days of further work on it. First they'll flash-draft this opinion piece, and then they'll revise it to make it as strong as possible.

"Much of what students know about the art of literary essay writing is transferable to any kind of opinion writing."

In life, as well as in the high-stakes assessments, students are often called to write opinion pieces where they draw on evidence and craft compelling claims from informational texts. To replicate these experiences, and to help students write off of informational texts in increasingly sophisticated ways, you'll ask them to plan opinion pieces where they draw on a variety of sources, both narrative and informational. Students will not need new narratives for this work. Instead, they'll use the narrative texts they studied in Bends I and II of this unit, as well as some of the texts on leadership they will have worked with during yesterday's minilesson.

Tackling Any Challenges that Come Your Way

CONNECTION

Describe how you spent the night thinking about the work students did yesterday and all the new situations they might encounter in the future.

"Writers, I don't know about you, but last night, I just couldn't stop thinking about those pieces we studied together. Petitions to the principal. Editorials on video games. Letters to the editor on peer pressure. Feedback to a museum. A graduation speech.

"I lay awake last night, tossing and turning, running through a list of ways what you know about writing literary essays might come in handy in the future: feature articles in magazines, reviews of restaurants and plays and books, nominations for awards, recommendation letters to help someone get a job, memoirs, advice columns. I could have kept listing different ways all night, and I'm sure you could come up with more, but I think you get my gist. There are just so many different ways you might need to use your literary essay skills, and your opinion writing skills more generally, in the future.

"I know I can't teach you everything you need to know about all the different kinds of opinion writing, but I think there's something I can teach you that might help when you encounter situations like these in the future."

❖ **Name the teaching point.**

"Today I want to teach you that you can't prepare for every possible writing situation you'll encounter. Instead you have to be flexible. When you face these new situations, you have to think, 'What do I already know that could help me here?' Then, you've got to apply that knowledge to the new situation."

TEACHING AND ACTIVE ENGAGEMENT

Teach through guided practice. Coach students as they read and analyze a possible scenario that will allow them to transfer what they know from writing literary essays.

"I'm hoping you'll help me try this. I've made this magical hat, of sorts, and I've filled it with a ton of different scenarios, all capturing ways you might use all your literary essay knowledge." I held in my hands a crazy hat, filled with scenarios

> ◆ COACHING

In this connection, you focus today's teaching on one of the most valuable things kids will ever learn—the skill of transfer. You acknowledge that you cannot teach them how to tackle every single specific kind of literary essay—or any other kind of writing, for that matter. But you can *help them develop confidence in their repertoire of skills that they can draw upon to become better writers—not just today, but tomorrow, and every other day.*

You could bring in a hat—maybe a top hat, a Cat in the Hat style hat, or a hat from your favorite basketball team. You could use a large box covered in fancy wrapping paper and bows. Or, you could design another storage vessel for the scenarios. Being able to draw out the scenarios makes this work more lively and exciting for your students.

I had printed from the online resources. "These are just the scenarios I could imagine, so I'm sure you'll come up with more. For now, though, let's get started trying one of these out. They all use those three pieces we read yesterday about leadership." I gestured to Ellis to come up and draw a scenario. With great fanfare, he reached into the hat and drew out a scenario, and handed it to me to project under the document camera.

"Will you read it to us, Ellis?" I projected the scenario, and he read it.

> Your local school board is trying to decide which leadership skills should be taught at your school. They want to hear from kids like you who have been studying a lot about leadership lately, to find out your opinion. They've asked you to give a three-minute speech about which leadership skills are the most important to teach. Prepare a speech that will really convince the school board of your opinion. Draw on "Maureen's Speech to the Graduating 5th-Grade Class," the "Persuasive Letter on Peer Pressure," "A Letter to the National Museum," and the "Panyee Football Club" video to help you.

"Whoa, there's a lot tucked into this task. Whenever you encounter a complicated invitation like this, it's important to take some time to understand it, to figure out what is really being asked. That's true whether you're working with a prompt for a test or a request from your boss to take on a new project. In these situations, it helps to reread what's being asked of you and to try to put it in your own words. Will you try with rereading the scenario with your partner, putting what's being asked into your own words?"

When faced with a complicated task—a prompt on a test, a group research project, or a request from a boss—students need to know how to unpack that task to ensure that they address every part of it thoroughly. When you ask partners to focus their attention on this prompt first, rather than allowing them to dive in to start writing, you teach them the importance of understanding the task at hand, and of taking the time to make sure they thoroughly understand what is being asked of them.

I knelt to coach partners. I listened while Evan asked his partner about an unfamiliar term. "What's a school board?" he asked.

"Umm . . . I think it's people who get to decide what is taught. Like, here it says they get to decide what leadership skills are taught. And they must listen to people, even kids like us, to get ideas," Latisha responded. Evan nodded.

"Now that you have an idea of what a school board is, see what you'll need to do. Try to put the other sentences into your own words," I said.

Evan and Latisha reread the prompt and decided that they were being asked to decide which leadership skills were the most important, and then write a speech that would convince other people who get to make decisions about their ideas.

Rally writers to consider what they've learned about writing literary essays that can also apply to this new situation.

I voiced over the class with a tip. "So, you've got your situation, and you made sure you understand what is being asked. Now you have to get ready to write something that does the job. The cool thing is that you're not empty-handed. You're carrying *everything* you know about writing literary essays. So right now, think, 'What do I know that could in some way help me here?' And, remember you can use the 'What Makes a Literary Essay?' chart to help you."

Students launched into conversations and I again listened to one, then another, coaching. I asked Amira and Jasper to share what they thought they could transfer from literary essay writing to this new scenario. "We said most of it

By reminding students to use the "What Makes a Literary Essay" chart from Session 1, you underscore the importance of drawing on prior learning to deal with a new writing situation. Your students have learned many skills, not just in this unit but in those that preceded it this year and in years past—but your students may need reminders to draw on all that they know.

transfers," Amira said. "Maybe not the author's craft part, 'cause that wouldn't really teach them about leadership. And it wouldn't make sense to name the author and the text."

"But we thought the others would work," Jasper said. "Like, we will still need an introduction. And we'll have to have supports with evidence or they won't believe us. And we'll need a conclusion to end."

"Hmm, . . . ," I said, taking in their thoughts. "So even though this scenario is totally different from a literary essay, you are thinking that you can still use almost everything you know about writing literary essays to help you. That's pretty cool, right?" I reconvened the class.

When you listen to your students thoughtfully and summarize their ideas in your own words, you not only reinforce their learning, but show them that they are being heard, their ideas have merit, and their abilities are respected.

Set students up to create a quick outline for how a writing piece to this specific scenario could go.

"Let's try out one more step that can help when you're tackling an unfamiliar situation. You can make a quick plan, sort of an outline, for how your writing piece could go. To do this, you have to think, "What would I write about first? Then? Next?" and you jot that down, making an outline for yourself.

"Ready to try it? Map out a quick plan with your partner. Give a little detail about what you'll write in each part." I gave students thirty seconds to begin planning, then I voiced over with a few tips.

"Think about your thesis. You might say, 'There are many important leadership skills, including A, B, and C.' Try it out with your partner." I left a minute for kids to try this, and then I continued.

"When you plan, it helps to think about the parts you'll need and what will go in those parts. Since this is like a literary essay, I hear some of you saying you'll need an introduction, some body paragraphs, and a conclusion. Work with your partner to brainstorm what should go in each of those parts." Students started brainstorming.

I called them back to share one possible outline for the piece I had prepared in advance.

"Here's one way the speech could go," I said. "See if this plan matches yours or if you set your plan up a little differently."

Fifth-graders are expected to provide logically ordered reasons within their opinion pieces. You are intentionally leaving your supports unranked, in any old order, so you can model for students how you rethink and revise your plan tomorrow.

Outline for a Speech to the School Board

Introduction:
- Hook the reader
- There are many important leadership skills, including honesty, positivity, and creativity.

Body Paragraphs:
- One important leadership skill is honesty.
  - Evidence
- Another important leadership skill is positivity.
  - Evidence

- A third important leadership skill is creativity.
  - Evidence

Conclusion:
- Restate claim.
- Ask the school board to take action on this.

Explain the next steps in this process: collecting evidence and starting to draft. Channel students to write-in-the-air the first few lines of a possible draft.

"Writers, the next step, after you have a plan, is to collect your evidence. You're pros at this from writing literary essays." I held up Layla's marked-up copy of *The Stranded Whale* from Bend II, showing the ways Layla had identified and recorded her evidence. "The only thing that's different is you have to find evidence from a few texts, not just one.

"Then, you start writing! Let's imagine you just reread the texts, found a ton of evidence, and are ready to start drafting. Will you take a few moments to begin writing-in-the-air the start of this speech? Remember to draw on everything you know about strong beginnings to do so. Write-in-the-air with your partner." I circulated the meeting area and coached writers as they talked.

"So we have to begin with something that gets readers to care and tell readers why the topic is important," Saul said to his partner Annie.

"Yeah, and then we need to write the thesis and sort of predict all the supports," Annie said.

"Can I pause you two for a moment? You've got all the right parts ready to go, but will you actually write your beginning in the air, saying what it would sound like just as if you read if from the page? Use the outline we made together as a guide." Saul and Annie nodded and started writing their lead in the air together. After a half minute, I drew the class back together.

Debrief. Name the process the students just worked through in transferable language.

"This is a process you'll need to use a lot, whether you're writing a petition, choosing the best books for a classroom library, or writing an editorial for a publication. Let me remind you of what you just did here that you could do anytime you're faced with a new situation. First, you studied the situation and made sure you really understood it. Then, you asked, 'What do I know that could in some way help me here?' and you thought about all the literary essay tools and strategies you could draw on. After that, you made a quick plan, an outline, for how the piece could go. Next, you'd probably want to go to both texts to start collecting the evidence you need. Then you started writing your essay, using your outline as a guide." I displayed a chart and pointed to each bullet as I talked.

It is important to help students distinguish between writing-in-the-air and summarizing.

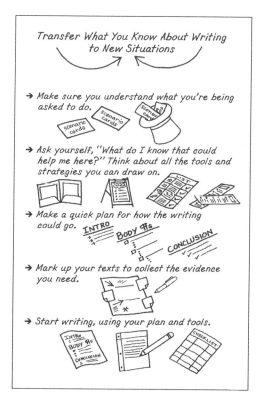

Transfer What You Know About Writing to New Situations

→ Make sure you understand what you're being asked to do.

→ Ask yourself, "What do I know that could help me here?" Think about all the tools and strategies you can draw on.

→ Make a quick plan for how the writing could go.

→ Mark up your texts to collect the evidence you need.

→ Start writing, using your plan and tools.

LINK

Channel partnerships to select the scenarios they'll work with today. Encourage them to draw on everything they know about literary essay writing as they approach these new scenarios.

"Ready to choose your scenarios? This will be kind of like the sorting hat in Harry Potter, but instead of sorting you into the four houses at Hogwarts, it will sort you into teams you'll work with later based on the scenario you'll study. Come up and draw a scenario with your partner. As soon as you get your scenario, get right to work with your partner using everything you know about literary essay writing to tackle that new situation."

I invited partnerships up to draw their scenarios from a hat.

It will take a little behind-the-scenes engineering to get all your partnerships matched with other partnerships. You'll find a selection of scenarios to choose from in the online resources. You'll want to limit the scenarios you provide students with, however, so that you're offering one scenario for every four students. Alternately, you could ask students to draw their own scenarios and form new teams with the four people studying the same scenario.

Possible Scenarios on Leadership

- Your school wants to help more kids develop leadership skills. They just can't figure out what skills are most important to teach kids. You're quite the expert now that you've read "Maureen's Speech to the Graduating Fifth-Grade Class," the "Persuasive Letter on Peer Pressure," and "A Letter to the National Museum" and watched the "Panyee Football Club" video. Will you help them figure out what they should teach? Prepare a report for your principal detailing which skills are the most important and why.

- A big election is coming up, and people in the community are trying to figure out what qualities they should look for in a new leader. You're something of an expert on leadership since you've read "Maureen's Speech to the Graduating Fifth-Grade Class," the "Persuasive Letter on Peer Pressure," and "A Letter to the National Museum" and watched the "Panyee Football Club" video. Your local newspaper heard about this and asks you to write an editorial expressing your opinions about leadership skills. Your editorial will be more persuasive if it's research based, so be sure to draw on what you learned in the articles.

- Your class is creating a special book bin called "Characters Who Are Strong Leaders." You need to choose one of the texts you've studied so far for this unit to put in this bin. Think about all the texts you've worked with: "Shells," the "Panyee Football Club" video, and the story you just wrote an essay about. Which text included the strongest leader? Then, write a letter nominating that text for inclusion in the special bin. Be sure to discuss why you'd choose that text over the other texts. Draw on the opinion pieces on leadership you read to help you ("Maureen's Speech to the Graduating Fifth-Grade Class," the "Persuasive Letter on Peer Pressure," and "A Letter to the National Museum").

- Your school board is trying to decide which leadership skills should be taught in school. They want to hear from kids like you, who have been studying a lot about leadership lately, to find out your opinions. They've asked you to give a three-minute speech about which leadership skills are the most important to teach. Prepare a speech that will really convince the school board of your opinion. Draw on "Maureen's Speech to the Graduating Fifth-Grade Class," the "Persuasive Letter on Peer Pressure," "A Letter to the National Museum, " and the "Panyee Football Club" video to help you.

- You're running for student council president at your school. You want to convince the other kids in the school that you'll be a strong leader. You think a speech is the perfect way to do this. Prepare a speech that will help you convince the other kids that you'll be a strong leader. Draw on what you know about leadership from "Maureen's Speech to the Graduating Fifth-Grade Class," the "Persuasive Letter on Peer Pressure," "A Letter to the National Museum, " and the "Panyee Football Club" video.

FIG. 15–1   The leadership scenario cards

Experimenting with Different Plans to Find the Best Fit

Y OUR STUDENTS ARE BECOMING PROS at planning how their literary essays will go. They know how to craft an interpretive claim, how to ensure it fits with the bulk of their text, and how to develop supports that fit with their claim. Once students have a thesis statement in hand, they generally have a clear plan for how their essay will go. An essay with the claim, "The Panyee Football Club overcame challenges because they did not let their space get in their way (Support A), they did not let other people get in their way (Support B), and, most of all, they did not let hard times get in their way (Support C)," gives students a clear outline for how an essay will go: start by writing about Support A, followed by Support B, and end by writing about Support C.

The pieces students develop today do not lend themselves as neatly to thesis templates, nor do they necessarily have parallel supports. This makes the work of organizing an essay more challenging. Because of this, you might find several students who need coaching to help them determine a thesis statement and to help them try different outlines for how their piece might be organized. These students might be using the thesis templates they used in Bends I and II and noticing that parts, ways, and reasons don't work in this new context. Or they may be creating an outline with parts that seem insignificant or disorganized.

MID-WORKSHOP TEACHING   **Planning with Flexibility**

"Writers, can I stop you for a minute? I was just working with Alissa, and I think she's trying something that all of you might benefit from. She's got the scenario where she's comparing and contrasting two texts, and she's trying out a bunch of different outlines to figure out how her piece might go. She made one outline, and then she tried out another outline that was totally different.

"First, she thought about *one way* her piece could go. She decided to start with her introduction, and then she thought she'd have one body paragraph that told about all the similarities between the two texts and another that told about all the differences. Then, she'd end with her conclusion.

"Then, Alissa pushed herself to try out *another way* her piece could go. She noticed her prompt talked about comparing the content *and* comparing the authors' craft moves, so she thought she could outline her piece another way. She'd still have the introduction and conclusion, but her body paragraphs would change. She'd have one

that told about how the content in both texts was similar and different, and another that told about how the authors' craft moves in both texts were similar and different. That essay would be pretty different from the first one.

"Once she had a couple of options, Alissa reread them closely to see which one might work best.

"This is work that literary essayists do all the time, right? When they plan, they try out all different versions—different outlines, different thesis statements, different kinds of evidence—until they find the one that works best for their audience and purpose.

"Will you try this out as you keep working? After you try one plan, try a few more, until you find one that's just right for your piece."

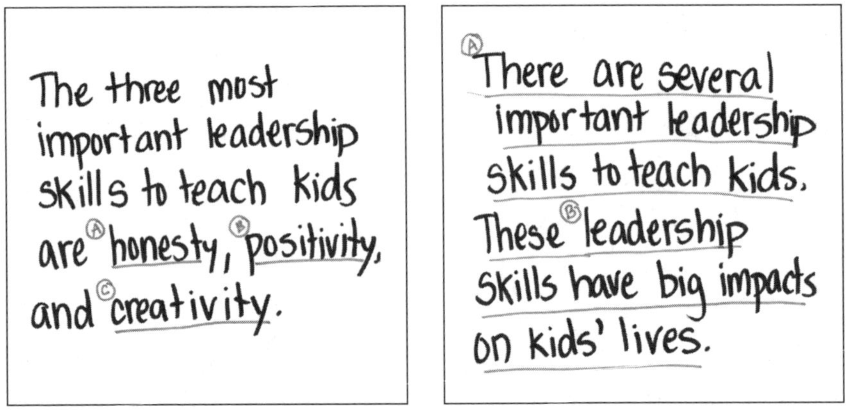

FIG. 15–2 A teacher created a visual to support a small group with different ways their thesis statements could go.

To start, you might name your teaching point. "Today I want to teach you that thesis statements can look all different ways. Sometimes, writers craft thesis statements with supports that match perfectly. Other times, writers develop thesis supports that teach important information—supports that are connected to each other in some way, but are not perfect matches."

Share examples to show students what you mean. You might say, "Take the scenario we were working with today. Earlier, we decided that we'd teach about three different leadership skills. Our thesis could sound like, 'The three most important leadership skills to teach kids are honesty, positivity, and creativity.' Those are three supports that match perfectly because they're all leadership skills. My essay would have three big sections, one for each leadership skill." You could display that thesis statement for students, underlining the three parallel supports to make them visible for kids.

Then, you might share an example of a thesis statement with supports that teach important information and are connected to each other in some way. "But that's not the only way I could organize this. Instead, I could say, 'There are several important leadership skills to teach kids. These leadership skills have big impacts on kids' lives.' Then, my essay would have *one* section that talked about the most important leadership skills to teach kids and *another* section on the impact those skills have on kids' lives." Display this thesis, marking the sections that would be developed later in the essay.

Next, you could coach students while they try this work with their scenarios. Help them to map out different thesis statements and think about how those thesis statements might help them forecast the parts of their essays. To a student just getting started, you could say, "Reread your scenario. Jot a list of parts that *could* make sense, parts you *could* include in your essay." To another, you might say, "You've got matching supports. Are there any other ways your essay could go? Any other parts that might be important to include?" If you see students comfortably planning out different ways their essays could go, you might encourage them to talk through their planning decisions, asking them to consider the importance of each part of their thesis statement.

Collaborating to Respond to a Challenge

Share a story about a time when you collaborated with others and it led you to tackle new challenges. Set students up to meet in same-scenario teams to compare strategies.

I asked the students to gather for the share, sitting next to the other partnership who had studied the same scenario. "Writers, can I tell you a story? Recently, I was getting ready to run a half-marathon, 13.1 miles. I had never run that much before, and I put together a plan for how to get ready. I mapped out how many miles I'd run a day, how fast I'd run them, even what I'd eat so I could run my fastest. I thought I had a pretty solid plan, so I brought it to share with a few friends who were also training for the race. It turned out their plans were a little bit different. Take my friend Megan, for example. She had a longer run every weekend, and I had saved all my longer runs for the week before my race. I ended up tweaking my plan, which made my training even better.

"I'm sharing this with you because whenever you're trying out something new, particularly when it's tricky, it helps to get together with others and compare strategies. Will you try this out with your same-scenario team? Get together, compare strategies, and see if you can collaborate to come up with the strongest possible plan to tackle your scenario."

Zoey, Latisha, Marco, and Adam were working on the scenario that channeled them to give the character Michael from "Shells" advice about how to be a better leader. Zoey and Marco were talking about their plan. "We thought we'd start by telling a little about the problems Michael has with leadership, and then we'd tell about the advice we'd share with Michael. We thought we'd give three leadership skills he should learn. And we'd end by telling him how to use that advice," Marco started.

Latisha said, "Ours is different. We wanted to tell about three leadership skills like you did. But we decided we'd give a leadership skill and then tell how he could use it. And then we'd do that again for the next two leadership skills."

"See if you can collaborate to come up with an even stronger plan," I suggested.

FIG. 15–3 Partnerships worked together to study Sana's outline and co-create an even stronger approach to the scenario.

USING WHAT YOU KNOW ABOUT LITERARY ESSAY TO PREPARE FOR A DEBATE

Writers, you know you can't possibly prepare for every writing situation you'll encounter, so tonight, you'll have to be flexible. Here's a new situation for you to try out:

> You are asked to take a side in a debate about which leadership skill is the most important: creativity or positivity. One side is arguing that creativity is the most important leadership skill, and the other side is arguing that positivity is the most important leadership skill. Choose a side, and prepare the argument you'll give in the debate. What reasons will you give? What evidence? Be sure to acknowledge the other side, the counter-argument.

Ga-In

Leadership Debate   3/7

Although creativity is an helpful

Claim leadership skill, positivity would do you better.

Reasons • Positivity is an important leadership skill because it would help your team.
• Positivity is an important leadership skill because it would help you.
• Positivity is an important leadership skill because it would help your creativity.

Evidence for Reason 1 • According to the Graduating 5th Graders speech, "leaders have positive attitudes, that others are drawn to people with positive attitude."
• According to the letter to the National Museum, "If you are positive, you can help the people you are working with stay motivated and 'positive.'"
• The Panyee Football Club demonstrates a perfect idea for positivity. Everyone in the village thought the idea of making a soccer team was dumb. But because they had positive attitudes they became champions.

Evidence for Reason 2 • According to the Letter to the National Museum, "If you are positive, you will make a better first impression."
• According to the "Letter to the National

Museum," "They look for the good in every situation and in every person."
• The Panyee FC transcript demonstrates that if you have a positive attitude you can make your dreams come true.

Evidence for Reason 3 • Would it be easier to be creative and positive or creative and not positive.
• The Panyee Transcript story was about boys dreaming to become soccer players when there was nowhere to play. They believed and was creative about it.

• I had a story. I had to make a poster. I was positive I could make a really good one. So I used my creativity to draw a crown.

Conclusion Positivity will get you through many things. You will be helping your teamates and yourself.

FIG. 15–4   Ga-In uses what she knows to jot debate preparation notes.

Here's the sample outline we wrote together today. You can use it as a model to help you:

Outline for a Speech to the School Board

Introduction:
- Get the School Board's attention.
- There are many important leadership skills, including honesty, positivity, and creativity.

Body Paragraphs:
- One important leadership skill is honesty.
  - Evidence
- Another important leadership skill is positivity.
  - Evidence
- A third important leadership skill is creativity.
  - Evidence

Conclusion:
- Restate claim.
- Ask the School Board to take action on this.

Transfer What You Know About Writing to New Situations

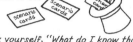

→ Make sure you understand what you're being asked to do.

→ Ask yourself, "What do I know that could help me here?" Think about all the tools and strategies you can draw on.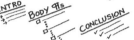

→ Make a quick plan for how the writing could go.

→ Mark up your texts to collect the evidence you need.

→ Start writing, using your plan and tools.

Logically Ordering
Reasons and Evidence

ear Teachers,

Today is another day on which we turn the reins over to you. Your students will probably benefit from an additional day to experiment with the different scenarios they worked with yesterday. While this work will feel like a fun game to your students, you'll know you are supporting your students as they strengthen their skills at transferring what they know about writing powerful literary essays over to any opinion piece.

The work of transferring what you know to a situation that feels new and novel is challenging, and it's bound to be a little messy. Don't get discouraged. As Grant Wiggins reminds us in his article "What Is Transfer?," your work today is giving students "practice in learning to play the 'messy' game, intelligently" (2010, 1). You are helping students practice their judgment as they make decisions about which skills and knowledge to use and when. Your work today, then, prepares students to more confidently tackle new situations in the future.

Below, we lay out one way a session addressing transfer might go. We've chosen to focus the content of this minilesson on organization, teaching students they can order reasons and evidence to best support their claims. This work is transferable to all the scenarios that students will encounter today. Of course, you'll want to adjust this plan so that it best meets the needs of your students.

MINILESSON

For your connection, you might want to discuss the homework students did last night. You could set your students up to share their homework with a partner, comparing the work they did to their partner's work and learning from one another. To lift the level of the work, you might suggest students focus their conversation on an area where you know they need additional support. For example, you might say, "Will you take a few minutes to share the debate plans you made last night with your partner? As you do this, really focus in on the outline you made. Discuss the decisions you made when you were setting up your outline, and then compare your outline to your partner's."

Alternately, if you have time to look at students' homework prior to today's minilesson, you might use the connection to highlight one student's work. You could project one student's outline and ask that writer to explain his process to develop the outline. Then, you could ask students to compare their outlines to the writer's outline, noting what's the same and what's different.

Then, you can give your students the teaching point for today, framing it in a way that is ambitious and worthy work for them. You might say, "Today I want to teach you that having a strong claim will only get you so far. What really matters is the supports and evidence you have to back up your claim, and, in particular, how you organize those supports and that evidence."

Next, transition to your teaching. To keep your minilesson brief, consider revisiting the scenario the class worked with yesterday, where together you planned a speech to convince the School Board which leadership skills are most important. To start, you could explain to students how you continued preparing for this speech after they left yesterday. You might highlight how you identified the three most important leadership skills, as well as relevant evidence from across the two texts that you could use to explain why those leadership skills were important.

Then, you might briefly demonstrate for students how you reread your supports, sorting them so they best support your claim. You could think aloud through a few possible scenarios. "I guess I could order them from the leadership skill you probably learn about first to the leadership skill you probably learn about last, but I'm not really sure that would make sense here. You don't necessarily learn leadership skills in a particular order. Or, I could order them from the least important to the most important leadership skill, because I've noticed that usually, the most important support comes last." Next, you could demonstrate how you revise your outline to include a more logical ordering of the leadership skills, thinking aloud along the way so students understand the process you're working through. Your revised outline could look something like this:

Revised Outline for a Speech to the School Board

Introduction:

- Get the School Board's attention.
- Name the three most important leadership skills.

Body Paragraphs:

- Third most important leadership skill (creativity)
  - Evidence
- Second most important leadership skill (positivity)
  - Evidence
- Most important leadership skill (honesty)
  - Evidence

Conclusion:

- Restate claim.
- Call the School Board to take action on this.

For the active engagement, you might ask students to practice a similar skill of sorting and ranking but to apply it in a slightly different way. For example, students could work with the evidence you found to support one of your bullets, sorting and ranking the evidence to determine which evidence to include and the best order in which to present the evidence. For instance, you might lay out all the evidence you've collected for your first support: *One important leadership skill is creativity*.

You might say, "I know that to really convince my audience, in this case the School Board, that an important leadership skill is creativity, I can't just throw evidence in willy-nilly. Instead, I've got to organize it. And sorting the evidence to see what evidence *really* fits and then ranking the evidence to decide the order that's *best* to present it in can help. Will you and your partner try this out right now with my first support?"

Then, you could lay out the evidence you've already collected for your essay. You might display the evidence on sentence strips or large Post-it notes so that kids can physically manipulate the evidence as they consider the best order in which to present it.

Evidence: One important leadership skill is creativity.

- Evidence A: mini-story about the Panyee Football Club building a pitch in the water when there wasn't space on land ("Panyee Football Club" video)
- Evidence B: Benjamin Franklin invented a creative solution to his problems with swimming. He designed his own swimming fins and sandals to help him swim. They didn't always work perfectly, but they were creative ("A Letter to the National Museum").
- Evidence C: "All across our history, people have had to make decisions that are not so clear-cut. Leaders are asked to do things that have never been done before" ("A Letter to the National Museum").
- Evidence D: The teacher conducted an experiment with kids to see if things were better when they were sad and bored all day or when they had a negative attitude ("Maureen's Speech to the Graduating Fifth-Grade Class").

Next, you could coach partnerships as they try this work. You might suggest students first sort the information, seeing what information actually fits the claim. Then, channel them to try ranking the information. You might say, "What if you could only choose *one* piece of evidence? Which piece of evidence do you think is the strongest? Why?" or "How would you order those three pieces of evidence in your piece? What order makes the most sense?"

To wrap up, you might ask one partnership to briefly share, highlighting the logical order behind their evidence.

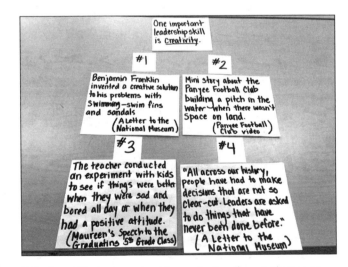

FIG. 16–1 Students sort evidence during the minilesson to determine the best order in which to present it.

In your link, you'll want to restate your teaching point, emphasizing that without strong supports and evidence, it's nearly impossible to convince your audience of your claim. Then, you'll want to launch students into their independent work. We suggest that you get students working with the scenarios for another day, so they have additional opportunities to practice transferring all they know about crafting literary essays to new contexts.

In the last session, students worked through a scenario with a partner, and today, you might choose to remove that scaffold. You could ask students to work on a scenario independently, meeting with a partner only after they've done some work making sense of the scenario on their own.

CONFERRING AND SMALL-GROUP WORK

For your conferring and small-group work today, you might gather small groups of students to support them in studying and continuing to learn from the mentor texts they examined in Session 14. To start, you could gather all the students preparing to draft one type of text—for instance, the petitions group—and say, "Let's study that petition about the lack of recess time. This time, instead of noticing how it has all the same moves as a literary essay, will you notice how it's structured? What are the big parts you can find? And, what work does each part of the essay do?" You might model how you do this work with one part of the petition and then rally partnerships to continue working through the petition, noticing the big parts and describing the work each part of the essay does in transferable language. This builds off of the work students did during the share in Session 14.

Then, you could coach students as they rethink their plans for their pieces in light of this new information. You could coach, saying, "How can you use what you noticed about the structure of the petition to make your outline even stronger?"

You might also spend time supporting students in transferring their learning from Bends I and II. For instance, up to this point you've taught students several different kinds of evidence they can include in their literary essays. As students plan, look for them to be transferring the work they did in literary essay to their opinion pieces today. For example, if you see a student only identifying quotes to add to his piece, you could remind him that opinion writers included varied evidence in their writing, and then coach him as he collects varied evidence to fit with his ideas.

Mid-Workshop Teaching

For your mid-workshop teaching, you might ask students to meet for a few minutes in their same-scenario groups. You'll want to select something for the groups to discuss, based on your observations of their work and initial conferences. For instance, if you notice several students with claims that feel weak or with claims that do not forecast their supports, you might say to the students, "Will you share your claims with one another? Give each claim a quick check. Does it address the scenario? Is it clear? Does it forecast your

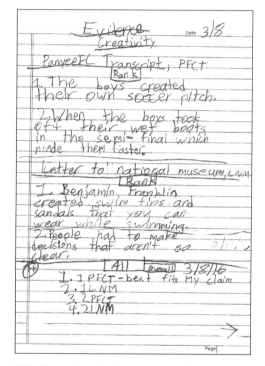

FIG. 16–2 Angelo determines evidence that could support his claim, and then ranks the evidence to consider which fits best.

supports?" Give the groups a few minutes together to talk, and then channel them to continue working with their scenario independently.

SHARE

In the next session, students will be flash-drafting an opinion piece based on one of the scenarios they've been working with over the past few days. To help students prepare for this, you might use your Share time today to get students to study all the scenarios they've worked with and to decide which of those scenarios they'd most like to bring through the writing process. You could explain to students that over the subsequent two days, they'll have the opportunity to collect additional evidence, flash-draft their piece, and make major revisions so their piece represents their best opinion writing. Then, give kids a few minutes to look over their scenarios and the work they did with each scenario. Channel them to choose one they'd like to develop into a writing piece.

Homework

Tomorrow, students will be flash-drafting the opinion pieces they selected to work with in today's share. Tonight for homework, you might want to give students additional time to prepare for drafting. You could suggest they try out different versions of their claim or outline, as you taught them yesterday, working to consider which best fits their text. Other students might need to collect additional evidence that fits with their claim, and students with a wealth of evidence might need to sort through that evidence to see which evidence *best* fits their claim. It's possible you'll want to give students a few possible options for how they could prepare themselves to draft.

Enjoy!
Katie and Mike

Session 17

Applying Your Past Learning to Today's Work

TODAY'S SESSION is as much about supporting students' drafting efforts as it is about supporting their independence as writers. If your students have grown up with Units of Study in Opinion/Argument, Information, and Narrative Writing, they've experienced what it is to be one's own job captain. They know how to get themselves going on a project, how to find the resources and tools they need to sustain that work, and how to create a plan for using those resources and tools to draft.

Even if your students haven't experienced the writing Units of Study, this session is designed to lead them through the writing process with greater independence, which is at the core of writing workshop. This will be especially important as students begin a kind of writing that in some ways will feel brand new. You'll remind them, as you have across this bend, that today's work builds on skills and strategies they've used before. Today you'll channel writers to think about all they know about writing in general, and about opinion writing in particular, so they can generate a plan and then draft fast and furiously.

The goal of today's session (and the goal of this bend) is transfer. Over the next two days, your students will take their opinion pieces through the writing process. They'll do this with increasing independence, making decisions about the tools that will most help them and decisions about how to revise and edit their piece. Today, you'll teach students to study charts and tools in the room to remind themselves of everything they know that could help them as they draft, to plan quickly for how they'll use those charts and resources, and then to draft fast and furious, bringing all they know to bear on their new draft. In the next session, instead of teaching students *one way* to revise, you'll set students up to work more independently, teaching students to use a writing checklist as a revision tool. This revision work requires students to draw on all they know and to determine how different items on the checklist apply to their piece.

Teaching students to transfer what they know to slightly different contexts helps to solidify learning and better prepares them to apply their opinion writing skills to future situations, whether they're working to advocate for cleaner parks in their community or responding to a prompt on a high-stakes assessment.

IN THIS SESSION, you'll teach students that writers draft a new piece of writing in the strongest possible way by drawing on all they know about other genres, in this case, opinion writing.

GETTING READY

✔ Display this unit's charts across the classroom so students can read them (e.g., "Template for Trying Out Possible Theses to Find the Perfect One" from Session 3; "Transitions that Spiff Up Essays" from Session 5; "To Craft an Angled Mini-Story . . ." from Session 4; "Kinds of Supports Literary Essayists Use" chart from Session 8; "Tips for Quoting a Text" from Session 9; "Ways Writers Unpack Evidence" from Session 9; as well as any other charts that your students regularly use) (see Teaching, Active Engagement, Link, and Conferring and Small-Group Work).

✔ Keep paper at hand, so you're ready to capture a student's plan for drafting (see Teaching).

✔ Recruit a student to demonstrate how they develop a plan for their drafting (see Teaching).

✔ Be sure your students have their writing notebooks and writing folders with them at the meeting area (see Active Engagement).

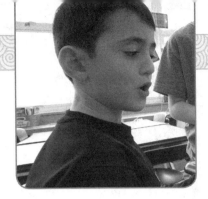

Applying Your Past Learning to Today's Work

CONNECTION

Share a story about a time you tried something new. Emphasize how you weren't starting from scratch. Instead, you built off of everything you already knew.

"Friends, I am a little sheepish to admit it, but I tried playing *Minecraft* for the first time last week." Students' eyes brightened with interest, and I continued. "Yes, it's true. So many of you have been talking about it, and I am always eager to try new things, so I played it. After all, I grew up with video games, and I thought it would be pretty easy for me to learn *Minecraft*." I paused and looked at the class dramatically. "But it wasn't. At first, it was really hard. I was like, 'Huh? What is going on in this game? What am I supposed to do? What are these monsters attacking me?' I really just wanted to give up." Several kids exchanged glances and nodded knowingly.

"But I didn't give up. I watched a quick tutorial on YouTube, and started playing again. Then, I realized that *Minecraft* was a lot like other games I had grown up with. The building part was a lot like a game I played called *SimCity*. Escaping the monsters was a lot like playing *Super Mario Bros*. I realized that if I drew from what I already knew about playing *old* video games, I could apply it to this *new* video game. Before I knew it, I had a little hut my avatar could sleep in at night, safe from the attacking monsters."

Draw a connection between your new experience and the drafting work students will do today.

"Obviously I'm not telling you about this because I just love video games. I'm telling you this story because it got me thinking about the pieces you're working on right now. Last night, you did a ton of planning and collecting evidence to get yourself ready to draft today. And, in some ways, I bet the drafting you're about to do feels totally new, 'cause chances are you've never written a piece *exactly like* what you're aiming toward today.

"But truthfully, you're not starting from scratch—not anywhere close to it. Just like I could apply all these skills from playing old video games into *Minecraft*, you too have got all these literary essay tools and all these drafting tools you can draw on that will make this new piece you're drafting pretty great, maybe even the best one you've ever written."

Make this connection your own. Substitute a story about anything you've done recently: trying a new video game, programming a website, cooking a new soup. Highlight to students how, instead of starting over and having to relearn every skill involved, you drew on all you knew to help you in that situation.

✦ **Name the teaching point.**

"Today I want to teach you that one way opinion writers—and all writers, really—get themselves ready to draft is by thinking back to all they know and all they have learned and by studying their charts and tools. Then, they draft fast and furious, using that prior learning to make their new draft even stronger."

TEACHING

Recruit a student to help you demonstrate one way a writer prepares to draft. Channel the student to demonstrate how he reviews his plan and uses classroom tools to help him draft.

"Mohammed volunteered to show you how he does this. Watch closely. Notice the steps he takes, 'cause you'll be trying this afterward." I asked Mohammed to join me, and he did, his writing notebook and writing folder tucked under his arm. "Mohammed chose the scenario about nominating a text for the 'Leaders to Emulate' book bin, and he decided that the 'Panyee Football Club' video is the one text that most belongs in the bin.

"So, Mohammed, are you ready?" He nodded. "Okay, so, first, it helps to do a little inventory, to think about all the stuff, all the tools that you've worked with that could possibly help you. That way, you know what you're working with. Let's look in your folder, first, to see what tools you have there."

Mohammed flipped through his folder. "Well, I've got some stuff in here. Here's the writing checklist. It could maybe help. And I've got this chart." He held up the "Transitions that Spiff Up Essays" chart. "Oh, and I guess I've got those pieces we looked at, the essays and editorials and stuff. Maybe they could help."

"Think about the tools outside of your folder," I suggested, spreading my arms wide. "Look around the room. What else could help you?"

Mohammed looked around the room. "For sure, the charts. I see a ton I could use."

I prompted him to say more. "For example . . ."

"For example, the one about mini-stories will help, because I want to include a mini-story about how the Panyee Football Club shows leadership skills. And I think the one about how to quote will help. I underlined a lot of lines I could quote. And maybe the one on unpacking evidence," Mohammed said.

"I hope you're studying Mohammed's moves carefully," I said, directing my attention to the class. "Did you notice how he did a quick inventory of the resources available to him, thinking about which ones would most help him as he drafts today?"

For this role, consider prepping a student in advance, so the minilesson runs more smoothly. You could pull a student aside for a few minutes in the morning to rehearse with her how the minilesson will go. Alternately, if you feel your students need more scaffolding, you might decide instead to model your own work, showing students how you review a plan and use tools to begin drafting.

For today's minilesson, you'll want to display the charts you've created across the unit. You may want to display both the anchor charts and the one-day charts. Students will draw on these charts today as they draft.

I looked back at Mohammed. "Alright, you've got a long list of stuff you could use. But tools don't do you any good if they just stay tucked away in your toolbox. They're only useful if you get them out and use them. Now, you've got to make a plan. How will you *use* these tools to help you draft?"

"Maybe first I'll reread that persuasive letter about peer pressure. I think that's kinda like what I'm writing," Mohammed started. I started jotting his plan so the class could see it.

I named the strategy Mohammed was planning to use. "Oh, so you're thinking you'll start by studying a mentor text, noting what that writer did that you could also try?"

Mohammed nodded. "Then, I think I'll start drafting. And I'll use the quoting and mini-story charts then to help me give better evidence. Oh, and the unpacking evidence chart to say more. And maybe when I'm almost done, I'll look at the checklist to see if I've forgotten anything."

Mohammed's Drafting Plan

- Reread persuasive letter on peer pressure.
- Start drafting. Use charts to help (quotes, mini-stories, unpacking evidence).
- Look at the checklist to see what else I still need to do.

Ask students to reflect on what Mohammed did that they could also try. Channel students to describe his process by naming what he did to get ready to draft.

"Wow, That's quite a process! Writers, will you, with your partner, quickly name what you just saw Mohammed do to get himself ready to draft? What did he do that you could also try?" I gave students a minute to talk, and then called everyone together.

"Give me a thumbs up if you said one of these steps: first, Mohammed thought about what his piece was. Then, he did an inventory of his folder to see what materials he could use. He could have studied his notebook too. Next, he scanned the charts in the room on the lookout for some that would help him. After he collected a bunch of resources that could help, he made a plan for how he'd use them to draft—what he'd do first, next, then, and so on."

ACTIVE ENGAGEMENT

Set students up to inventory the resources available to them. Channel them to make a plan for how they'll use those resources to draft. Encourage students to jot those plans as to-do lists.

"It's your turn to try this. Take a few minutes to first do an inventory of the stuff you have that could help you draft. Look in your folder and your notebook. Look at the charts around the room. Figure out what can help you as you draft today. When you've got a sense of your resources, make a plan. How will you use those resources to help you create the best possible draft?"

You'll want to make sure this process goes quickly. Asking the students a few questions can help. You might also restate what a student shares with greater clarity, saying things like, "So what you're saying is . . ."

It's possible that students have misplaced some of the resources you've distributed across this unit. Consider carrying extra copies of these resources with you as you coach students today. If you notice, for example, that students no longer have a copy of the Opinion Writing Checklist, you might give them a new copy to work with.

I coached students as they worked independently to develop their plans. Skylar had two piles of resources growing in front of her. "Oh, my, you certainly look like you are thinking carefully about your tools and resources!" I said. Skylar nodded. "I'm sorting the stuff that will help and the stuff that won't," she said.

"Let's look at one of the resources that you put in the 'will help' pile. Pick one we can think about first." Skylar grabbed her rough-draft literary essay about *The Stranded Whale*. "Hmm, . . . your rough draft. How could you use that to help you as you draft today?"

"Um . . . I could reread it," Skylar said. "You *could* reread it," I said, "but how will that rereading help you draft?"

"I guess if I reread it, I could see the things I did well in my literary essay," Skylar said. I left wait time and gestured for her to continue. "Maybe I could mark those things with Post-it notes so I remember to try them in my editorial today."

I encouraged Skylar to keep planning this way, by studying a tool and considering how she could use it, and then I moved on to coach another student.

After a few minutes, I voiced over, "Be sure to jot your plan down. It's like a to-do list. That way, you can mark off the steps as you draft."

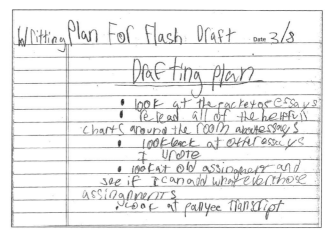

FIG. 17–1   Alain lists several steps he'll move through while drafting.

LINK

Restate the teaching point. Rally students to head off and draft, using the resources they identified to help them create the best possible draft.

"Writers, whenever you're getting ready to draft, remember that you're not starting from scratch. You know a ton about drafting, and you're equipped with a bunch of tools that can help you. So, today, and whenever you are ready to draft, it can help to first take a little inventory, to think back over all you've learned and all your charts and tools. Once you've gathered some resources, you can make a plan and start drafting, using those tools to help you. Using all that prior learning can really help you make your draft much stronger!"

"You've developed powerful plans, so I don't want to keep you here at the meeting area for a minute longer. You'll want to move through your plan today, so that by the end of today's workshop, you've got the strongest possible draft of your piece you can. And, if you finish drafting, you can start your revision work."

"Off you go to put your plan into action!"

Supporting Students in Transferring Their Knowledge to a New Writing Challenge

TODAY, we suggest you focus your conferring and small-group work on supporting students in transferring the repertoire of writing work that you've taught so far this unit. That is, you may find some students who need support strengthening their claims, others who may need to link their elaboration back to their claim, some who need support determining how to structure their new writing piece, and still others who need work bringing forth all their new learning about conventions as they draft. As you confer today, you'll want to keep an eye on all of these needs and more, reminding students to draw on what they know by referencing your earlier charts and teaching whenever possible.

Help writers strengthen their claims.

A strong claim is central to a strong opinion piece. If a writer crafts a claim that is wishy-washy, filled with lots of tentative language, or lays out a claim with supports that are overlapping, her entire piece is weakened. Therefore, as you confer with students today, you'll want to pay special attention to the claims students develop. As students draft, you might study the room quickly, on the lookout for any students who could use additional teaching.

As you confer with students to help them craft their claims, be sure to reference earlier charts. You could refer to the "Template for Trying Out Possible Theses to Find the Perfect One" chart from Session 3 and the "Kinds of Supports Literary Essayists Use" chart from Session 8. You might also want to carry a copy of the Conferring and Small-Group Work section from Session 3, "Coaching to Develop Strong Claims," which outlines predictable problems with thesis statements and tips you might share with students.

MID-WORKSHOP TEACHING
Filling the Room with Powerful Lines

"Writers, I almost didn't want to stop you, you're so focused on your drafting. You've got all these tools out to help you—some of you have even stood up to walk around the room and study our charts—and you should be proud of the way your drafts are coming together. I thought we could all pause, just for a minute or two, and you could share some of the most powerful lines you've written so far. Take a minute to reread your piece, and find the one sentence that shows your best work today. Maybe it's a sentence that will pull your readers in, or a sentence that captures precisely what you're trying to say.

"I'm going to be a conductor, holding an imaginary baton. When I gesture toward you, read your line loud and proud, so the rest of the class can marvel at the writing work you're doing." I mimed pulling out my imaginary baton and began to gesture to students one at a time. They filled the room with their key lines.

"One reason the Panyee Football Club should be nominated for the Local Leaders award is they understand the power of teamwork."

"Teaching kids leadership skills today will set them up to be better leaders in the future."

"There are similarities and differences in the leadership skills the two texts teach about."

"Just incredible, writers! Back to drafting, and use all the tools you have to create more lines like the ones you just shared."

Help writers link their elaboration back to their claim.

Take stock of the elaboration work students do. You might notice students who elaborate on their ideas, but who don't link their ideas back to their claim. That is, as you study student elaboration, you may need to ask yourself: is this writer's elaboration helping to convince an audience of a claim? To address this in a small group, you might say, "I want to teach you that elaboration isn't just giving more evidence. Elaboration is about helping readers understand *how* your evidence links back to your claim." Then, you might refer to the "Ways Writers Unpack Evidence" chart from Session 10. You could briefly show students how read through a paragraph of the class essay on "Shells" from Bend II that is filled with elaboration, noting when your elaboration is just saying more and revising it so that your elaboration explains how your evidence links back to your claim.

Help writers use what they know about writing conventions as they draft.

In their seminal book, *The Power of Grammar: Unconventional Approaches to the Conventions of Language*, Mary Ehrenworth and Vicki Vinton write about the importance of helping students transfer previous learning about grammar and conventions to new contexts and pieces. To support this, they suggest introducing a language convention for the first time near the end of the writing process, when students are editing. Then, Mary and Vicki recommend revisiting that same convention the next time students are drafting, teaching them that now, they don't have to wait until editing to use that grammar or convention rule. They can start using it right away, as they draft.

If you are conferring with a student and notice he is not drawing on all he's learned about grammar and conventions, you might share a tip. You could say, "I want to teach that yesterday's editing becomes today's drafting. What I mean is that once you've learned about a grammar or convention rule, and you've edited for it, you don't want to wait until editing to include it again. You can start when you draft, using everything you know about grammar and conventions as you write." Then, you could act as a coach as the child drafts a little bit of his piece, whispering tips along the way. "Add those quotation marks . . . Remember where the comma goes."

Becoming Feedback Partners

Channel students to name the work you usually do during one-to-one conferences. Explain that students can do similar work as they work with partners.

I asked students to break from our typical routine and join me on the rug for the share. "I do writing conferences with you guys all the time. With your partner, will you name how a writing conference with me usually goes? What do I do first? Next? Then?" I gave students a minute to talk, and then I asked Layla to name the steps.

"You always start the same way—'What are you working on as a writer?'—and then you ask us more about what we say," Layla said. "And you always give us a big compliment. It makes us feel good."

I signaled for Roland to add on. "Plus you teach us something new. And you have us try it in our own writing."

"You can do this same work when you're sharing writing with your partner. You can do a little research, give your partner a big compliment, figure out what they need help with, and then teach it to them."

Rally students to work with partners as critical friends, giving honest and actionable feedback about one another's writing.

"Your work with your partner will be most helpful if the feedback you give—both your compliment and your tip—is honest, and if it's about things your partner can actually take action on and improve in his or her piece.

"Are you ready to try this? Decide which partner will be the teacher first and which partner will be the writer. Teachers, get things started by asking a question, maybe 'What are you working on as a writer?' or 'How's it going?'" I knelt down to coach partnerships as they got started.

After a few minutes, I channeled students to jot down their feedback on a Post-it note and leave it on their draft to guide their upcoming revisions.

FINISHING DRAFTING AND PUTTING PLANS INTO ACTION

Today, you started flash-drafting your new opinion pieces, using charts in the room, checklists, and other tools to help you create the best possible draft you could. You also met with your partner, and your partner gave you some honest feedback about how you could improve your draft.

Tonight, work to make your piece as strong it can be. You might need to finish drafting, following the plan you created during the minilesson today to create the best version of your draft you can. You might need to try the feedback your partner gave you, revising your draft based on that feedback to make it stronger. Or, you might know another way you can strengthen your piece! Whatever you choose, you should have a solid version of your draft done when you get to school tomorrow.

Analyzing Writing and Goal-Setting

IN THIS SESSION, you'll remind students that writers sometimes pause to consider progress, using a checklist to assess their own growth and set goals. Then, they work purposefully to accomplish those goals.

GETTING READY

✔ Copy the Grade 5 and Grade 6 Opinion Writing Checklist for students (see Teaching and Active Engagement).

✔ Be ready to project a section of the Opinion Writing Checklist (see Teaching and Active Engagement).

✔ Mark up a sample of your writing against the checklist to share with students (see Teaching and Active Engagement).

✔ Create a chart titled "Using the Writing Checklist in Even Smarter Ways" (see Teaching and Active Engagement and Link).

THINK OF A GOAL YOU'VE SET, or a New Year's resolution you've made. Perhaps it was to finish your degree, buy your first home, or read all of J. K. Rowling's books. Most likely, setting that goal was a great first step in your journey to achieve it, but only a step. As football coach Tom Landry put it, "Setting a goal is not the main thing. It is deciding how you will go about achieving it and staying with that plan."

Too often in the classroom, work around goals ends with goal-setting. Students set goals and record them in their notebooks or on a class chart, and then they continue with writing as usual, leaving behind the goals they've set. When you ask, "What are you working on as a writer?" that student will usually be able to articulate a goal. However, when you follow up, saying, "How's it going? What progress are you making? What's been tricky?" you often hear crickets.

Today's teaching seeks to remedy this. First you'll teach students how to use the Opinion Writing Checklist more effectively to set goals. Then, you'll communicate to students that goal-setting is about much more than just setting goals. You'll teach students that the real work begins once goals are set—when writers begin working intentionally toward their goals. You'll emphasize the significant changes writers can bring about when they work diligently to accomplish their goals.

Your coaching will be critical as students set goals and work toward them today. Students may feel that goal-setting is just about improving deficits or fixing the areas on the checklist where they've marked "Not Yet." As you coach, you'll help students to see that writers can also set goals about things they are gesturing toward, and that they can then work hard at those specific aspects of writing until they become strengths. Channeling writers to set goals related to work they are already approximating can help all writers to develop strengths.

Across the session, you'll help students cultivate a habit of mind around goal-setting that they will carry with them to new situations. Your teaching today supports students in more confidently setting and working toward goals that matter in the future.

Analyzing Writing and Goal-Setting

CONNECTION

Make connections between the work students did in the previous session—drafting their opinion pieces using all they knew—and today's work: using a writing checklist in more skilled ways.

"You know that when you want to get better at something new and challenging, one way is to draw on everything you already know. Yesterday, for instance, you thought about all you knew and about all the charts and tools that could help you. Then you used your knowledge and tools to help you draft fast and furious. Using that prior learning helped you make your new draft even stronger.

"I want to remind you of another way you can get better at something new and tough. You can set big goals, goals that are sky high, and then work incredibly hard to meet those goals. By deciding on specific ways you can get better, concentrating your energy on those goals, and then by working like crazy on them, you can dramatically improve your practice.

"I know you've worked with the writing checklists earlier in this unit." I held up the Opinion Writing Checklist. "Teachers designed this checklist to be an incredibly useful tool, one that would help students to set crystal clear goals, with the expectation that students would then work toward those goals. But the thing is, it seems like you're using this checklist more like a shopping list. Have you seen people use a shopping list? They just check, check, check things off as soon as they put them in their cart, and then they never think about them again." I acted out this work as I described it. "When you use the writing checklist this way, things get checked off, but your writing doesn't really get better.

"I've been working with this checklist a lot, and I thought I could share some tips with you that might help you use it even better, so it really helps you tackle this new, tough work."

❖ **Name the teaching point.**

"Today I want to teach you that to get dramatically better at something, you need to work at it deliberately. As writers, you can use a checklist to help you study your work, find evidence of what you're already doing, and identify goals worth working toward. Then, you work like crazy toward those goals."

◆ COACHING

It's important to be honest with students about what they're doing well and what they can do even better. Here, you tell students about the less effective ways you've noticed them use the writing checklist. This connection will be even more powerful if you substitute examples from your own classroom. Do your students check off all the boxes without even glancing at their piece? Do they check off things they've done in one tiny place, even if they haven't done them repeatedly? Use specific instances based on what you've noticed about your students' use of the writing checklists across this unit and in prior units.

TEACHING AND ACTIVE ENGAGEMENT

Teach through guided practice, coaching partnerships as they use the Grade 5 and 6 Opinion Writing Checklist to self-assess their work and set goals.

"Ready to try this? To start, I'll coach you and your partner through using the checklist super effectively, and I'll tuck in some tips along the way. After a bit, I'll pass the reins over to you, and you'll have to keep using the checklist and studying your work on your own. Here goes."

I projected the Grade 5 and 6 Opinion Writing Checklist and asked students to pull out their copies. "It's hard to go through the whole checklist at once, 'cause it's got a ton on it. Instead, it helps to zoom in on one section, and then to read that section and say it in your own words. Will you zoom in on 'Elaboration' first? Find it on the checklist, read it with your partner, and put it into your own words. Get started." I listened to partnerships as they rephrased the "Elaboration" strand of the checklist into their own words.

Coach partnerships as they study one partner's work, looking for evidence. Share an example of how you marked up your piece using the checklist, and rally kids to do the same.

"Now that you know what's expected of fifth- and sixth-graders for elaboration, it's time to study your own writing. You can't just check off 'Yes,' and say, 'I did it!' without really studying what you did. Instead, you have to reread your piece carefully and look to see if you can find proof of where you did this work described on the checklist. Once you find that proof, it helps to mark up your writing in the margins or on the words that show proof. Let me show you what I mean."

I projected a piece of my own writing to show students an example of what I meant. I explained how I had marked up the evidence I found in my piece by underlining and annotating in the margins.

"Underlining and annotating worked for me," I said, "but you'll probably develop your own system. Maybe you'll use different colors to show the different parts of the checklist, or perhaps you'll make little flags out of Post-it notes and use them to mark up where you find evidence.

"Will you and your partner decide whose work you'll study first? Together, read the piece, looking for evidence of elaboration. Mark up anything you find." I coached partnerships as they started.

"You've found evidence. Now it's time to score the work. Remember that a 'Yes!' score means you can say, 'Yes, I've done all the parts of this, and I've done it all across my writing.' A 'Starting To' score means you've done it sometimes, or you've done parts of it. A 'Not Yet' score means you haven't done it yet. 'Starting To' and 'Not Yet' are great scores to have in some ways because it means you've got some work identified you can do. You've got one minute to give the writing a score."

If most of your students are writing at or near grade level and are meeting many of the expectations on the Grade 5 Opinion Writing Checklist, it makes sense to share the Grade 5 and 6 checklist today, so all students have next steps. If most of your students are writing below grade level, you might substitute the Grade 4 and 5 checklist. It's discouraging for a student to score his or her writing and have all "Not Yets." Alternately, you might choose to give different checklists to different students in your class."

Elaboration and Craft can be tricky for students because these categories can't always be pinpointed to one exact part of a piece of writing; they weave across the piece. We chose to focus our coaching on elaboration, but you should substitute for a different category if your students have different needs.

Opinion Writing Checklist (continued)

	Grade 5	NOT YET	STARTING TO	YES!	Grade 6	NOT YET	STARTING TO	YES!
Ending	I worked on a conclusion in which I connected back to and highlighted what the text was mainly about, not just the preceding paragraph.	☐	☐	☐	In my conclusion, I restated the important points and offered a final insight or implication for readers to consider. The ending strengthened the overall argument.	☐	☐	☐
Organization	I grouped information and related ideas into paragraphs. I put the parts of my writing in the order that most suited my purpose and helped me prove my reasons and claim.	☐	☐	☐	I organized my argument into sections: I arranged reasons and evidence purposefully, leading readers from one claim or reason to another.	☐	☐	☐
					The order of the sections and the internal structure of each section made sense.	☐	☐	☐
	Development				**Development**			
Elaboration	I gave reasons to support my opinion that were parallel and did not overlap. I put them in an order that I thought would be most convincing.	☐	☐	☐	I included and arranged a variety of evidence such as facts, quotations, examples, and definitions.	☐	☐	☐
	I included evidence such as facts, examples, quotations, micro-stories, and information to support my claim.	☐	☐	☐	I used trusted sources and information from experts and gave the sources credit.	☐	☐	☐
	I discussed and unpacked the way that the evidence went with the claim.	☐	☐	☐	I worked to explain how the reasons and evidence I gave supported my claim(s) and strengthened my argument. To do this I may have referred to earlier parts of my text, summarized background information, raised questions, or highlighted possible implications.	☐	☐	☐

Name the process you just went through in transferable language.

"This feels a ton more purposeful than just crossing things off of a shopping list, huh? Let me say back what you did, and then you'll go through these steps on your own." I revealed a new chart and named the steps on the chart.

Set up students to choose another category on the checklist and to work through the checklist steps on their own.

"Ready? Pick up your own essay, choose a category on the checklist—maybe one you're not sure you've totally done yet—and dive in. If you get to step five, repeat the process! Use this time to see what you're already doing as a writer and to figure out what you haven't done quite yet." I gave students a few minutes to work on their own, to study their own writing and note their own strengths and needs.

Roland had selected Craft from the checklist. "I'm looking at the first part, where it says, 'I made deliberate word choices and chose when to quote words to have an effect on my readers,'" he said.

"Does your essay show this? If so, where?" I prompted.

"There's some here where I said Mom's kisses 'didn't have the safe, solid feeling they'd had before.' I thought that would be good for readers," he said.

"You found one example of craft in your piece. Mark it up. To check 'Yes!' you have to have several examples all across your piece. Keep checking all across your piece for more evidence of craft," I coached.

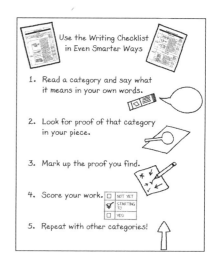

Students will not have time to go through the entire checklist at this time, and that's okay. Your teaching today supports students in using the checklist as a more effective tool for self-assessment and goal-setting in the future, and it sets students up to be in charge of their own writing lives. These are worthy goals for your young writers.

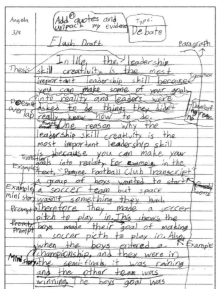
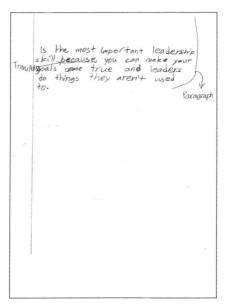

FIG. 18–1 Angela marks up her flash draft.

LINK

Explain that writers also use the checklist as a tool for goal-setting, and add an additional step to the chart. Rally writers to set goals and work toward those goals.

"Today, you'll be in completely in charge of your own writing. This is the last day you'll have to work on this piece, and you'll have to make decisions about what you need to do to make your writing as strong as you can. Having some goals in mind that you can work toward will help."

I revealed two more steps on the chart.

Using the Writing Checklist in Even Smarter Ways

1. Read a category, and say what it means in your own words.
2. Look for proof of that category in your piece.
3. Mark up the proof you find.
4. Score your work.
5. Repeat with other categories!
6. **Set goals worth working toward.**
7. **Work toward your goals.**

"Take a minute to set some goals. Look at your checklist. What goals do you want to work super hard toward today? Look at your 'Not Yets' and your 'Starting Tos' scores because those are great things to turn into goals. Mark up your goals on the checklist or jot them down so you've got a plan for your writing work today.

"Remember, you're in charge of your writing today—and every day. As soon as you've got your goals, head off, get the tools you need, and start working to make your piece even better than it is right now."

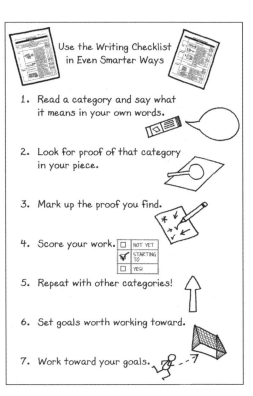

Use this time to coach students who linger in the meeting space, helping them to set goals worth working toward and develop a quick plan for how they'll work toward those goals. Look ahead to the conferring and small-group work section for tips about how this coaching could go.

FIG. 18–2 Sivan lists a variety of goals he'll work toward to strengthen his piece.

Supporting Self-Assessment, Goal-Setting, and Progress toward Goals

I F YOU HAVE *Writing Pathways: Performance Assessments and Learning Progressions, Grades K–8*, you'll want to take a careful look at Chapter 5, "Self-Assessment Checklists: The *What*, the *Why*, and the *How*." This chapter provides a more in-depth look at writing checklists that can be used with students across a variety of genres: information, opinion, and narrative. It explores additional ways to help students deepen the work they do with writing checklists.

It's no small feat to teach your students how to set and work toward ambitious, attainable goals. While some students may quickly identify needs and begin working toward those goals, other students may require more support and coaching. You might decide to split your conferring time today, using the first part of the workshop to help students as they self-assess and set goals, and then shifting your focus to helping students work toward rigorous goals during the second half of the workshop.

Supporting Self-Assessment and Goal-Setting

First, you could look to see if any students are lingering at the meeting area, still self-assessing. Ask yourself: Has a student slipped back into old habits, checking items off the list without searching for proof in her piece? If this is the case, you might pull up next to the student and say, "Where's the proof you did that? Are there any other places where you've tried this? Does that one example really show mastery?" Encourage the child to continue this work as she self-assesses.

You may find some students who feel discouraged when they look across their checklist and see that most of their checks are for "Not Yet" and "Starting To." If you see a student like this, you might pull up close and give a little pep talk. Emphasize how noticing what you need to get better at is a good thing because it gives you a path for how to improve your writing. You might say, "Once you've found some areas where you can improve, you have a course forward for *how* to improve. You know what work you can do. That's something to celebrate."

Other students might jump confidently into goal-setting, but when you look at their goals, you notice that they are small. Perhaps a writer has decided to add the transitions *one reason* and *another reason* across her piece or has decided on one part of

---

MID-WORKSHOP TEACHING
Being Your Own Problem Solver

"Hold on, friends. I'm a little confused. I see some of you just sitting and staring at your pieces, and I even see some of you with your hands up. It's like you're waiting for me to come over and solve your problems." I acted flabbergasted about what was going on. "You can't sit and wait for me. You've got to be your own problem solver. You've got to take responsibility for solving your own problems.

"Let's try this. Sara, will you share the problem you're facing, and then will the rest of you imagine that you're Sara, and you have to solve this problem on your own?"

Sara said, "Well, I don't know how to make my conclusion better. It feels boring. I'm stuck."

"All right, problem solvers. Be Sara. How could you solve this?"

The kids named several possible solutions: reread to figure out what you're really trying to say in the essay and then write about that in the conclusion; look at the checklist to get ideas for what you could include; study mentor texts to see how they wrote their conclusions, and try to write one like that; try out a bunch of possible conclusions without worrying about which is best, and then choose the best one; meet with your writing partner for feedback.

"Back to writing, and this time, don't just sit there waiting for your teacher to solve your problems. Be your own problem solver!"

---

her introduction she needs to strengthen. Gather writers like this together and offer them a few quick tips on developing high-priority goals. You could display a mini-chart that captures your teaching:

Develop Goals that Really Count!

- Look across all the possible goals on your writing checklist.
- Ask yourself:
  - What does this text *most* need?
  - Which goals will make my piece much better?
- Choose goals that lead to *big* changes.

Then, coach students as they study their writing checklists and prioritize goals that will have a bigger impact on their piece.

Supporting Work toward Goals

Once your students have set goals and headed off to revise, you'll want to support them as they work toward those goals. Some students might have solid goals but feel unsure how to work toward them. You might teach these students by referencing your teaching from the previous session. You could say, "When you drafted your piece yesterday, you drew on everything you knew about good essay writing, and on all the tools in your toolbox to help you. You can do the same when you work toward your goals. You can take a goal and say, 'What tools do I have that could help me work toward my goal?' Then, you can use that tool to help you." Next, you could coach students as they revisit their literary essay tools and apply them to this new context.

Other students might be making tiny changes to their piece, inserting a word in here or there and thinking that they are making major revisions to their piece. You'll want to remind these students that revision involves making significant, large-scale changes to a piece. Share a few examples of what you mean by large-scale revision. You could highlight how when writers revise an introduction, they might try out three or four different versions to see which work best. They could experiment with several ways to precisely word their claim, making sure it captures what they're trying to say about the text. Then, you might contrast this with the work you're seeing students do, saying, "Do you see how this is different from the work you're doing today, poking a word in here and crossing a word out there? Large-scale revisions lead to large-scale improvement." Then, coach students while they choose one of their goals and revise their piece in dramatic ways.

Partner Work to Celebrate Progress toward Goals

Celebrate the work students did revising toward their goals. Encourage partners to reflect on their writing progress.

"By setting goals, and working toward them like crazy, you've been able to dramatically improve your writing in the span of one day. Before we move on, let's take some time to reflect. In a minute, I'll ask you to share the work you did today with your partner. Explain to your partner what you worked on and what you got better at, and point out some specific places in your piece where you tried that work. It might sound like, 'Today, I was working on . . . and I became better at . . . and here's where I tried it . . .' Look at your writing, and get yourself ready to share."

I gave students a minute to reread their work in silence, and then I said, "Start reflecting. Celebrate what you worked on and the growth you made as a writer!"

SESSION 18 HOMEWORK

 ## DESIGNING YOUR OWN HOMEWORK ASSIGNMENT

Tonight, you're the boss. It doesn't make sense for me to give everyone in the class the same homework assignment right now, since you're all at different places with your pieces. You know best what you need to work on tonight. This is the last day you have to work on your opinion piece to make it the strongest you can.

Right now, will you make a decision about what's next for your project? Do you need to make sure you're really explaining all the evidence you're including? That your transitional phrases help link parts of your essay together? That you made deliberate word choices to have an effect on your readers? Something else? Whatever you decide, will you make a small box on the top of your draft and jot your homework assignment inside it? Then, get started working on your plan.

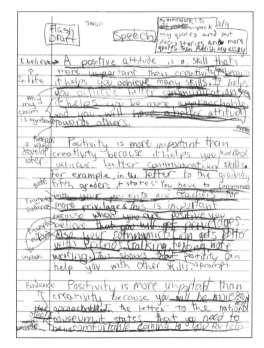

FIG. 18–3   Sivan creates his own homework assignment.

Becoming Essay Ambassadors

IN THIS SESSION, you'll teach students that once people develop expertise, they can take that knowledge to a broader audience and share what they've learned with others. One way they do this is by hosting small groups of interested participants.

GETTING READY

✔ In advance of today's session, you'll need to set up times for the writers in your class to teach what they've learned to students in other classes. We suggest reaching out to third- and fourth-grade teachers. Ideally, each student will be able to work with a small group of three to five students during today's Share.

✔ Prepare a chart titled "We're Experts On . . ." and be ready to add ideas students generate (see Connection).

✔ Be ready to project the demonstration writing materials you used with a small group of writers. We suggest showing your teacher plan, your demonstration writing, and a mini-chart (see Teaching).

✔ Create a list of students' names and the classroom each student will be teaching in. Be ready to project it or display it on a chart (see Share).

ODAY MARKS THE LAST DAY IN THIS BEND and the culmination of this unit. Over the past four weeks, you've taught students how to read texts analytically, developing more nuanced, text-based ideas as they reread. You've taught students to design strong thesis statements and to support those thesis statements with varied evidence: with mini-stories, quotes, parallel lists, and an analysis of author's craft. You've taught students to think more critically about the supports and evidence they include and to make critical decisions about how to order their supports and evidence. You've taught students how to write about a variety of texts: videos, short stories, memoirs, nonfiction texts, and more. And, you've taught students to transfer all this learning over to new contexts, so they can confidently carry what they know into any opinion writing scenario they encounter in the future.

Instead of teaching another minilesson, detailing another specific opinion writing strategy, we encourage you to change course. Today, we suggest you hand the reins over to your students. "You've got such expert knowledge now," you might say to your students, "and it would be a real shame if our unit ended with all that knowledge staying trapped inside your brain, if you kept all you learned to yourself." Then, you'll empower students to design small groups on opinion writing topics for other kids at the school. We imagine that during today's session, students will develop their own small groups to plan what they'll teach and how they'll teach it. Then we imagine students will create tools to use as they teach. Finally, during today's Share, you could send students off to third- and fourth-grade classes around the school to become ambassadors for teaching and writing strong literary essays. Each of your fifth-graders would assume the role of teacher, pulling together a group of three to five students and teaching a small group for them.

Today's session will require some preparation, but it will be entirely worth it when you see your students taking on the role of teacher and leading seminars on topics of their expertise. Reach out to your colleagues to coordinate times for your students to visit. We suggest that you arrange for your students to visit lower-grade classrooms, but you could also arrange for students to teach other fifth-graders or for them to lead small groups for their families during a parent celebration. Ideally, students will lead their small groups in a timely fashion, either at the end of today's session or tomorrow. Their teaching is designed to be quick and dirty. Think of it more as a rough-draft teaching than as a final, polished product. Because of this, we recommend you channel students to do their teaching quickly, so they only spend this one day planning how the groups will go, rather than stretching the planning process across several days.

> *"Marvel at students' sophistication of language, the specificity of their teaching points, and their ease at discussing Opinion Writing strategies."*

Take some time to scuttle from room to room while your students are teaching. Marvel at the sophistication of their language, the specificity of their teaching points, and their ease at discussing opinion writing strategies. Your students have come a tremendous way as opinion writers over the course of this unit, and they are ready to transfer their new skills to confidently tackle any situation that comes their way.

Becoming Essay Ambassadors

CONNECTION

Rally students to generate a list of matters they are experts on related to literary essays and opinion writing.

"You've become experts on a ton of things over the past few weeks, matters related to literary essays specifically, and things related to opinion writing generally. Will you and your partner take a few minutes to brainstorm things related to literary essay and opinion writing that you feel like you now control? You can use the charts in our classroom to remind you of things we have studied." I listened to kids talking and jotted a list of what I overheard.

We're Experts On . . .

- Growing big ideas
- Writing thesis statements
- Writing mini-stories
- Choosing really strong quotes
- Figuring out the authors' moves
- Using the writing checklist
- Editing our writing
- Writing quick speeches, editorials, and more!

"Whoa! This list is already filling the chart, and I bet you could keep listing more."

Emphasize that experts share their knowledge. Explain that students will teach small groups to share their expert knowledge about opinion writing with others in the school.

"Here's the thing. Experts don't keep their knowledge to themselves, bottled up inside their brain. Instead, experts share what they know. Some give talks and lectures, others write books. Some go out into the world and take action. Some become ambassadors for a cause. A ton even teach what they know, holding classes or small groups on topics of their expertise.

"You've got such expert knowledge now, it would be a real shame if our unit ended and all that knowledge stayed trapped inside your brain, if you kept all you learned to yourself. I thought instead, today, you could use that expert

The topics your students generate might vary from the lists generated in our pilot classrooms. That's wonderful! Celebrate the topics your students are experts on, and add them to your chart. Your students will be able to confidently lead seminars on those topics. If your students' list feels a little incomplete, you might also add a few items to the list that students do not generate by pretending that you heard students say those topics.

This is a rigorous timeline, but it's also entirely attainable. The teaching your students do today will be rough-draft teaching. Their plans, tools, and visuals won't be perfectly polished, and that's alright. Students are solidifying their learning across this messy process.

knowledge to become ambassadors of essay, to teach small groups of third- and fourth-graders in our school what you know about essays. They could really learn a lot from you. Are you up for it?" The kids nodded enthusiastically. "I bet you're already thinking about what you could teach. You'll have to get right to work, because they're expecting you in fifty minutes."

❖ **Name the teaching point.**

"Today I want to teach you that experts share their knowledge with the world. Some do this by becoming ambassadors of sorts, setting out to teach others topics they know and care a lot about. To prepare for that teaching, they think about *what* exactly they'll say, and plan *how* the teaching will go."

TEACHING

Share an example with students of how you planned a small group for a group of literary essay writers. Emphasize the process you went through as you were planning.

"You know I lead small groups with you all the time, right? In the past few weeks, all of you have had a chance to work with me while I teach you something in a small group and then coach you as you try it out. Quick, will you remind your partner how those strategy groups usually go?" Students turned and talked, naming the typical parts of my strategy groups.

"Thumbs up if you said one of these parts. I usually start by naming what I'll teach you—teachers call that the *teaching point*, since it's the *point* of our teaching. Then, I give you an explanation of how to do the work, or I show you how I do it in my own writing. After that, it's your turn to try it. Oh, and you said I usually give you tips as you're trying things to help you do the work even better.

"Those small groups would *not* go well if I went in empty handed, if I brought you together and said, 'Umm . . . Well, I guess I want to teach you something . . . Hmm, . . . I think maybe I could . . . No, that's not it . . .'" I dramatized this, playing up my lack of preparedness, and the class laughed alongside me. "That wouldn't work well, right? Instead, I come in with a little plan. Let me show you what I mean."

I projected a simple template I often used to plan how my small groups would go. "See how I start by listing that teaching point, the big thing I want to teach you? This was for a strategy group on quoting, and I decided to teach one way writers find the best possible quotes: by rereading all their quotes and sorting them to see which best fits their claim. That was my first step, figuring out *what* to teach you.

"Then, I had to figure out how to teach this to you. I decided I'd use my own writing to teach this. I collected three quotes in my booklet so I could show you how I read all three of those quotes and then decided which was best. And I made a little chart that said the teaching point and gave a few tips." I projected my booklet, followed by my mini-chart, so students could see the tools I had made to prepare.

Alternately, you might decide to turn the teaching and active engagement portion of the lesson into an inquiry, and gather students around a video of a teacher leading a strategy group. There are several videos you could choose from on our Vimeo site at www.vimeo.com/tcrwp. You might set students up to watch the video with an inquiry question in mind. For instance, you might say, "What do teachers do as they lead strategy groups that you could also try?" After students watch the video, you might collect their responses. Students might suggest that the teacher clearly names a teaching point, repeats the teaching point multiple times over the course of the lesson, gives a little demonstration, gets the students active right away trying the work, and gives students tips while they work. Then, you could channel students to plan their own strategy groups, applying all they learned in the video to their work.

> Teaching Point: Writers choose the most powerful quotes. One way they do this is by rereading all their quotes and sorting them to see which best fits their claim.
>
> Teach:- Model with three quotes, thinking aloud about which is best
>
> Coach:- Coach writers as they sort Quotes and rank them.

FIG. 19–1 A teacher shares her small-group planning template.

"That was my next step, figuring out *how* I wanted to teach you and making some materials to help me teach and you learn."

Restate the small-group planning process you went through using transferable language.

"So, these small groups require a little preparation. To start, I choose something to teach, something that's important for all of you to learn. Then, I figure out *what* exactly I want to teach you about that thing. After I know what I want to teach you, I figure out *how* I'll teach it, and I make any tools or charts that will help me."

ACTIVE ENGAGEMENT

Rally students to select one expert topic on which they'd like to lead a seminar. Coach students as they start planning out how their strategy group will go.

"Ready to try this? Choose a topic. Maybe it's one that's on our 'We're Experts On . . .' chart, or maybe it's something else you're experts on. Once you've got it, start figuring out what you want to teach about that topic. It might help to think about what I've taught you and what you've tried in your own writing to get ideas for what you could teach. Or think back to what you shared at the beginning of this minilesson. Jot what you're thinking in your notebook."

Tony had already jotted "author's craft" at the top of his page when I knelt down next to him. "Great, you know your topic. Now you've got to figure out *what* you want to teach about that topic. What are you thinking?" I asked.

"About the techniques," he said. "What about the author's techniques do you want to teach?" I asked.

"I guess I want kids to know that authors use techniques and that kids can figure out what those techniques are if they read some of the books." I gave him a thumbs up and moved on to coach another writer.

After a few minutes, I voiced over, "Remember, experts not only think about *what* they'll teach, they also think about *how* they'll teach it. Make your plan. How will you teach? Will you teach by using your own writing? By showing an example in a mentor text?"

I gave students another minute to brainstorm, and then asked them to share with their partners their plan so far. "Share what you've got so far with your partner. And, if you're feeling stuck, see if your partner can help you."

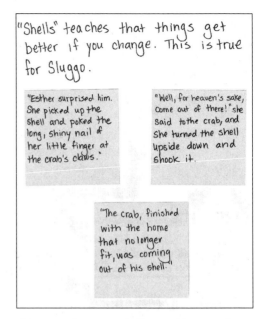

FIG. 19–2   Resources to be used in a small group

Here, we suggest that you channel students to plan and teach their own seminars, so each student gets a chance to be an expert and teach others. You might decide to modify this and ask students to plan and teach a seminar with their partner.

Students need to make quick decisions about what they will teach. Be ready to make suggestions to students, saying, "The mini-stories you crafted were so focused. You could definitely teach about that." Or, "Remember how you helped Khalid choose the best quotes? I bet you could help third-graders do that too."

LINK

Channel students to work intensely to plan out how their small groups will go and to create tools and visuals to support the audience they will teach.

"Essay ambassadors, there's no time to waste. The third- and fourth-graders are expecting you in forty minutes! You'll have your own group of kids to work with and teach, and you'll need to be prepared when you meet with them.

"Use this time now to do whatever you need to do to get ready. You might need to spend more time figuring out *what* you'll be teaching your group. Or, you might jump into *how* you'll teach it. Make a plan, and then create any writing or tools or charts you need to help you. I'll leave chart paper and markers up here in case you want to make any tools to take with you. Off you go!"

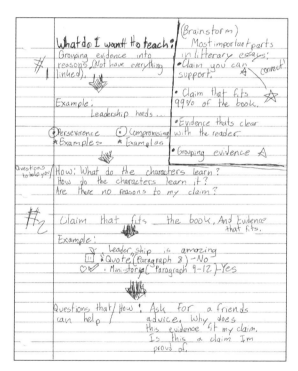

FIG. 19–3   Kelly quickly revises her plan for her small group.

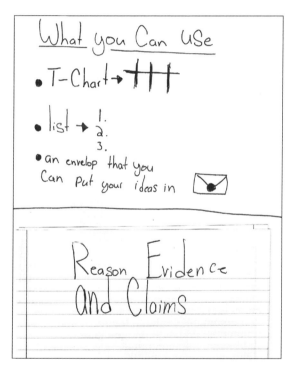

FIG. 19–4   Carolina creates a chart to teach her students about tools they can use to develop claims and collect evidence.

Helping Students Prepare to Teach

YOUR STUDENTS only have a limited amount of time to prepare for the small groups they'll teach during today's share. To quickly and dramatically lift the level of work your students are doing, you might focus your energy today on voicing over tips to the entire class and leading quick one-on-one conferences with kids.

Here are some tips you might voice while students are working, based on what you notice about your students' planning and preparation:

◆ "Make sure your teaching point is brief and clear for your audience. It should give them a little information, not just tell the topic. Like a thesis statement, you might try it out a few ways until you get it *just right*."

◆ "Think about your teaching. Do you want to show the kids how you do something in your own writing? Do you want to show an example from one of the mentor texts you've studied? Whatever you decide, mark up the parts you'll use so they're easy to find when you're teaching. I use Post-it notes to mark up the parts I'll reference."

◆ "Make sure your planning is laser-focused. You've just got twenty minutes left to get ready to go."

◆ "Teachers don't just plan for what *they* will do. They also plan for what their *students* will do. Make a plan for what you'll ask your students to do or write. They should have a lot of work to try."

◆ "Look at the charts in the room to get ideas. It helps if your chart has a title and some steps or bullets that your students can follow."

To keep your conferences brief, you might ask students what they need. You might say, "What's feeling tricky? What could you use some help with?" This kind of questioning sets the tone for the conference and invites students to set the agenda. It also helps to streamline the time you spend teaching, because you don't need to spend time researching—you can jump right into something the writer needs help with. You'll probably want to carry the small-group planning tools you shared with students during the minilesson with you as you confer today. You might also find it helpful to carry other small-group charts and tools, so you can share a range of options with students as you confer.

Whatever you decide, keep today's conferences brief. Determine what the student needs support with, give a tip, and coach the writer for a minute while he starts trying the tip. Then, move on to another writer, and repeat the process.

MID-WORKSHOP TEACHING   **Rehearsing for Teaching**

"Have you ever been part of a dress rehearsal for a play or musical or concert? In a dress rehearsal, you try things out exactly the same way you're thinking they'll go during the actual performance. The dress rehearsal gives you a chance to see what's working and what you need to tweak.

"Just as actors rehearse for a play, teachers rehearse for their teaching. I'm thinking that doing a little rehearsal might benefit you all. To try this, you'll need to gather everything you have so far to use with your small group, and then meet with your partner. Decide who will go first, and that person should get started teaching right away. If you're the audience first, notice what the teacher does well, but also be ready to give the teacher feedback on what he or she could do differently, what he or she could change."

After a few minutes, I voiced over. "It's almost time to switch roles if you haven't already. Take a minute to share feedback before you do. What did your partner do well? What could they do a little differently?"

A few minutes later, I said, "You've got fifteen more minutes to prepare, writers. Take your partner's feedback, and use it to make this small group the best you possibly can."

Bringing Small Groups to a Broader Audience

Emphasize the importance of the teaching work students will do shortly. Then, send students out as ambassadors of essays into the other classrooms to teach their small groups to other kids.

"Essay ambassadors, you're about to bring the third- and fourth-graders an incredible gift: your knowledge! These small groups you've planned will help those kids learn even more about opinion writing, and they'll lift the level of the opinion writing they do from here on out.

"I've got you all set for the classes you will teach in." I projected a document that listed each student's name and the classroom he or she was teaching in. Five or six kids were headed to each classroom to teach. "I'm really wishing I could be in thirty places at once so I could sit in on all of your small groups and learn from you. I'll jump from class to class to see as many of you as I can.

"Ready? It's time to gather your plans and tools and head out around the school. You've got this!"

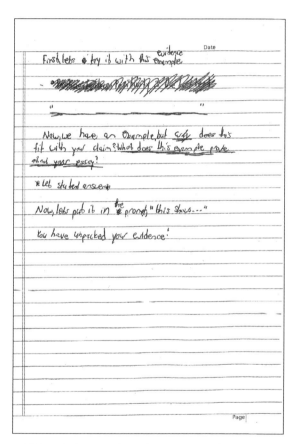

FIG. 19–5   Olivia generates a plan for her small group. (See additional plans on the online resources.)

Munro's Petition
Munro Louis

In life leadership skills are important for kids to learn. In fact these skills are key to being positive and the importance of being positive.

I believe that leadership skills should be taught in schools. Leadership doesn't mean you're ambitious. It means that you work as a team you are responsible and most of all you have a creative imagination.

One reason why that leadership shills should be taught in schools is because it teaches us to work as a team. Although this may sound crazy what I'm going to tell you but TEXTING, SOCIALIZING IN CLASS, NOTE-PASSING all fall into the category of teamwork. And teamwork helps us be good no, great no, fantastic Leaders. This shows that you are building skills that teachers call "disruptive to teaching" while we are actually practicing to be leaders.

Another Way leadership should be taught in schools is that you learn to be responsible. There are several ways how leadership skills can teach us to be more responsible. One way is in the text <u>Dear Graduating Fifth Graders</u> it explains "If you want to succeed you need to be a strong leader. This shows that by being a strong leader you are a good role model, you are happy, making good decisions and having fun. This doesn't mean that you are ambitious or being the ruler of everything.

A final reason why leadership skills should be taught in schools is it means you have a creative imagination. According to the text <u>A letter to The National Museum</u>" it tells us that you have to be positive to people so that they come over and tell you what they need help with and they can trust you to tell them the correct answers. Being a leader is exiting but also takes al large amount of creativity to make those ideas possible. This shows that it takes a lot of work to accomplish tasks that are hard. Take Leonardo Da Vinci as example. When people were still using catapults, which were over around 500 years ago he invented the first man, automated machine gun, which we still use <u>TODAY</u>! Obviously he was very creative. This shows that the guy was a hard, hard, hard worker because he created things in so many different areas of science.

In conclusion people should be taught leadership skills not to be powerful but to be smart with their creativity and to make things useful for people. Leadership skills teach responsibility, it teaches us teamwork and most of all it teaches us to have a creative imagination.

FIG. 19–6   Munro's petition on why people should be taught leadership skills.

Debate Essay

By Elizabeth

In the world, something is always better than something else. Positivity and creativity are both very important leadership skills, but I believe Positivity is better because when you have positivity, ideas are more creative and positive, keeping positive can make it so you don't give up, and lastly because keeping positive usually has a better outcome.

One reason on why I think positivity is the most important leadership skill is because ideas are usually more creative and positive. In the film "Panyee FC" It states that all of the boys loved to watch soccer from their TV. But one day, one of the boys had the idea that they should make a team of their own. The other people in the village heard their plan, and thought it was plain stupid. There wasn't any space. They all sat around, doubt and any happiness had been washed away. Then one of the boys suggested if they didn't have any space for a pitch, they'd make their own. Happiness came back, determination laced with it. Even though the villagers thought their idea was stupid, they got the idea to make their own pitch. They kept positive through all the hard work and they made one. It was shady, but durable. This is important because it shows the boys kept positive when others didn't believe in them, and it boosted their creative ideas to make a raft of their own.

Another reason on why I think positivity is the most important leadership skill is because keeping positive can make it so you don't give up. In the text "The Stranded Whale" by Jane Yolen, the protagonist Sally was being teased when she spotted a whale lying on its side. Sally didn't take a moment to stop and think, she raced down the dune stripping off her shoes, book bag, sweater, and she raced to the whale. Abandoning them in the sand, the boys also helped out dipping their sweaters in the ocean to help the whale. "We need help, I said. Josh raced off, to an emergency phone halfway along the beach, maybe half a mile away. The policeman who answered said he'd call the Coast Guard, though it took them twenty minutes to get to us, so we kept wetting down that whale, one sweater, and two sweaters at a time." This shows that Sally and the boys didn't give up and just wait for help. They kept positive, helping the whale with a sweater or two at a time. Josh even raced to the emergency phone which was half a mile away, just to save the whale. This also shows they didn't give up.

Last, but not least on why I think positivity is the most important leadership skill is because keeping positive usually has a better outcome. In the speech "Dear Graduating 5th Graders," the author explains one of their experiences. She explains that her teacher gave them a challenge to spend an entire day acting sad, and bored, and then the next day spend it smiling and saying hello to everyone. On the first day, the author explains "When we saw other students in the hallway, we looked away. When we all talked in class, we all talked about how miserable we felt going through life with a negative attitude." And then on the next day, "I remember walking down the hallway and saying good morning to a group of first graders. They all smiled back and said good morning to me! Now, when I see those first graders in school, I always stop to talk with them and ask them how they are doing." If the author met these first graders on the first day of the challenge, I can infer that she'd look away and tell them how miserable and bored she was, and those first graders may have reacted the same way. But since that did not happen and it happened on the second day, the outcome was much different. They all smiled back, and reflected the same positivity the author gave to them back to the author. I used to think that the phrase "What you put out in the world comes back to you" wasn't true, but now I realize it is.

In conclusion, these are all the reasons why I think positivity is the most important leadership skill. While positivity and creativity are both very important leadership skills, when the day comes that you are a leader, you may have to choose which one you go by. The choice is up to you.

FIG. 19–7   Elizabeth's essay in preparation for a debate.

Persuasive Letter

Archer

Dear voters,

    If an important candidate is running for an important position in an election, don't zero in on how he/she looks, acts, or speaks. This is how the candidate influences you into voting for them, even if they're not responsible. While they present themselves during speeches, try to look for 4 leadership skills that I will call the most vital leadership skills a leader could have. As a voter, try to look for a candidate with a positive attitude, a creative mind, a streak for being persistent, and most importantly, a trustworthy candidate. You, as a voter should never THINK you know who you're voting for, you should KNOW who you're voting for. The famous leaders in all of history had these skills to be a leader, and your candidate should have these leadership skills also. Always look out for the qualities that separate a follower from a leader.

    Look for a candidate with a positive attitude. This is one of the most important leadership skills. This skill blooms in everyday life to being a leader. In other words, people with positive attitudes are more successful than negative people, says "the Letter to the National Museum." One example to support this is "It gives a better first impression…"- "the Letter to the National Museum" says this because first impressions are important. Research by "Brain Games" shows that people pay attention to the first reactions/words the people do. First, "Brain Games" took identical twins and said a series of words but in a different order. The most convincing order was from strongest to weakest. This shows how a positive attitude gives an upper hand on winning a election. This is one leadership skill you should look for.

    Look for a candidate with a creative mind. Creativity helps in everyday life to making a political stand. A good candidate has creativity, and this enables them to "Make unclear decisions for the community." To say more, creativity proves to be useful when deciding a big plot for the community. This can be clarified as a trait that enables the leader to keep the community under control, even in hard times. To add on to this, creativity comes to make solutions to many, general problems. It will allow the candidate to not panic but keep control of the community.

    Look for a candidate with a persistent way. They will never give up and will stand for the community in times of need. They will remain loyal to the people. A persistent person makes a good leader because they are the foundation of the whole community. If the community starts to waver, you can count on the candidate's cool, collective power to keep the community from falling apart. If he/she will do so, expect the community to persevere through the corresponding hardships.

    Finally, look for a trustworthy candidate. It is easier to rely on a leader that is brutally honest. The community can look up to them as a great leader. Also, more trustworthy people are successful, says "the Letter to the National Museum," and "Speech to Graduating Fifth-graders." These two resources tell a lot about how to be a leader. To say more about this, it turns out that all great leaders in history have this, and if your candidates don't have this trait, then don't vote for them.

    To sum it all up, the perfect leader is one that has a positive attitude, a creative mind, a persistent person, and a honest person. Look for these leadership skills to vote. I guarantee your choice was the best.

FIG. 19–8 Archer's persuasive letter to voters about what to look for in a candidate.

REFLECTING ON GROWTH

Writers, you have made tremendous progress over the past month. Tonight, take some time to celebrate your growth and reflect on the progress you've made. Bring home your on-demand assessment from the very start of the unit and the writing piece you just finished. Reread those two pieces. You could start by reading your on-demand assessment, noticing what you were doing and not doing in that piece. Then, you could read the writing piece you finished yesterday, noticing the ways in which your writing has already gotten better.

After you study your writing, write long in your notebook about the progress you've made as a writer. Here are some questions you might use to guide your reflection:

- What's been easy for you as a writer in this unit? What's been challenging?

- In what ways is your writing better now than it was a few weeks ago?

- How have those changes strengthened your writing? How have they helped your readers?

- What goals do you have for your writing work moving forward?

- How has this unit changed you as a writer? as a person?

Happy reflecting!

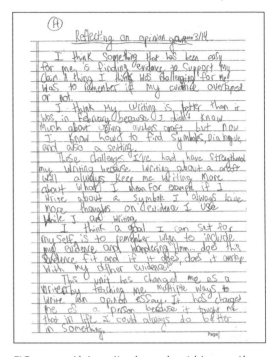

FIG. 19–9 Alain writes long about his growth as a writer.